ALSO BY ALEXANDRA MARSHALL

THE SILENCE OF YOUR NAME

ARROWSMITH
PRESS

ISBN: 978-1-7346416-8-4

Boston — New York — San Francisco — Baghdad
San Juan — Kyiv — Istanbul — Santiago, Chile
Beijing — Paris — London — Cairo — Madrid
Milan — Melbourne — Jerusalem — Darfur

11 Chestnut St.
Medford, MA 02155

arrowsmithpress@gmail.com
www.arrowsmithpress.com

The thirty-seventh Arrowsmith book was typeset & designed
by Ezra Fox for Askold Melnyczuk & Alex Johnson
in Freight typeface, a font by Joshua Darden

Cover Art by Kristen Mallia, Mallia Design

Parts of this book first appeared in different form
in the following publications:

"The Afterlife of a Suicide" in The American Scholar;
"The Ultimate Alchemy" in Ploughshares;
& "And Then What?" in Lit Hub.

THE SILENCE OF YOUR NAME

The Afterlife of a Suicide

ALEXANDRA MARSHALL

for my granddaughters

Alexandra and Julia

Sound scatters light through darkened ages, come to
shed the silence of a trance –
your name

bears silence past dreaming, past ages past,
past reckoning years, past recreating
past abandonment.

Come over children's voices one muted glance calls
come. Come anyway,
come one step across chasms come between

come home.

Abena P. A. Busia
Testimonies of Exile

THE ULTIMATE ALCHEMY

We were children of privilege: Tim devoted his spring break to the voting rights march from Selma to Montgomery, and I was soon to set off for Asia and Africa to learn the essential life lesson, for a white person, of being the minority race. I'd worked hard to convince my parents that a round-the-world air ticket was a better investment than graduate school – and I was right – but in this finite summer interval Tim and I were imagining our future together. He was a tennis pro at a club in the town of Old Lyme while I studied dance at the prestigious program based at Connecticut College a few exits north. Whenever I could get away to Tim, I did, and in these treasured weeks we spent many tender hours lying by the open doors of the former hayloft in his cousin's partly renovated carriage barn, listening to the mezzo-soprano horns from the trains hugging the shore of that scenic coastline as they trailed into the distance.

In my dance class that morning, while a company member demonstrated the contract-and-release at the core of the technique, Martha Graham – herself – stalked among us, wielding a pointer to adjust our form. It was both terrifying and thrilling to be in the spectral presence of a dance pioneer, and while I doubted I'd ever achieve the perfection she demanded, my extracurricular identity as a dancer had gotten me through high school and college. Still, the abrasive Rolling Stones anthem "(I Can't Get No) Satisfaction" was that summer's hit song, and it was probably because I'd already decided to suspend my rigorous training for freeform travel that I felt the limits of that exclusive community. How much more was there to say about the Achilles Tendon when, four months earlier, Governor George Wallace refused protection to Dr. Martin Luther King Jr. and his legion of supporters, including Tim, on their 54-mile march to the state capitol?

Tim spent his first year out of college teaching at Andover, where his New Haven neighbor, Yale's Rev. William Sloane Coffin Jr., had begun his career as an activist chaplain. And that fall he would enter Union Seminary on a Rockefeller Fellowship to explore the ministry. A religion major, Tim's thesis topic was Nietzsche's construct of the creative/intuitive power of Dionysus and the critical/rational power of Apollo. I'd studied Nietzsche, sort of, but as a French major I was assigned the masters of literature, like Proust, of roughly the same era. Tim's vocation to the ministry wasn't yet declared, but it didn't escape my notice that the family plot in Old Lyme's Duck River Cemetery was down the road from the classic white church founded in 1665, exactly three hundred years earlier, by a preacher named Moses Noyes, Tim's maternal ancestor.

If I'd had any idea it would ever be relevant to recall the details of the only time I was in that cemetery with Tim, I'd be able to chronicle it like a historian. Instead, let's picture Tim in his tennis whites and me in a coverup over my black leotard and tights, with my brown hair fixed in its tight dancer's bun, Tim's blond hair sun-streaked to make his eyes – his mother's cobalt blue – even brighter. So we're in stark contrast, but as we strolled by, did we bother to notice the irony in the name of the narrow road bordering the cemetery's near side, Bittersweet Lane, or the sign marked No Outlet?

On that afternoon, Tim and I were a pair of tourists as we walked among the gravestones in the yew-hedged section of the cemetery, straight ahead from the gate, overlooking a pond edged with water lilies. From the lineup of matching white marble gravestones we read aloud the names and dates of those who came – and went – before, stopping still before the miniature marker shaped like the others. I asked about the baby, his sister, whose inscription reads "Katharine Lee Buxton, died in infancy," but all Tim knew was that she'd lived for three months, long enough to be given the nickname Kitty. He had only heard "crib death" concerning the loss of this firstborn child, and was told nothing of the grief of the young woman, his mother, married at nineteen to an obstetrician nearly twice her age.

To the left of Kitty's was the marker for Tim's grandmother, Helen Gilman Ludington Rotch, a *Mayflower* descendant and one of Boston's civic leaders. At her death she was a board member of Americans for Democratic Action and had been president of the Massachusetts League of Women Voters, the organization founded at the national level by her older sister, Katharine Ludington, the suffragette for whom baby Kitty was named. Tim honored this history, and with his voting rights activism in the Civil Rights movement he had embraced this legacy.

But next to his grandmother's conventional upright marker was a pink marble slab that lay flat like a blanket. This tombstone bore the inscription "In Loving Memory of JOSEPHINE NOYES ROTCH" and, below it, "Wife of Albert Smith Bigelow." I found the cryptic inscription "In Death Is Victory" a forlorn choice for a girl whose dates revealed that she'd died at twenty-one, my own age, but when I asked Tim what it could mean, he said he knew nothing about the death in 1929 of his mother's oldest sister.

It would be another decade before the lurid circumstances of Josephine's death were to become quite public in a bestselling book. Although it generated aftershocks that reverberate to this day, the story was so untold that her four younger sisters didn't know it. Tim's mother, Helen, was only ten at the time and would claim to "barely remember" the big sister she called Dodie, whose High Society wedding and private funeral had both taken place in that church up the road from the cemetery.

We moved along. And while Tim and I might have speculated about the impact of the losses of the young bride and the infant who died before their mothers, or been curious to investigate what happened to that young widower bridegroom, we were feeling too alive that day to brood on death's mysteries. Which of us – who on earth – could have predicted that the next stone to be placed in that plot, just five years later, would bear my young husband's own name and telescoped dates?

In the Boston of inherited wealth, the five fetching Rotch daughters were raised in a Commonwealth Avenue mansion in the same posh neighborhood as the Bigelow and Crosby families. The eldest daughter, Josephine, was engaged to marry Albert Bigelow the day after his graduation from Harvard.

But the previous summer, when Josie and her mother sailed to Venice to shop for her trousseau, she was introduced to Harry Crosby. He and his wife were there to recuperate from the Four Arts Ball in Paris, where they lived in a deluxe, frenzied version of bohemian exile, in willful violation of Boston etiquette. In Venice, Josephine entered into an obsessive affair with Harry that ended, six months after Josie and Bert's picture-perfect wedding in June of 1929, in Josie and Harry's murder/suicide.

Harry was a half-generation older than Josie and Bert. Having impulsively joined the Army Ambulance Corps out of St. Mark's School, deferring Harvard in order to fight in France, he was nearly killed, on what he ever after called his "first death day," in an explosion during the Second Battle of Verdun. He was just nineteen then – "Won Oh Boy!!!!!!! THE CROIX DE GUERRE. Thank God," he wrote home – but that permanent trauma defined him. Today we would understand Harry's reliance on alcohol and drugs as self-medicating the terror of his war experience, but with his return to the decorous world of Boston, only his mother excused his habitually eccentric attire and rebellious behavior. Several semesters at Harvard were condensed into a "War Degree" that left him unsuited for employment, and his college record was such an embarrassment to his father that they sank into a mutual disdain from which they never recovered. Harry pursued and married the former Mary Phelps Jacob Peabody, nicknamed Polly, who submitted to his demand that she use the excuse of her first husband's drinking (which wasn't considered a good enough reason) to divorce Richard Peabody, the father of her two children.

In their escape to Paris, Polly and Harry became locomotive partiers, their drugs and alcohol paralleling the prominent French writers – the "morbid poets" Baudelaire and Rimbaud – who had engaged in their own darkly ecstatic preoccupations with death. The Crosby couple founded a press in order to publish their own poetry and diaries, and Polly was renamed Caresse to mark the publication of her first book of sonnets. The Black Sun Press soon featured elegantly crafted editions of work by the literary expatriate circle in Paris including James Joyce, D.H. Lawrence, Hart Crane, Oscar Wilde, T.S. Eliot, Ezra Pound, and Kay Boyle, whom Harry deemed the greatest female writer since Jane Austen. They published Proust too.

When Harry first encountered Josephine in Venice he was reading

Nietzsche's *Thus Spake Zarathustra*. He was so enthralled by the message "die at the right time" that he wrote in his journal, "Die at the right time, so teacheth Zarathustra and again the direct 31-10-42. Clickety-click clickety-click the express train into Sun." This date represented the projected shortest distance between the orbits of the earth and the sun, so October 31, 1942 was the day, at Harry's urging, that he and Caresse had already selected for their own elaborately imagined double suicide. Upon meeting Josephine – "Enter the Youngest Princess of the Sun!" – Harry claimed her as his newest recruit, while introducing her to the "black idol" opium that he and Caresse had discovered a few years earlier on their travels to North Africa.

When their bodies were found, the news was suppressed in the Boston papers. The New York tabloids freely speculated, but because Harry was the nephew and godson of J.P. Morgan, Jr., the kindly "Uncle Jack" whose generosity Harry often sought and always abused, the *Times* gave the story fourteen cautious paragraphs under the headline "COUPLE SHOT DEAD IN ARTISTS' HOTEL" with the restrained subheads "Suicide Pact Is Indicated Between Henry Grew Crosby and Harvard Man's Wife" "BUT MOTIVE IS UNKNOWN."

Tim died in Ghana. He and I were barely into our Operation Crossroads Africa program when an unspecified fever initiated a rapid decline that dead-ended seven days later with him cutting his own throat. Although his mother never asked to learn more than what I reported to our gathered families – when I know I mentioned the breadknife because my own mother definitely heard it! – on several subsequent occasions Helen ruefully admitted to me her reflexive need to redefine the cause of Tim's death as a tropical disease. By her consistently brave example I gradually became alert to the function of denial as a constructive force. Yet without understanding its origins in her buried family history, I didn't know how or why to penetrate the destructive aspects of that denial. I felt so relieved by her lack of blame, of me, that I willingly honored her preference for a modified version once I understood that this was what she could live with. She didn't seem to realize that by her firm resolve not to speak of the trauma – and because I loved her – neither could I.

But then six summers later, while I was leading another group of Crossroads volunteers, this time to a project in the Netherlands Antilles, I received a letter from Helen where her usual happy chronicle of family news was interrupted by her acute distress at a just-published excerpt appearing in the *Atlantic Monthly* from a forthcoming biography called *Black Sun*. The book by Geoffrey Wolff told the story of Harry Crosby and the flamboyantly reckless life that ended with his shooting his lover and then himself in a laboriously chronicled murder/suicide pact. His lover's name was revealed to have been Josephine Rotch Bigelow. That the scandal had been so successfully concealed that nearly fifty years later this came as *news* to the dead girl's four younger sisters was instantly translated into their collective outrage against the biographer.

At the time of Josephine's death, her sister Lydia was nineteen and had been Josie's maid of honor in that wedding day lineup of twelve bridesmaids and fourteen groomsmen, including Bert's Harvard classmates with storybook names like Roosevelt, Carnegie, and Tiffany. I'd seen the classic formal engagement photograph of Josie displayed on the grand piano, but understood neither the facts nor this utter rejection of them by her younger sisters. In the view of Lydia, Katharine, Helen, and Phoebe, Wolff had grievously slandered their dear Dodie by telling the tragic story of Harry Crosby's foreshortened life and foreshadowed death. It seemed that the family had long ago made its peace, so to speak, by not ever speaking of it.

In Helen's second letter to me about the *Black Sun* excerpt she wrote:

> We gave Phoebe a copy of the Geoffrey Wolff *Atlantic* article. She was incensed [sic] by it and wrote the *Atlantic* a letter which they forwarded to Wolff. He couldn't have tried very hard to reach members of the family. He claims his book is an artistic study of suicide, but from that article I'd say it was a gossipy scandal. I hope his book won't be widely read. He seemed a bit nervous and replied immediately. He probably thinks we want to sue. If it's a study in motives and Crosby's personality, why does he have to mention any names?

In a follow-up letter to me, Helen made reference to her cousin's son Townsend Ludington, the owner of the Old Lyme carriage barn, whose two uncles, Nick and Wright, having introduced Josephine to Harry in Venice, then claimed her dead body for the family from the Bellevue Morgue:

> Towny had read that article in the *Atlantic* and had not been familiar with the story. It's too bad to bring up the old scandal. It bothers Lyd the most of all because she was so close to Dodie. I was so young, I didn't really know her at all.

But the publication had prompted the sisters to invite their former brother-in-law, Bert Bigelow, for an afternoon visit to Hill Top Farm. Bert returned to the place where he and Josie had spent their honeymoon, bringing his second wife, Sylvia Weld Bigelow, to whom he'd been happily married for forty-five years. From Helen's upbeat report I could picture them sitting together in the semicircle of Adirondack chairs overlooking the riding ring and the fields beyond, sipping iced tea with mint from the bed by the back porch of what had once been the cook's farmhouse.

In more prosperous times, the Rotch girls had enjoyed The Farm's all-day recreational opportunities, including horseback riding, tennis, and a nine-hole golf course. Their massive Stone House with its gracious veranda overlooked the large lake, and their guests were accommodated in several other noteworthy houses on the property, including the diamond-paned Colonial homestead trucked up from coastal New Bedford, where their paternal ancestors – "the Royal Family of New Bedford" – owned two of the three merchant ships from whose decks the tea was famously dumped overboard into Boston Harbor.

As a girl I'd had no frame of reference for the depth of this layered world, nor as a young woman did I grasp the poverty at the heart of the wealth. I was told that after their mother's death their father married his longtime mistress, to whom he bequeathed his fortune when he then died a few years later. He rendered his surviving daughters land-poor by leaving them Hill Top Farm without the means to support it, but I saw the Rotch sisters as survivors and greatly admired everybody's favorite Aunt Lyd, the second oldest after Josephine. Although *Black Sun* became a bestseller when it was released later that summer, I doubt that this reversal or any of the book's grisly particulars came into their conversation that afternoon, since the purpose of that get-together with Bert was to share their common fury – kill the messenger – at the biographer.

Of course I felt pressed to know more, so first thing after returning from my Crossroads project on the tiny Dutch island of Sint Eustatius I bought *Black Sun* to find out why Helen and her sisters were so agitated. Because I knew from seeing Josephine's gravestone the day Tim brought me to the Old Lyme cemetery that she was twenty-one when she died, I noted the early error when Wolff wrote, on page 4, "Harry was thirty-one; Josephine twenty-two." Although I've read *Black Sun* numerous times by now and have no reason to doubt Wolff's otherwise careful research, the mistake helped me see why Josephine's sisters felt entitled to protest his scarce effort to portray her.

On the night of Harry's death, Caresse called upon Archibald MacLeish, the Boston lawyer turned poet and another Black Sun author during his Paris sojourn, to sit with Harry's body at the Bellevue Morgue. Forty-four years later MacLeish reported to Geoffrey Wolff in an interview, "As I sat there looking at the corpse, seating myself where I wouldn't have to see the horrible hole in the back of his ear, I kept saying to him: you poor, damned, dumb bastard." Harry's "phony mysticism" fueled his inferior poetry, according to MacLeish, whose own poems Harry revered second only to T.S. Eliot, ahead of e e cummings. MacLeish defined Harry as "the most literary man I ever met, despite the fact that he'd not yet become what you'd call a Writer." He had tried unsuccessfully to convince Harry to follow Rimbaud's example: relentless excess lived at the service of his art rather than for its own sake. He found Harry's poems "too long and too diffuse and too careless." "The manuscripts seemed to me unmade beds."

After Harry's death MacLeish wrote a poem about Harry called "Cinema of a Man," a quietly enigmatic series of images. But e e cummings came in for the kill, with this:

                    2 boston
     Dolls;found
     with
     Holes in each other

     's lullaby and
     other lulla wise by UnBroken
     LULLAlullabyBY

                    the She-in-him with

        the He-in-her (&

        both all hopped
                        up)prettily
        then which did
        lie
        Down,honestly

        now who go(BANG(BANG

If *Black Sun* is a record of the inevitability of Harry's suicide, in the privately published counterpoint *Josephine Rotch Bigelow* memorial book created for family and friends, Josie was lovingly portrayed by her mother as "an unusually lively and vigorous baby" who "only missed being born on the Fourth of July by a few hours, and all her life she insisted on celebrating her birthday on the Fourth, which seemed, somehow, to be a fitting date for one of her temperament."

Mrs. Rotch observed that her first daughter had "an extraordinarily definite and marked personality, from the day of her birth, difficult to handle, but never uninteresting." "I think no one who saw Josephine dance when she was about eleven years old will ever forget her – she was so full of the joy of life, so naturally graceful, and had such a vivid, dramatic way of throwing herself into it."

One of her teachers wrote to Mrs. Rotch, "I have always loved and admired your Josephine. Hers was the leading mind of her class, whose mature judgment was always the standard that challenged my very best endeavor. To me she seems a spirit of fire made of substance none may presume to comprehend."

Mrs. Rotch's sister, Katharine Ludington, described her niece in the graveyard at Old Lyme: "She never seemed to have any thought of the cemetery as a melancholy spot, perhaps because she had been brought up on the old traditions and anecdotes of the place and the humor of the earlier stones with their astonishing cherubs and epitaphs." Indeed, in a remark with resonance for me, she added, "Her husband says that on his first visit there she took him to the old cemetery to see where the members of the family were buried, and there was never a question where she would want to be laid herself."

Each of the candid photos of Josephine as a child reveals this high energy, and there is an echo of it, and more, in the studio portraits from her adolescence. Her mother's muted grief is most evident in her reminiscence, "Constantly in trouble through her contrariness and her power of inventing mischief, she was always ready to admit that she was in the wrong. She would storm and weep, but before night she had either come to make up, or had left a note on my pillow saying she was sorry and would 'try to be good.' When she was about twelve, she gave me a framed motto, 'Lead thy Mother gently down life's steep decline...'."

It would be a distortion to imagine Harry meeting his match when he encountered Josephine, but his friends had observed to Harry how in the portrait of "the Fire Princess" that he displayed on his desk in a silver frame, and which was in his wallet when he died, Josephine's features so closely resemble his that they look like brother and sister.

His one sibling, a sister nicknamed Kitsa, married and later divorced one of his friends, Robert Choate, whose influence as managing editor at the *Boston Herald* was why the news of the scandal went almost entirely unreported in Boston, other than to note that the bodies were found clothed. But Choate had also been Harry's chief enabler in the pursuit of Josephine, offering them his house near Josie and Bert's Beacon Hill apartment and, in the week preceding the murder/suicide, by accompanying them from New York to Detroit, by train, on an impromptu escapade.

In his diary Harry described how, on that return trip, "she cries many opium pills and all night we catapult though space J and I in each other's arms vision security happiness." In his entry for December 6, back in New York, he wrote, "J sick as a cat from the opium," with the notation "1 West 67," the address of his friend Stanley Mortimer's frequently borrowed studio at the Hotel des Artistes. It was there that, four days later, Josephine and Harry met for the last time.

According to another of Harry's lovers in Paris – one who had refused Harry's repeated invitations to die with him – he loved Josephine mostly because she loved him. Other friends condemned his "Youngest Princess," blaming the victim for calling Harry's bluff by demanding that they die together. In the assessment of Archibald MacLeish, "This whole thing caught up with Harry; he'd built it up, the black sun, a philosophy with edges of demonology in it; he peddled it to an awful lot of girls. This one, apparently, took it seriously. Then he was faced with a situation from which there was no escape whatsoever. He couldn't walk out of that place alive."

The New York tabloid details included Harry's red-varnished toenails and the tattooed soles of his feet, one with a cross and the other a sun-symbol. Josephine wore her orchid corsage and he his black carnation, and her look was characterized by the deputy medical examiner, in recording her death as a homicide, as "the expression of smiling expectancy on the dead face of the beautiful young wife, indicating that she had gone to her rendezvous expecting a caress, not deadly bullets."

In Josephine's final love letter to Harry she wrote, "Death is *our* marriage." But this rambling prose poem reads to me like a sadly girlish inventory of what they loved in common: orchids, caviar, champagne, the number 13, and the color black. It has a "Sound of Music" banality to suggest, tragically, that they were no match for each other.

While there was no mention of opium in the medical report, an empty quart of scotch was found with their bodies. The *New York Daily Mirror* revealed the alcohol content of the dead couple's brains – hers twice his – and declared "Jo-Jo Bigelow" almost literally "dead drunk." The medical findings also concluded that Harry had shot Josephine first and then himself, but not until several hours later.

I was shocked to read this account and wished Tim were alive to absorb with me the secret history of the dead young woman the family never referred to. By comparison to this scandal, Tim's own violent death by suicide was in such a different category that it could seem almost unwilled. Was this what his mother preferred to believe about him, and believed?

In the family plot in the Duck River Cemetery, Helen placed Tim's grave next to baby Kitty's, with room for her own one day between her son and the valiant mother for whom she was named. Josephine's pink stone marker had been set in place nearly fifty years before the publication of *Black Sun*, but the horror was fresh.

After their reunion in 1976 I never heard Helen mention Bert Bigelow again. Nor in the Afterword to a subsequent edition of *Black Sun* published twenty-seven years later, in 2003, did Geoffrey Wolff display any increased interest in either Josephine or the husband she betrayed. Instead Wolff defended himself against the reviewers who had faulted him for writing about such a minor writer as Harry Crosby rather than the significant literary figures of the day. To *TIME* magazine's criticism that Wolff's excuse for the book was its "gossip," he justified his research methods by answering, "The gossip in Black Sun is substantiated hearsay," a claim seemingly addressed to Josephine's angry sisters – two of whom had since died – but which would not have satisfied them.

My own persistent efforts to comprehend and absorb the trauma of Tim's suicide would have been rewarded by seeking out Bert, instead of only discovering his heroic story seventeen years later by way of the prominent *New York Times* obituary marking his death at age eighty-seven.

In the sixty-four years beyond that December day in 1929 when his wife lied about the purpose of her visit to New York, I learned that Bert charted his exemplary life with a stunning modesty. In the volumes of crimson-bound *Harvard Class Reports* for the Class of 1929, Bert's detailed chronicles tell of a life of deep personal fulfillment and great public courage. With Bert's commitments to peace and social justice he could have been Tim's mentor.

In 1959 Doubleday published Bert's account of his nonviolent civil disobedience in *The Voyage of the Golden Rule: An Experiment with Truth.* "Nonviolence is the noncreation of antagonism," Bert wrote, defining the Quaker creed he'd embraced several years earlier when he and his wife Sylvia hosted two "Hiroshima Maidens" for a year during their multiple plastic surgeries to correct for the disfiguring injuries caused, at age seven and thirteen, by the bombing of Hiroshima. "What response can one make to this," he wrote of these Japanese survivors, "other than to give oneself utterly to destroying the evil, war, that dealt so shamefully with them, and try to live in the spirit of sensitivity and reconciliation which they displayed?"

Bert's own experience of that war was dramatically circular, beginning with his enlistment in the Navy the day after Pearl Harbor was attacked and concluding as Captain of a destroyer escort approaching Pearl Harbor on August 6, 1945 when the first news was released of the atomic bomb exploding over Hiroshima. "Although I had no way of understanding what an atom bomb was I was absolutely awestruck," he wrote, "as I suppose all men were for a moment. Intuitively it was then that I realized for the first time that morally war is impossible."

This realization in 1945 prompted him in 1958 to set out, with a crew of three, on the 30' sailing vessel *Golden Rule*. This was a peace action to protest the U.S. government's planned nuclear test explosions announced for that April at Eniwetok. In his letter addressed to President Eisenhower, Bert explained that, by sailing from Hawaii into that prohibited area two thousand miles away, he and his crew intended, "come what may, to remain there during the test period, in an effort to halt what we feel is the monstrous delinquency of our government in continuing actions which threaten the well-being of all men."

Bert wrote, "We were willing to face death – sure. But, like thousands of men, and in other countries women and children, I repeatedly faced death during the war." This deliberative consciousness of lives beyond his own was the simple definition of Bert's courage, and his heroic modesty remains uncommonly winning.

He and his crew outfitted and provisioned the *Golden Rule* and, after a series of judicial maneuvers and counter-maneuvers, the vessel set off. It would ultimately fall to the U.S. Coast Guard to forcibly intercept the *Golden Rule* on the high seas, charging criminal conspiracy for violating a nautical technicality: "the registration numbers on the bow were three-eighths of an inch too short and not parallel with the water line." For this fabricated infraction Bert and his crew were sentenced to sixty days in the Honolulu City and County Jail, by which time the nuclear tests were scheduled to be completed.

In a front-page box this notice ran in the *Honolulu Observer*:

Too late to classify: FOR SALE One 30-foot pacifist ketch, scarcely used. Asking price: $16,000. Registry letters 'Golden Rule' canted one-sixteenth inch, but otherwise fully approved by the U.S. Coast

Guard for sailing anywhere (except Eniwetok area). Contact owner, Albert S. Bigelow, Honolulu City Jail ... any time, day or night, within next 48 days.

More than fifty years later, in 2011, the boat was found derelict in a California boatyard. Since restored by the organization Veterans for Peace, the *Golden Rule* has been rededicated, as a means of instruction against the manufacture and use of nuclear weapons, to its original mission.

In his book Bert wrote that his teachers in the practice of nonviolence were William Penn, the Quaker founder of Pennsylvania who went to jail six times "for deliberately being in kindly disobedience to government"; the Quakers who had given up slave-owning a hundred years before the Civil War and conscientiously violated the Fugitive Slave Act in assisting runaways; the lesson of Gandhi's political revolution that "nonviolence creates the climate and atmosphere for freedom of the spirit"; and the revolutionary example of nonviolent resistance in the Montgomery, Alabama bus protest led by Dr. Martin Luther King Jr.

As Bert defined Dr. King's rationale for nonviolent resistance, "This method permits a struggle to go on with dignity and without the need to retreat. It is a method that can absorb the violence that is inevitable in social change whenever deep-seated prejudices are challenged." In the presidential election of 1956, when Eisenhower was reelected in a landslide, Bert wrote in Dr. King's name as his candidate for president.

Four years later, a young John Lewis, the brave and beloved longtime Congressman from Georgia, described his seatmate on the bus as "a big rugged-looking guy from New England who looked as if he belonged on a sailing ship a century ago," an impression that might have described the whaling forebears of the wife of Bert Bigelow's youth. This bus ride was in May of 1960, and the then middle-aged Bert was one of the original thirteen Freedom Riders with Lewis, a twenty-year-old college student, when they set out from Washington to New Orleans to test a Supreme Court ruling banning discrimination in interstate public facilities.

Congressman Lewis wrote in his 1999 book *Walking With the Wind: A Memoir of the Movement* that when the bus made a rest stop in Rock Hill, South Carolina, Bert put himself between Lewis and the group of white teenagers who went after him. "It had to look strange to these guys to see a big, strong white man putting himself in the middle of a fistfight like this, not looking at all as if he was ready to throw a punch, but not looking frightened either."

As Lewis described it, "They hesitated for an instant. Then they attacked Bigelow, who did not raise a finger as these young men began punching him. It took several blows to drop him to one knee." A white policeman finally intervened, but Lewis and Bigelow refused to press charges, invoking the governing principle of nonviolence that defined the Freedom Ride's sponsoring organization, the Congress of Racial Equality. Before moving on, though, Lewis got his cup of coffee in that "whites-only" waiting room.

From there the bus passed through Georgia without incident, but further along in Anniston, Alabama, it was attacked by a mob of Klansmen, many still in their church clothes. They firebombed the bus and held the doors shut to prevent the Freedom Riders from escaping.

The excuse offered by Birmingham's Police Commissioner Eugene "Bull" Conners for the lack of police presence was that it was Mother's Day, but when the fuel tank exploded, dispersing the mob and allowing the riders to evacuate the bus, the fiery explosion captured by a photographer for the *Anniston Star* was a transformative image. This alarming picture of the Greyhound bus in flames finally succeeded in bringing the country's attention back to earth after the more prominent – dominant – competing story of astronaut Alan Shepard's travel in space.

It was five years after the Freedom Riders, in March of 1965, that Tim coaxed a friend to ride the "freedom train" south to Alabama for Dr. King's march from Selma to Montgomery. This nonviolent demonstration for voting rights inspired, and defined, Tim's own foreshortened ministry dedicated to the Civil Rights and antiwar movements. He would follow in these footsteps, and I know that if Tim could also have known of Bert Bigelow's courageous commitments, he would have been motivated and sustained in his own vocation.

Instead, when Tim brought me to stroll among the grave markers in the family cemetery in those last summer weeks before my departure for the rest of the world, as we began to imagine what would turn out to be our own abbreviated marriage, it didn't occur to either of us to wonder about that dead bride or her widower-bridegroom.

That is, if Tim had known to investigate the man whose own identity was lost to the family of the impetuous bride who gave up her life so inexplicably, he would have honored, and been instructed by, Bert's dedicated work for peace and justice. I can also imagine that if I'd been given the story of Josie and Bert, and come to know Bert in my own life as a young widow, I might not have felt so uniquely unaccompanied. More, in my own emergent political life I too would have had the chance to follow Bert's lead. With the profound example of the rest of his life, Bert Bigelow had performed the ultimate alchemy: turning violence into nonviolence.

If the Rotch sisters seemed unburdened by their sister's violent death, I myself have felt oppressed by the unanswerable question of what pushes – or pulls – a person to suicide. This mystery has repeatedly been my subject as a writer, but my sequential attempts to write the novel I always called *The Child Widow* failed one after the other, inhibited by my persistent wish to make suicide seem less deliberate. I finally collapsed my unrequited energy into an urgent short story I called "Child Widow" and believed with its publication that I could finally consider that awful ambition fulfilled.

But then came Tim's mother's obituary notice in the *Boston Globe* following her peaceful death several years ago at age ninety-two. The four sisters by whom she was predeceased are named – Josephine, Lydia, Katharine, Phoebe – and her survivors are listed as a daughter and two sons, eight grandchildren and a great-granddaughter. With no mention of Tim.

Of course I wanted to know which of Tim's siblings – or if Helen herself – had excluded him from her obituary. But as I readied myself to confront them, my deeper and preeminent discovery was that the permanent shadow of Tim's story cannot be erased, which meant that by default it now belonged – as it has always belonged! – to me. This commissioning represented a challenge, but it was primarily a liberation. Having reimagined Tim's suicide through the distorting lens of his family's enforced denial, I was now both permitted and obliged to remember it, and to write it, the way it happened. I was made able to name Tim among those by whom his mother was predeceased.

My new narrative recounts my husband's bleeding to death at the age of twenty-eight. It tells how, thirty years later, when Tim was dead longer than he'd been alive, I returned to Ghana and, unannounced, was welcomed back to the town of Wenchi by the same Chief and Queen-Mother as had received us just three days before Tim ended his life. At last able to reconnect with those whose own lives had been haunted ever since by the mystery of the unresolved death of their foreign guest, I was given access to the depth of my shame at not having come sooner.

With the example of Bert Bigelow's long life of remarkable service to the unrelenting values that he acquired the hard way, there is a lesson. Turning violence into nonviolence is another way of saying that, by embracing sorrow, and in refusing the easier option of denial, a greater opportunity is created: the transformation of grief into love.

MIXED MARRIAGE

Ours was a mixed marriage between the Fifties and the Sixties, so we weren't just "engaged" but *engaged*. But you wouldn't have learned from the four paragraph notice in *The New York Times* – "Parents Reveal Betrothal of Miss Marshall" – that, while identified as a debutante, twice, I had recently returned from that post-college year spent mostly in Asia and Africa.

I was "presently employed at the Japanese Consulate in New York" while my future husband, Timothy Lee Buxton, was identified as having been awarded a Rockefeller Fellowship to Union Theological Seminary. ("At present he is in his second year of graduate work at the seminary.") It didn't mention that Tim was a voting rights activist counseling the troubled consciences of boys in the process of becoming draft dodgers. Nor that his parents' addresses, "Dr. and Mrs. C. Lee Buxton of New York and New Haven, Conn." signified the end of their marriage.

The *Times* might have referenced Dr. Buxton as the physician in the *Griswold v. Connecticut* Supreme Court case whose recent 7-2 ruling made physician-prescribed contraception legal in the United States, but couldn't have known that he was *presently* a patient at the Bloomingdale Asylum to treat his self-diagnosed "nervous collapse." The announcement stated "The wedding is planned for Dec. 30," a date just seven weeks later. Back in 1966 the timing might have implied that I was pregnant, although the rush was only to qualify for Union's married student housing. A studio apartment was suddenly free in the new yellow brick building on Riverside Drive, overlooking Grant's Tomb.

While I was away Tim and I had come to know each other more deeply by the old-fashioned means of letter writing. My searching letters to Tim and his in return were the anchor-lines that held us securely. Even on the other side of the world I wasn't immune to the infectious enthusiasm that got Tim elected as that year's class president. His competitive drive was embedded in the fun he was having, and generating, whether in the classroom or on the tennis court. Within his family he was a devoted big brother, including, if necessary, to his own troubled father.

Having attended the *Griswold v. Connecticut* arguments before the U.S. Supreme Court, I thought of Tim's father as a superhero. And yet, Tim's letters reported Lee's having recruited him into the intimacies – *Oversexed v. Frigid* – of his parents' unhappy marriage, and his breakdown when Helen left him.

By the coincidence of my mother's close friendship with Helen's sister Phoebe, when my brother and I were kids our family was invited for an extended visit to Hill Top Farm. It was a hellish day's drive from New York back then, so it felt like heaven to get there and run around the vast property, trailing behind our friends and their cousins. Tim was the oldest of the nine grandchildren but had been sent off to tennis camp instead of enjoying Hill Top's camp-like activities supervised by his exuberant aunts. It was in this advantaged context that we and our parents were introduced to the rest of the gregarious Buxton family, and why I felt when Tim and I met that I already knew him. It felt familiar, too, when the next day Tim drove me from my college town near Boston to The Farm that I hadn't known was nearby, for a visit with his Aunt Lyd. The reversal of fortune wasn't acknowledged as we sat at her kitchen table in the former cook's house, and when afterwards she and Tim played a medley of show tunes on the grand piano that crowded the small living room, I was enchanted. My mother saved the note Lydia wrote to her to report that, during our impromptu supper, Tim was "stealing sideways glances" at me.

But in those seven weeks leading up to our wedding my mother expressed her concern about Tim's father's condition being hereditary. I'm not sure how much my parents knew (or from what source) about Lee's prolonged stay in this famous nearby psychiatric hospital, but I chose to dismiss their discomfort about Tim and his prospects – that is, their fears for me and mine – as precisely the political and social conservatism that Tim was gently helping me to outgrow. Yes, I too was sometimes intimidated by the close father-son bond that made my parents uneasy. The intensity of their dialogue at the dinner table was as if they spoke a coded language. And though Tim expressed no desire to study science and had no discernible aptitude, it was nevertheless assumed – by his wanting to heal political wounds – that he would eventually become a doctor like his father.

Still, charisma wasn't a contagious disease. I believed, and argued, that Lee's volatile example provided ample negative reinforcement for Tim. Exactly because of Tim's intimate knowledge of his father's acute condition, I was confident he would surely never let that happen to him.

The previous March, while I was in Africa imagining joining the Peace Corps, Lee wrote in a letter to Tim:

> That was a great visit yesterday. We really covered a lot of ground and, incidentally, found out a lot about each other. I wish you'd go ahead and marry Alexa – after all, why bother to wait. You'd be a lot happier + so would she. I hope you don't worry about this nervous collapse being hereditary, because one can be sure it isn't. It's environmental and I hope none of you get caught up in a combination of things the way I did.

In needing to provide an answer to my mother's worry about the impact on Tim of Lee's chronic instability, wasn't Lee's own reassurance definitive? No matter what, on the *Heredity v. Environment* argument, wasn't he the doctor?

In fact, Tim did "get caught up in a combination of things" the way his father did. Similarly, Tim's own personality's persuasive enthusiasm combined with a darker dread, a misleadingly thin membrane over an intelligence that couldn't keep up with itself. I watched Tim strive, without grasping that his ambition was a fear of failure.

But, ah, what energy! Of course he could be nearly impossible to keep up with, which I learned at the top of Aspen Mountain on the first morning of our honeymoon when I saw the signpost for "Ruthie's Run" and recognized it from the *Sports Illustrated* list of America's Ten Best Ski Runs.

Not even my dancer's legs could sustain me in my crisis of faith – in him and in myself – as I struggled against my urge to refuse to race him through those celebrated corkscrew turns. And yet I loved following Tim down that mountain and being challenged to stay with him, and succeeding.

The weather that week was bitter cold, but at our inn at the base we generated plenty of heat. By a roaring fire in the lobby I remember Tim sitting with that week's *TIME* magazine, its black and white cover proclaiming GOD IS DEAD in reference to the very theologians Tim was studying at Union. The argument didn't impact me, but neither was I bothered by that. It still seemed normal back then for men to pursue cosmic concerns, and for women not to.

Our *Times* wedding announcement included the piously still-life Bachrach studio portrait of me in the long slim silk dress hastily crafted from the ivory kimono fabric that was a gift during my time in Japan. My father never talked about his wartime enemy, but during his service as a naval officer in the "Pacific Theater" my pregnant mother left their Upper East Side apartment for her childhood home on East State Street in the Pennsylvania coal and steel town where my parents were born. Though they had grown up in the permanent shade of the Great Depression, they were the relatively secure daughter and son of Sharon's banker and surgeon. I was fifteen months old when I met my father for the first time – so, yes, I look hesitant in that photo with him in his dress uniform – and can only imagine the loss to me of my cozy world when my parents moved back to New York. That is, I regard myself as a New Yorker, but I am stamped by the basic hometown values on which my parents were raised.

My father had been recruited out of law school to the world-famous firm Cravath, Swaine + Moore, to which he returned after the war's interruption and came to be regarded as its most stubbornly diligent worker. My lonely mother told me that when they were newly married she'd head downtown to Grand Central Station, where, under the vaulted turquoise ceiling with its gold-etched constellations, from the marble staircase balcony she would survey the bustling travelers as they crisscrossed the rotunda, imagining the lives they came from and/or where they were going.

Her acute self-doubt was justified, but with the birth of my brother and our move to the city's nearest suburb, her life as a homemaker undercut her ambitions rather than freeing her to explore them. With our upgrade to a grander house with an attic apartment for a live-in housekeeper, the compensatory rewards of my mother's consuming volunteer work looked limited, no matter how worthy the causes. Throughout the years of my bratty adolescence her chief asset remained her remarkably durable sense of humor, no thanks to me. But every time my dad's secretary called to say he wasn't going to make it home for dinner, she poured herself another tumbler of the J&B scotch that came, like our milk, in half-gallon bottles.

Our cultural life was curated by the Book of the Month Club and those who assembled the *TIME-LIFE* series of classical and semiclassical albums. But I saw all the hit Broadway musicals, graduating to Leonard Bernstein's theatrical "Young People's Concerts" when I was fourteen. I couldn't consider myself rebellious when my little brother's mischief-making escalated into the petty crimes for which he was later punished with enrollment at The Choate School – "Willy needs a father figure!" – where things only got worse. An early instance of his bad-boy behavior occurred at age six when, while I was sitting for my half of the pair of pastel portraits of us that my mom had commissioned, my brother pocketed the artist's gold watch.

Jay Hyde Barnum was a children's book illustrator who had asked me to pose for several little girls in a book published that year called *Pierre Comes to P.S. 20*, so my pride turned to humiliation when he phoned my mom after our sitting to report his watch missing. At first denying having stolen the watch, Willy finally gave in and led us to a spot in the yard where he'd buried the evidence. I remember feeling frightened as much by my mother's rage as by my brother's crime, a dynamic that became all too familiar. And, predictably, because I was unable to sympathize with my mother's incapacity as a single parent with no clue how to help my struggling brother, I idealized my father's devotion to his work as the top of the corporate law pyramid. Given the power disparity in their roles, it was a no-brainer to choose his over hers.

At our Formica kitchen table on one of those nights when it was just us two, Mom admitted that she could not have considered boarding school for me because she knew that, once I got out the door, I'd be gone. I would often use the excuse of homework to escape these conversations, but that time I stayed because we both knew she was right. Although I wanted her to be happier in her own life and shared her aching for a deeper connection with me, her frustration was a free-floating burden that neither of us knew how to address. I resembled my father except for being short, like her, so she taught me by example to stand up straight and look taller. This worked so well that, in seventh grade at my new all-girls private school where I was a day student, when I discovered the modern dance program offered as an alternative to gym, I already carried myself like a dancer.

It was love at first sight. My teacher noticed my "Buddha-like" pliés and, even as a beginner, she encouraged me to audition for the Dance Club. She commuted the short distance to Dobbs Ferry from the city, where she performed with a small dance company whose posters decorated her office. Miss Clifford showed me how choreographing a dance was like any other assignment: you get an idea and find a way to express it.

One year our spring concert's theme drew on the popular book of captioned photographs called *The Family of Man*, and instead of one of the upbeat choices I choreographed a solo from the stark image captioned "I Am Alone with the Beating of My Heart." My score was a recording of the whooshing sound of an actual heartbeat, a choice that sounded spooky but was inspired because that pulse illustrated the contraction and release of the spine to which my arms and legs were attached and moved as extensions. My performance was followed by the silence that can either signal success or failure, an ambiguity my mother reported as having been reinforced at Intermission by the other mothers' attempts to console her. Did my being alone with the beating of my heart mean I was brokenhearted?

I was a year younger than most of my class and wasn't as ready for college as they were, but because my mother's own college ambitions had been thwarted by the Depression, she needed me to proceed on schedule, and so I did. I shouted "Then *you* go!" as I sent in my application to Wheaton College, which my dad's sister had attended for only nine days and left because she was homesick. I wanted the time to Find Myself, as my indulged generation put it to our parents who didn't have that luxury.

Perversely, when in that spring of my senior year I wrote an English paper about *1984* and *Brave New World* I realized, too late, that I was a good student and ready to learn after all. At Wheaton I also discovered a very good dance department, plus the New England Conservatory in nearby Boston for master classes, so I had what I needed. I majored in French because it had fewer requirements than English and gave me more time in the dance studio, but, more, because of my summer job after freshman year as an *au pair* in Paris. I fell in love with the language in the form of a boy with the romantic name of Jean-Loup Valentin. Initiated by his French kisses, we corresponded during the academic interval of my sophomore year, when I learned how to be passionate on paper in order to make absence its own form of presence. I also contrived a way to return to another job in France, to him, for consecutive summer romances.

Three years earlier, at fifteen, I'd been given the gift of "The Grand Tour" with my best friend Jean, by her world-traveler parents. From Ancient Greece to Byzantium to the European Renaissance I experienced the world's wonders: Delphi, Hagia Sophia, the Sistine Chapel. My travel diary details the exotic ingredients of our daily meals as we made our way from the Parthenon to the Eiffel Tower, from *moussaka* to *Crêpes Suzette*. On this journey I intuited the circular definition of wanderlust according to Henry Adams, as I would later discover in his memoir *The Education of Henry Adams*: "The habit of expression leads to the search for something to express."

During my travels in East Africa on my round-the-world ticket I'd visited Tim's boyhood buddy in the town in the southwest corner of Uganda where Waldie served as a Peace Corps Volunteer. He remembers from our conversations my earnest desire to define my future, while my own memory is clear that I wanted to do exactly what he was doing. One night I was riding on the back of Waldie's motorcycle on the 100-kilometer route from the larger town of Mbarara back to Rukungiri. When the headlight failed, we sat by the side of the road in the utter darkness, finally lying in the red clay gutter to wait until dawn. A lioness was rumored to have killed someone in the vicinity, which Waldie gently told me to account for our need to stay awake. The compensation for me was in looking up into the wide universe of more stars even than van Gogh had painted with his mad "Starry Night" vision. Whether innocent or ignorant in my trust, my discovery was that I lacked fear. No rescuer came along the empty road that night, but neither did the lioness.

This experience was a version of the one I'd had a month earlier, in broad daylight, a thousand kilometers to the east in the newly named East African country of Tanzania. Inside the volcanic Ngorongoro Crater lived the highest densities of lion prides on earth, and migrating herds of zebras and wildebeests streamed across that expanse. Back then a safari was less hyped than today, so when the guide casually delivered a cheetah outrunning our Jeep to bring down a gazelle, we foreign tourists were put in our place in the food chain. It was exhilarating, but that's not what I'm referring to as the parallel moment of clarity to that starry night.

It was at the nearby Olduvai Gorge in the Great Rift Valley where, just five years before, the paleoanthropologists Louis and Mary Leakey had found a skull and the hand and foot bones of what they called a twelve-year-old girl. In heralding the discovery, the National Geographic Society had brought the news to the attention of its subscribers, and there I stood, nearly two million years later, another girl, a descendant. At the center of our human universe I felt the same comprehensive calm as under that canopy of stars. It's as close as I've ever come to religion.

So my restlessness wasn't altogether quieted by my extended travels during that year, but I was also glad to return to Tim. His year was made difficult by his father's hospitalization at the Bloomingdale Asylum in nearby White Plains, where Tim visited him twice-weekly. In a letter from there dated December 18, 1965, six months after the Supreme Court victory, Lee wrote to Tim:

> I fainted (not really lost consciousness I don't think) in the living room + dining room yesterday + now I'm confined to my room. Not a bad idea when you look over the clientele here – however that's not what I'm writing about. [He then details the "expanding subdural hematoma they'll have to drain," but isn't concerned.] No, what I'm worried about is that damned intentional polyp. I'm terribly anxious to get it operated on because, frankly, I don't want them to find a malignancy in it, to say nothing about the fact that this kind of post-op care is so messy. Aren't human beings absolutely incredible! Here

on one Sat. night I try to commit suicide + and on the next want to stay alive.

Lee was still there three months later when, in a letter that is heartbreakingly parental in tone, Tim wrote to his father:

> We think one helluva lot of you Doc + by God we're pulling for you. But <u>Please Never</u> forget that our love is not based on your success but on your concern + dedication to us – to caring, to being yourself – Please <u>never be afraid</u> in the next 40 years of your life, of being yourself – not a super man!! Love, Tim

It was later that month, while I was in Uganda, that Lee's letter said "I wish you'd go ahead and marry Alexa" and "I hope you won't worry about this nervous collapse being hereditary, because one can be sure it isn't."

Lee's long recovery was still ongoing when we married that next December, but his absence likely made it easier for Helen, if harder for Tim. The wedding reception took place at our country club in the former mansion of Frank Jay Gould, son of the notorious Gilded Age robber baron, Jay Gould, who was a founding member of what was then called The Ardsley Casino. As we came from the church a sudden heavy snowfall made it difficult to navigate that steep driveway, but everything else went according to plan, notwithstanding that the planning competed with Christmas week, which was normally my mother's favorite time of the year.

We settled into our studio apartment on a fold-out couch, and I went back to my job at the Japanese Consulate, devoting my long subway commute to dutifully scouring the glossy women's magazines for the casserole recipes they featured. At the end of that semester we headed to California, where Tim paused his seminary studies to take an intern year position as assistant to the popular Dean of Stanford's Memorial Church. In that year of student protests spreading across the country from Columbia to the University of Michigan to Berkeley, Dean B. Davie Napier preached up a storm, and the pews of "Mem Chu" were filled to capacity by students and faculty who, together, increasingly turned against the law-and-order university administration.

I had been hired as the "resident assistant" to the Director of the Bechtel International Center, a job that came with a sunny apartment in the Mediterranean-style villa at the heart of the Stanford campus. Every morning I would open the doors to the California sunshine and plug in the first of the 75-cup pots of coffee that I kept fresh all day for the foreign students who came by for the nonstop programming as well as for ping pong. An informal international food festival developed when I proposed that they write home for the recipes of the foods they missed most. Region by region, it was a way to demonstrate common origins among ethnicities at war with each other.

One afternoon a middle-aged visitor staying in the I-Center's guest room timidly knocked on the door to our apartment to ask if I had an iron so she could press the beautiful multicolored ceremonial dress that was wrinkled from her long travels. I set up the ironing board and we conversed over tea while she stood to press the delicate fabric. She'd come to Stanford to attend an institute on education, and I learned that back in Samoa she was the director of a teachers' college. When she then made reference to her husband and I asked what he did, she replied, "He's the King."

One of our students started a foreign film series in the I-Center's atrium, and he became a campus celebrity when he ran for student body president as a self-described one-armed Italian Communist. Giulio Cesare won the election over a topless dancer named Vikki Drake, whose campaign posters all disappeared within minutes because they featured her extracurricular work at an East Palo Alto strip joint. Since just two years earlier the activist David Harris won his own election for student body president – his power enhanced by that of his wife, Joan Baez – the contest between Giulio and Vikki provided comic relief, especially in light of the ongoing protests against the Vietnam War that provoked the Stanford administration to further alienate the students and faculty with its actions. The more press-worthy clashes took place up the Bay in Oakland – and we joined those crowds of demonstrators too – as, week by week, President Johnson's prospects for reelection grew weaker.

At Memorial Church the Dean was asked to perform the wedding of a freshman student named Peggy Rusk, the daughter of LBJ's Secretary of State, Dean Rusk, then an object of fierce antiwar protest. Just three months after the *Loving v. Virginia* Supreme Court decision legalized interracial marriage, Peggy was marrying a "Negro." Rusk refused to walk his daughter down the aisle that day, but the marriage endured for the next forty-four years, until Guy Smith's death.

Then on March 31st came LBJ's announcement that he would neither seek nor accept the Democratic nomination, which was the lead story for just four more days, until the murder of Dr. Martin Luther King Jr. eclipsed everything. That spring Tim taught an extracurricular course at Mem Chu called "Seminar in Black and White," assigning for discussion Claude Brown's *Manchild in the Promised Land* and Eldridge Cleaver's *Soul on Ice*. Cleaver was a jailed member of the Black Panther Party in Oakland who wrote, "From my prison cell, I have watched America slowly coming awake." He described the nonviolent movement that Tim had joined in Selma as a step toward the violence that Cleaver came to see as necessary.

At the same time, Cesar Chavez enlightened the country to the economic injustice suffered by migrant workers by leading the California grape boycott. Chavez was on a hunger strike that he ended after nearly a month by breaking bread with Bobby Kennedy at his side, wearing the emblem of the National Farm Workers Association. Chavez refocused the struggle between violence and nonviolence with this statement: "I am convinced that the truest act of courage, the strongest act of manliness, is to sacrifice ourselves for others in a totally nonviolent struggle for justice." The Central Valley was another point of resistance against injustice, another way to honor Dr. King's values.

But then California's Primary Day came just twelve weeks later. We watched Kennedy's victory speech and headed to bed not knowing that, in a few minutes, our candidate for president would be mortally wounded, that dream yet another nightmare. It seemed appropriate, while being awful, that the Democratic Convention held in Chicago that August saw blood in the streets.

After that year of full engagement it was hard to leave California, but we drove back to New York, where Tim finished his last year at Union and I got a Masters in French from Columbia's Teachers College. I'd forfeited my passion for dance, unable to prioritize that demanding discipline in the twenty-two months of my marriage. In Kyoto I'd studied Classical Japanese Dance long enough for my teacher to put me into a public recital, but that fixed form of dance was isometric exercise compared to Martha Graham's exacting technique. Perhaps I'd been convinced by my dad, in our only "what I want to be when I grow up" conversation, that I should pursue "something you can go back to once your kids get to be school-aged." At the time my father's ever practical advice sounded sensible and even somewhat progressive, compared to the alternative of being a stay-at-home mom forever. The liberation was coming, but not soon enough.

Tim's father was healthy again and, back at Yale, he had surprised us with his sudden announcement that he was getting married. The divorce that precipitated his collapse had yielded a romance with a woman whose first husband, also a doctor, was killed by a swarm of bees while clearing a roof gutter at their home. Her four bereft children were wary of their mother's whirlwind courtship and remarriage, but Tim and I flew in from Stanford for the joyous wedding weekend, and were optimistic. By the time of our return east it was clear that, while Lee Buxton was indeed a charmer, as a father and stepfather of eight he was doomed to fail. Tim's siblings had always felt that Lee was only ever interested in parenting Tim anyway, and when his second son flagrantly took up with his beautiful new stepsister, Lee retreated to the vodka bottles he hid in the basement.

In spite of Tim's earnest coaching, he could see by Lee's self-medicating that his father was sliding toward another collapse. Intervening once again on his own behalf, this time Lee checked himself into Tompkins One, the psychiatric ward of his own Yale New Haven Hospital. During an urgent family therapy session intended for crafting a workable plan for Lee's release, Tim and I were present for a stunning reversal. Like a door on a hinge, the psychodynamic shifted, and in a resolution that defies logic – not to mention the Hippocratic Oath to do no harm – at the end of that meeting, a second family member also became a resident there.

Only four years earlier, in 1965, Lee had been profiled in the *New York Times* in a prominent "Man in the News" feature to accompany its extensive coverage of the *Griswold v. Connecticut* Supreme Court ruling. Under the headline "Gentle Crusader" the story was told about how Dr. C. Lee Buxton, Chief of OB/GYN at Yale and the medical director of Planned Parenthood's New Haven clinic, provoked his voluntary arrest by providing birth control to married women, in deliberate violation of an ancient Connecticut statute known as the Barnum Act of 1879.

This law was named for the circus entrepreneur PT Barnum, who began his career in 1835 with the $1000 purchase of a slave woman named Joice Heth. Barnum began exhibiting her in sideshows around the country by promoting her as the 161-year-old former nurse to George Washington. Soon she was earning him $1500 a week. Barnum became a politician and later served multiple terms in the Connecticut state legislature. The law enacted as the Barnum Act stated that "any person who uses any drug, medicinal article or instrument for the purposes of preventing conception shall be fined not less than forty dollars or imprisoned not less than sixty days," further finding that "any person who assists, abets, counsels, causes, hires or commands any offense may be prosecuted and punished as if he were the principal offender."

It was the violation of this law for which Dr. Buxton and Estelle Griswold, the medical and executive directors of the Planned Parenthood League of Connecticut, were arrested and fined. Found guilty as accessories, when their conviction was upheld by the Connecticut Superior Court, their lawyer Catherine Roraback appealed to the U.S. Supreme Court, which heard the "right to privacy" case on March 29-30 of 1965.

When the Supreme Court handed down its 7-2 decision in June, Dr. Buxton said to the press, "All doctors in Connecticut may now prescribe child spacing techniques to married women when it is medically indicated." And while this victory for women and their physicians certainly represented a great advance over the criminalizing Barnum Act, as I sat with the defendant's family and listened to the oral arguments in the great chamber of the U.S. Supreme Court, I was aware of myself as Tim's twenty-one-year-old girlfriend for whom, as a New Yorker, access to contraception was easy.

Honored for his patient care and research on infertility, Lee's most recent book was called A *Study of the Psychophysical Methods for Relief of Childbirth Pain*, providing alternative means of relieving "pain and sorrow" during childbirth. His was a bold argument against both Freud and the Catholic Church – for what he termed a harmful straining to find the pain beneficial – in favor of the new practices he'd observed in clinics, mainly in Europe, that met Lee's goal of providing "sympathetic obstetrical care." He believed "the psychological advantages seem to be such that some type of psychophysical preparation techniques should become a permanent aspect of obstetrical care." He didn't live to see Natural Childbirth realized in America, but he envisioned it.

In the summer of 1967, Tim and I had been married six months when Lee presented me with a copy of his book, signed "Doc" and inscribed "To Alexa Buxton with love and anticipation of someday being assisted by her into the state of grandfatherhood." It would be another three years before Tim and I reached that "someday" decision, but in that moment with Lee I felt the same love and anticipation.

It was just two weeks after Lee's release from the hospital that he suddenly developed severe systemic health complications. Tim was summoned to New Haven and was by Lee's bedside, at home, when his father died. After these years of marital turbulence and the consequent collapses despite the pioneering career for which he'd been justly celebrated, Lee's unexpected death at age sixty-five was a jolt.

When Tim phoned with the news I taxied across town in the middle of that night to be with Helen, and witnessed the only open grief I ever saw her express. At nineteen she'd dropped out of Bennington to marry Lee, age thirty-four. Following the loss of their first child, Kitty, Helen had raised their subsequent four children as a full-time mother. Now that after her divorce she was enjoying the first independence of her life, at age fifty, with her own apartment and a job as the receptionist in a Manhattan doctor's office, she let me see the cost of those years with a man who was both heroic and antiheroic.

She had left Lee because she felt they were "destroying" each other, a bitter conflict that Tim was recruited to mediate. I never witnessed their struggles, but Tim's sister later told me that their troubled marriage had begun inauspiciously, when, as the newlyweds drove off after their wedding, Lee pulled off the matching hat to Helen's "going-away" outfit and tossed it out the car window, pronouncing, "That's that."

At some point during the overnight after Lee's death, as we were sitting together in her living room, Helen pulled a Bible from her bookshelf to show me her list of the readings and hymns she'd chosen for her own funeral service. I felt more than a little uncomfortable in being invited to imagine her death, but I recognized her need to both grapple with and deflect the end of Lee's life. I said I'd tell Tim where to find these instructions. It would have been absurd even to contemplate the possibility that she would live for another forty-two years while Tim would die exactly one year later.

But then, because it was Helen's nature to reject unhappy thoughts, she reached for her souvenir from a recent trip to the Soviet Union, the set of painted wooden dolls nesting one inside the other in diminishing sizes, pretty women wearing gaily patterned headscarves. She was animated in describing the Russian film version of *The Brothers Karamzov* that was nominated for that year's Academy Award for Best Foreign Film. The travel adventure seemed to symbolize her newfound, hard-won freedom, so she was seeing through the Iron Curtain's current political leader, Leonid Brezhnev, to a romanticized version of what had existed under the Tsars. She had loved her time in Moscow and St. Petersburg so thoroughly that she asked me if, when Tim and I had children, they would call her *Babushka*, the Russian word for Grandmother. Helen's beautiful bright blue eyes sparkled in anticipation of that happy day. Of course I agreed.

Tim eulogized Lee in a service at Yale's Battell Chapel, and his ashes were buried in a prominent place in the Grove Street Cemetery established in 1796 as the New Haven Burying Ground. That July date was the day when, a year later, Tim lamented that he would never play tennis again and asked, if I were pregnant, if I'd get an abortion.

While at Union Tim was inspired by Yale's Bill Coffin and Stanford's Davie Napier to imagine himself an activist college chaplain like them. He knew Bill began his campus ministry at Andover, the brother school to Phillips Exeter Academy, and I assume this played into Tim's accepting the invitation to expand Exeter's three-man religion faculty. Tim was joining his new friend Chris Brookfield, along with a worldly Dominican priest named Dan Morrissey (recently come to Exeter from Paris at the urging of Ambassador Sargent Shriver) and the conventional Episcopalian school minister, Ted Gleason, whose open home attracted a cadre of forty "deacons" to engage with social justice concerns by way of a "peace and love" liturgy that was typical for the mid-Sixties. In the language of such hyper-entitled institutions, Tim was pronounced a good fit.

With my own fresh degree from Columbia I applied for a job in the Academy's French department, but I was told during my interview, conducted in French, that school policy prohibited hiring a teacher's wife because this would skew the voting in faculty meetings. Instead, I filled a vacancy at the Exeter Area Junior High School and taught French I, II, and III to 125 students in back to back classes. This was Exeter's final year as an all-boys school before its reluctant faculty was forced to succumb to coeducation. Tim reported being regularly unsettled during those faculty meetings by the grudging complaints that bringing girls to campus meant having to install bathtubs and extra electrical outlets for their hairdryers.

I quickly came to see that elite world from the perspective of the misfits, the troubled boys sent too far away too young. They reminded me of my own brother Willy (who became Bill at Choate and resumed Will with his escape to Colorado) on whose behalf my mother felt justified in writing a scathing letter to Choate's headmaster, Rev. Seymour St. John, accusing him of "wanton cruelty" for crushing her son's already fragile self-confidence. I respected Exeter's principled principal, but I worried about the Exeter boys who fell short of the Scholar/Athlete ideal, some of whom coped heroically in their efforts to meet the Academy's demands. They didn't know me except as a faculty wife who baked cookies for them.

Compared to Tim's team-taught seminars around the oval Harkness Table for which the Academy was prized, my days were a blur of improvisation. According to the Direct Method theory of language learning that I'd been taught, my students would learn French by osmosis. The threshold of my classroom was like a border crossing where, on the other side, we all assumed new identities. I encouraged my students to give themselves French names, giving me 125 additional names to learn, and tried hard to embody the enlightened new methodology. I had no idea if it was working, until one day in late October when a student stopped me out in the corridor where he could ask his question in English. He was still wondering, "What's this *je suis?*"

"What's this *I am?*" was my question too, and I didn't have the language to answer it either. So the following Monday I started over with all my classes – "Hello out there!" – and from then on we all had an easier time, and a lot more fun.

I managed to keep up my hectic pace, which that fall included helping

Tim plan for his ordination to the Congregational ministry, a joyous ceremony featuring the gospel hymn "Oh Happy Day" and bouquets of the balloons that had become a feature of liberal religion. Tim's devotion to the father he'd recently lost was the subject of his ordination statement, but the liturgy was an authentic celebration.

In a pained letter aimed at resolving the hurt caused by his skipping out during the ordination, Tim's brother admitted, "I do not understand a great deal about us and myself. It's both tiring and scary." He himself was an artist, but he was conscientiously trying to honor Tim's desire to be ordained while being just as earnestly mystified by why anyone would choose such a path. In this same letter written seven months before Tim's death, Tim's brother reported on a kitchen table conversation that he and I had on that ordination day. He wrote: "She is very happy + loves you + loves being your wife."

I cling to this testimony because I know it to be altogether true. And yet, in this confined prep school world, I missed the larger lives Tim and I had enjoyed in both California and New York, the "cultural exchange" that was intrinsic. In our attic faculty apartment, the door next to Tim's study opened onto a dormitory hallway. We'd cheerfully painted its four rooms ourselves when the Academy declined to, but I graded my papers at that kitchen table. Tim's Christmas vacation began a full week before mine, and while the inequality of our roles went without saying, why was I the one staggering up those four flights with a tree and the dry cleaning and two bags of groceries? I'd stopped at the State Liquor Store to buy a bottle that I set down on the top granite step just wrong – the bottom cracked and its contents drained down the stairwell – so I wasn't in the holiday mood to arrive home to find Tim entertaining two advisees who had already had time to go home for vacation and get kicked out again.

When spring finally came to New Hampshire, so did the inaugural national Earth Day on April 22, an environmental protection initiative that Exeter faculty and students viewed as a teaching opportunity and energetically embraced. The campus was again mobilized two weeks later, when on May 4 at Kent State University, students protesting the escalation of the war against Vietnam with the invasion of Cambodia were fired upon by the Ohio National Guard, killing four and wounding nine others.

Phillips Church was at the center of the response at first to Earth Day and then to the national outrage sparked by the Kent State violence against the student demonstrators. There were teach-ins and calls for justice, and as was true in the Civil Rights movement, the religion department became a recruitment center for political action.

During these same weeks, the campus was visited by Rev. Dr. James H. Robinson, who was promoting Operation Crossroads Africa, a program he had founded in 1958 and which President Kennedy later credited as "the progenitor of the Peace Corps." The premise behind Crossroads was more specific, however. Dr. Robinson was the grandson of a slave, and his explicit goal was to bring an interracial group of American and Canadian college student volunteers to Africa in order for all to experience a reversal of the First World's majority/minority race structure. The lesson in this opportunity resonated with me because, in Asia and Africa, on my own, I'd already learned there's no better way to be taught Civil Rights.

Serving Dr. Robinson lunch on our barely used wedding china at our narrow secondhand refectory table, as he described the projects planned for that summer to build with the help of local counterparts a community center or housing or a medical clinic, I felt recruited. I thought of Tim's good friend Waldie and the rewards he both gave and gained as a teacher in Uganda, and how, as a guest in Rukungiri, I'd imagined applying for Peace Corps service. When I asked Dr. Robinson if it might be possible for a married couple to be co-leaders for Crossroads, and he said it might be, I saw how much I wanted that eight-week journey into the unfamiliar. The unfamiliar was what, on my previous travels, I'd already learned to test, and trust.

After our lunch with Dr. Robinson I constructed reasons why Tim should want to go to Africa. I talked about the legacy of Dr. King and how Crossroads was an expression of those values to which Tim was already committed. He'd only been to the British Isles and Western Europe, so I described the wide-open sky and its horizons. I told him about the thousands of migrating animals I'd seen cross the Serengeti Plain, as if they roamed the entire continent. He'd given himself a Pentax, and in the past year in New York spent many hours at the Bronx Zoo making striking black-and-white animal portraits that carefully excluded evidence of their captivity. "They'll be free!" I made him this promise, sweeping my arm around our living room decorated with his framed prints. Like a tour guide I said, "You'll see!" and urged, "Trust me!"

The prospect of Crossroads got me through the daily demands of being a faculty wife with a teaching job in a world that bore no resemblance to Tim's. Having followed him to and from California, wasn't I now giving him a life-changing experience? Wouldn't we both profit?

In spontaneously asking Dr. Robinson about co-leading a Crossroads group, I didn't realize it was already assumed by Tim's colleagues that he would teach in Exeter's summer school program. Now that we were married, it didn't occur to us to spend a summer apart, so Tim sent in his Crossroads application while keeping that teaching option open in case Crossroads didn't work out. I never doubted the outcome. Weren't we the perfect team? Tim's Civil Rights activism surely met the aims of Crossroads, and my travels and work at Stanford's International Center were qualifications beyond the fact that, as Dr. Robinson noted at our lunch, I was more than able to cope with an assignment to a Francophone country. It gave me hope to think that, as a break from this world where Tim had already proved himself indispensable, we could venture out.

Still, the application process was demanding. I wouldn't know until reading Tim's orphaned journal after his death that he'd felt "nervous" about the day of interviews at the Crossroads office in New York. My own un-ambivalent experience highlighted the dinner held that night, a warm gathering with the other potential leaders that took place in an apartment furnished with museum-like glass cases containing exquisite examples of African sculpture. This collection was curated by Susan Vogel, the art historian wife of Jerry Vogel, who was the deputy director of Crossroads. We sat in small groups and ate groundnut stew – peanut soup – the staple dish of West Africa. This meal struck me and a number of the others, including some returned Peace Corps Volunteers, as the next best thing to being there.

Between the end of the school year and the start of Crossroads, we went to Maine's Monhegan Island, where Tim was invited to preside over a wedding. The guests were an assembly of artists, the most prominent among them Jamie Wyeth, who made his dramatic entrance from a motorized cart, carrying his wife in his arms, her pale blue sundress trailing to cover her paralyzed legs.

Tim wore a purple necktie he'd bought for the occasion of this first chance to put into words his own definition of marriage:

> May you enjoy each other's company, forgive each other's faults, love and cherish each other through all times and occasions. Whatever befalls you, think of it together, share each other's interests, agree with appreciation and disagree with tolerant understanding. Always strive to keep alive the glow of great adventure. To you will come sunshine and shadow, times together and apart, joys and sorrows, privileges and obligations, but through them all may a larger and richer life be yours.

In pronouncing the couple husband and wife, Tim exhorted:

> Go forth now together into the world with the care and love and joy of all of us. Sanctify all life through your immediate lives. In your special ways make life whole, and through the example of your love, heal this broken world.

He'd glued these words into a little typed booklet that I would later discover tucked inside a back pocket of the generic spiral notebook he brought to Ghana. The wedding took place on June 20, in a living room overlooking the open water where the lobstermen who were guests along with the artists sunk heavy wooden traps to fish out a living. It was an Exeter connection that had prompted this invitation to Tim to feel free to tinker boldly with the ancient language of wedding ritual.

The ceremony Tim wrote doesn't mention "the gift of children," but our own planning included the decision for me to stop taking the birth control pill that had been my daily companion for longer than we'd been together. If after three and a half years "it was time" for us to have children, I conceded that there were worse places to raise them than on a campus where, for the other half of the year when the students weren't there, the faculty kids had the run of the place. A number of these boys and girls were in my own classes in the public school, but unlike the sons and daughters of those affiliated with Pease Air Force Base, the area's chief source of employment, I got the impression that the faculty kids were only marking time until they got old enough to move up. I couldn't exactly argue in those parent-teacher conferences that Exeter's French Department wasn't substantially better resourced than mine, since mine was just me.

Tim's plum-colored necktie was conservative, for him, whose tie collection became famous on campus as a way to mediate the student rebellion against the Academy's dress code. The faculty couldn't seem to cope with a lowering of that standard while preparing for coeducation, so Tim's solution was to gather ugly neckties from thrift shops. He wore a new one every day, and the boys followed suit. The necktie rule remained in place, but Tim provided a way to abide by the letter of the law while violating its spirit.

I was flattered when in my school principal's letter of recommendation for my Crossroads application, Frank Kozaka wrote, "Mrs. Buxton has an inner core of toughness." I knew this was the truth because of how hard I worked to convince my middle school students to give French the chance it deserved to change their lives the way it had mine. Maybe it was my "inner core of toughness" that had carried me through my own pre-adolescence, but I could sense that they knew I understood they were at the utter mercy of their hormones. They were juvenile enough to play dress-up in acting out the dialogues we improvised in the classroom but sophisticated enough to try out their emerging language skills on our field trip to an authentic French *bistro* near Harvard Yard. I adored this about them.

"VIENS! VIENS!"

Our four-day Crossroads orientation began five days after the Mohegan wedding with a lecture about medical issues and money. Tim recorded in his journal "another funny-frightening account of what can go wrong with us – sample 15 of 19 in Sierra Leone got Malaria last summer." About managing our funds I noted that "they made Tim sign all the traveler's checks which doesn't seem fair but which is a relief since I trust him more than I trust myself with this type stuff." My own rationalizing contrasts with Tim's revelation that he felt "overwhelmed at what a leader is expected to do." His insecurity was reinforced the next day when the volunteers arrived. After our first meeting, a guy with relevant experience in Africa whose younger sister was assigned to us – by an awkward coincidence they were the son and daughter of the superstar President of Princeton, Tim's alma mater – took Tim aside to tell him he feared that Tim was "too heavy-handed." In Tim's clear desire to hold the group together and/or keep it from falling apart, he was trying too hard.

Tim wrote in his journal that this criticism "bowled me over," a reaction that surely undercut his confidence in the following day's "group formation" sensitivity training with professional facilitators guiding us through exercises about race. When "The shit began to fly!!!" Tim wrote that he became "especially depressed because the problem was indirectly a comment on my 'leadership' or at least on the concept of leadership."

But he also reported receiving the implied criticism as "a crucial lesson – Don't be too ponderous too soon!" – and credited me – "Lex said some beautiful things about independence and cooperation in marriage and in a group!" – with helping to address, and release, the tension. After adjourning, a game of Frisbee also seemed to serve its recreative purpose.

Throughout the orientation there were meetings with local Ghanaians who were both entertaining and informative about the customs of their culture. We learned about the universal meaning of names (such as that a female born on a Wednesday, like me, is named Akua) while being told at the same time that although the deposed leader Kwame Nkrumah's name represents a ninth child born on a Saturday, since he was actually an only child born on a Friday, he was probably just named for a friend. The flexibility of this formula was like adapting a recipe to incorporate available ingredients, and it resonated because of the way I'd been forced to transfer the skill of improvisation – a value in modern dance – to my French classroom. I was also intrigued and impressed to learn that the ancient Ashanti culture is matrilineal, and that a Queen-Mother has real power. As an American girl reflexively adhering to the dregs of Fifties assumptions in that summer of 1970, eighteen months before *MS.* Magazine's inaugural issue, I was balancing between two discrepant standards of behavior: assertive and submissive.

While Tim concealed the depth of his anxiety from me, I could see that he was preoccupied and discouraged. His journal analyzed the participants by searching for their strengths, but of our final leaders' meeting before heading to the airport, Tim wrote, again, that it was characterized by "incredible nonchalance – beginning late, fielding questions revealing how little leaders know about what they are to do."

At JFK airport we had what he experienced as "a long time of waiting – anticipating + it not coming or coming but never as expected – I've got to learn NOT to anticipate and to just roll with what happens." And when twelve hours later our plane touched down in Dakar for refueling, Tim noted, "Dakar itself was not what I expected – having heard that Dakar was a great cosmopolitan city I <u>anticipated</u> what the airport would be like + it was far more drab + modest – But for the group the <u>idea</u> of arriving was so special – cameras everywhere and shouts from Blacks about <u>We're home</u>. I felt strangely out of it – like I didn't have a part in <u>being home</u>."

My own note says simply: "It was neat arriving at Dakar, very dry + brown + Muslim looking."

We had been educated and motivated in a talk given by Willard Johnson, a charismatic Crossroads staff member about whom I wrote, "I am in awe of his ability to speak, his brilliance with words but his interjection of personality, humor, experience, dreams, scholarship." Willard was an African American who talked of the particular relationship of Blacks to Blacks. Tim described him as "a huge tall thin powerful-looking man with a hypnotic face and voice. He spoke of the Black man 'going home' + the whole notion of America and Africa – his last words – go to Africa, enjoy it, do what you are going there to do, but don't pollute Africa in the process." In speaking to the Black participants, I heard him addressing whites too. He said this relationship to Africa was also *possible* with whites.

During orientation our twin-bedded college dormitory room was a staging area for supplies – eight weeks worth of water-decontaminating tablets – and a stack of cartons for Willie Laast, our Ghanaian fixer, from Jerry Vogel, the Crossroads rep who would spend the summer traveling around the continent from project to project to keep things on track. We spent very little time in that room, clearly insufficient for either of us to know enough about what the other was feeling.

From the airport in Accra our Ghana I and II groups were brought by bus to the Ministry of Education Hostel, where men and women were directed to separate quarters. My journal for our first afternoon reports "slept talked relaxed" while Tim's account tells of a trip to the beach with one of our volunteers and two other guys. Without being warned against swimming in the Gulf of Guinea, Tim discovered, "the undertow was subtle and wicked – I nearly drowned. I swam + swam and kept getting farther from shore – I almost panicked. I reached the beach exhausted + afraid."

When Tim described this, my first thought was of another time he'd told me about when he and his father were walking along together on a Connecticut beach and Lee abruptly plunged into the water. Recognizing that Lee intended to let himself drown, Tim went in after him and brought him to shore. Because Tim was an athletic and confident swimmer, he wouldn't have been properly intimidated by this steel gray water whose waves crested at an ominous distance from the beach. He seemed not to have noticed, the way I would have, that although there were plenty of other people at the beach, they only waded in up to their ankles.

After an egg curry dinner that night at a restaurant called the Spread Eagle, Tim and I went off to our separate dorm rooms. Through the open windows I too could hear the talk from the porch, where the Blacks from both groups had gathered to caucus, to share their experiences of this return to the land of their ancestors.

Tim told me the next morning that he had drifted off but awoke again some time later to hear the other group's leader propose a plan to reformulate the two groups according to race, one Black like her and one white like us. This was in direct violation of the founding mission of Crossroads, but it was only abandoned when Joan, a girl from our group, refused to go along. Overhearing their deliberations made Tim feel so "anxious + depressed" that he "got 3 hours of sleep after a LONG day." Where was I? Sound asleep.

The next day we were moved to the more accommodating International Student Hostel, but where, again, there wasn't a room we could share. Our restricted time together focused on the negotiations for visa extensions from both the American and Canadian embassies – "(stuffy cold American ambassador + Canadian high commissioner great, funny, charming)" – and arrangements for transportation from Accra to Kumasi, where we would be privileged to witness the installation of the new King of the Ashanti people, the *Asantehene*. We looked forward to this but, more, to leaving Ghana II behind and getting established in our village. It wasn't easy for these task-driven North American college students to relinquish the need to perform, no matter how often we'd all been told the construction project for which we would eventually break ground was only part of the reason for our being here.

But then Tim developed a sudden fever of 103.2 and was taken to the Legon University Hospital, where he was admitted with a diagnosis of "slight" malaria despite the fact that this was still only Day 3 and we'd been told that malaria has a 16-day incubation period. The next morning I hitched a ride to the hospital, and wrote:

> *Tim better, cheerier temp 100 but had diaherrea (better learn to spell this I guess) 27 times during the night because water he was given to drink by the quart was unboiled.*

This was the morning of July 4th, and we'd been invited to the residence of the American ambassador for an Independence Day hot dog cookout for 200 people, where the only Blacks beyond our Crossroads groups were the Ghanaian servants. I left the gathering to visit Tim again at the hospital, relieved to find him steadily improving. He said he'd been told several times here that he gets too wound up about things and doesn't relax enough, which shows up more in this culture. His journal concurred:

> I feel better now except that I have learned a sad lesson about myself. First I am now almost well – thus I wasn't very sick – yet I cried (although I did 'adjust' to the hospital alright). In fact a Ghanaian fellow patient I have just spoken with does not think I have malaria at all – so what does this do for me? I don't know.

He added:

> Again I am so glad Lex is here – to learn from and with + to share – I feel so strongly we will each grow together too – Just seeing her every day does so much for me – the whole world moves from black + white to color (even literally – always bright wonderful colors!)

With his trademark humor restored, he concluded:

> I have made my own diagnosis. I have had MINI-laria.

I ended my own day's report by writing "I miss Tim." The Tim I missed was the "Mr. Buxton!" who was so beloved by the Exeter boys he championed that they shouted his name like cheerleaders and were dressed like him, like teammates, in their own flamboyant neckties. I missed the Tim strong enough to sustain his father, pleading with him to heal in a heartbreaking correspondence they both saved. I missed the Tim who also understood and honored his mother's need to be independent, the Tim who could play the piano for hours from a book of 500 show tunes, who was also a fiercely athletic competitor. I even missed the Tim whose journal over-analyzes our Crossroads participants according to their Frisbee skills.

I missed the charismatic Tim who wasn't afraid of the truth, who convinced his pal Charlie to join him in riding the Freedom Train to

Alabama, who joined the clergy with a desire to follow Dr. King, not in bringing religion to the people, in bringing the people to religion. The Tim who talked me into getting married, who was old-fashioned enough to be concerned that if my parents knew we were having sex they wouldn't respect him. I missed the Tim with too tender a heart.

I missed the Tim whose journal during our year at Stanford reveals:

> I'm still very young. I want more than anything to be capable of wisdom yet I am so full of the love of wisdom (in men I can read or listen to) that I am blinded to what I realize now to be the long road one must take to reach wisdom. I still enjoy tasting the fruits – someday I must learn to plant the tree.

Even now, all these decades later, I examine his Ghana journal entries looking for signals I missed at the time, and I quote them because, tragically, they're all there is to chronicle the decline that dead-ended six days later. I decipher these reflections hoping to find, if not an explanation, at least a farewell.

> I had <u>expectations</u> early this morning (again – again – expectations – anticipation, the lesson is there! I think of Hesse + the journey to the East + the man not having faith in the group (what was its name?) The faith + trust of Journeying rather than planning each step + evaluating it) of a happy reunion and the drive to Kumasi. Yet again reality corrects dreams – another doctor came in at 9:30 – looked at my record + told the nurses in my presence that he hoped the temperature would stabilize now that it had gone to 98.4. He said that should take a day + then I could leave Monday. I gulped and said I had been told by Dr. Balfor (?) (the doctor who had seen me) that an early departure might be possible – the doctor frowned and after a long discussion he decided to allow me to go taking some pills with me to prevent relapse. The others were waiting in the bus – and then!! more to learn from – getting signed out + filling prescriptions took an hour + 1/2 while people waited helplessly – Lexa was impatient the whole thing was horrible + I was so disappointed that I felt sick again – Finally we were freed + the reunion was a bust because it had taken so long to get out – everyone was staring vacantly – no one asked me if I were sick, had been or how I felt now. I was anonymous –

Although that second doctor preferred – and it was surely preferable – to keep Tim under observation for another day, he was released to travel upcountry with us in the relative luxury of a new Mercedes Benz bus with "Harmony" written across its front in sky-blue script lettering. My own journal's shorthand description naively oversimplified:

> up + bus arrived + Kwabena arrived (counterpart) + got packed + to hospital for 1 1/2 hour wait for Tim's discharge – whew. He was ready to go except for pills + payment + doctor's OK but anyway I'm glad he is out and feeling well enough to wonder why he wasn't made a fuss over + I wonder too.

In recounting that journey Tim wrote:

> The 6-hour trip was very bearable + short compared to expectations (again! the doing is fine – but the damn thinking!) I thought it miraculous but after 30 trips to the john just the day before I felt no urges + my stomach is fine. I liked being with the people again.

Yet here is his last regular journal entry from that night, July 5th:

> tonight again no sleep – mind racing until it seems to want to burst – restless jumping around – nightmares – double fear of relapse fear for Lex –
>
> I even said a long <u>prayer</u> out loud + <u>really</u> meant it. I get SO WORKED UP!! I show it only by tightness but otherwise I am getting better – tomorrow the great ceremony!!

But then in attending these festivities Tim became further dehydrated, and overwhelmed by the heat and the crowds. Did sunstroke get added that day to the accumulation of challenges to Tim's deteriorating resistance? In writing "otherwise I am getting better – tomorrow the great ceremony!!" did he believe it himself? He would make a few more entries in his journal, but this day marked the end of his narrative.

Instead, after a handful of blank pages he wrote:

<u>In mid Stream</u>
teaching
theological rapping

        spurts of real generosity
        preaching
        speaking publicly
        organizing

And farther along this memo to me:

        LEX
        Our traveler's checks in Blue case
        passports together
        health cards in side pocket
        arrange to have traveler's checks
        in another name.

Then a next-to-last lucid page:

        Problems for doctors analysts etc.
        of the symptoms + clues, which
        leads through to the core + which
        is peripheral? or do they all lead
        to the same core.

        Is losing hold the same as
        cowardice or insanity? To what
        degree is one responsible?
        Wouldn't it be ironic
        if the only way to lose self-
        consciousness were utter
        unconcern for how one is received
        as in madness.

        The concept – reality connection
        + unconnection.

And now Tim's final notation :

        night and day
        to separate them if they

conflict – you then run the
risk of schizophrenia.

Some thoughts about disassociation
and disintegration of personality

The "dream" theory that dreams are
among other things a release of
energies, impulses, perceptions
which otherwise would build up
to be unbearable is fascinating
My experience 7/6/70 – no
sleep images come anyway – which
way greatest impact – in conscious
mind or through dreams -
which the best prognosis?

no paranoia
no hates
anxiety about next things
feeling of tightness inflexibility
in regard to new things
reaction + adjustment time longer
subtleties disappearing
concentration?
will?

Every survivor craves a suicide note, and I have come to accept this as
Tim's even though, composed four days before he ended his life, he already
seems to have left me behind. Still, as a last word isn't "will?" preferable
to his instruction about arranging to have the traveler's checks in another
name, when they ought to have been in both our names in the first place?

Though I can't know the meaning of Tim's cryptic "will?" I've tried to
remain open to the question he posed. My eclectic bibliography chronicles
this diligent search, but it remains unanswerable. When even in my final
impressions of Tim I could still recognize the strong son who had guided
his adored father through his remarkable public life and into a peaceful

private death, I am left to wonder how this could be.

The "tightness inflexibility" for which Tim criticized himself was concealed even then, in his own last analysis. In pursuit of answers to my questions about what happened and why, I would later come to rely on intensive talk-therapy to deliver what I could live with. It did.

One afternoon a psychoanalyst friend and I were power-walking the circumference of a large New England pond, the dirt path widening and narrowing as if a metaphor for our conversation as it shifted between the gravity of our life stories and the ways a change of season announces itself. The forsythia was emerging from tangled branches into what looked like spiky yellow coronets, and we could almost hear music. I asked Anna – named for Anna Freud in the Vienna of her birth – for her definition of suicide. I'm not even sure what I wished for from her just then, but she gave it to me:

> "In the moment when Tim pressed the breadknife to his own throat, he had sufficient ego to kill himself but insufficient ego to *not* kill himself."

For "the great ceremony" in Kumasi the procession of mourners and the parade of celebrants were intertwined, moving slowly across the clay bowl of the city center. The robes of black-on-black stamped *Adinkra* cloth observed the passing of the previous king of the Ashanti, while the vividly colored woven *Kente* celebrated the installation of his nephew, Jacob Matthew Poku, a British-educated lawyer, who was serving as Ghana's Ambassador to Italy when he was chosen to become the fifteenth ruler of the Ashanti Empire. The newly installed *Asantehene* assumed the name Nana Opoku Ware II and was displayed for this occasion on a canopied platform, seated on the stool that symbolized his power, his bare arms and hands dressed in the gold bracelets and rings mined from these rich lands. There were other white people among these tens of thousands come to mark this royal occasion, but we were like specks of flour folded under to disappear into a velvety batter.

We stayed overnight in Kumasi at the University of Science and Technology, in a dormitory building that felt like a skyscraper compared to the modest guest hostels in Accra. Tim and I shared a room at last, but we squandered the opportunity for intimacy with his criticism of me for losing track of $40 of group funds and my accusation that in his self-obsession he was acting just like his father. After an hour of trying to convince him to rest and relax he seemed less tense. So when he said, "In a way I hope you're not pregnant," I didn't reply, although I wrote in my journal, "In a way I hope I am and wonder actually if I might be."

Our ride to Wenchi the next day was in the bed of a 4-ton lorry. Tim rode in the cab with the driver, but the rest of us experienced the shocking novelty of hiding under a tarp when a cloudburst turned the road to mud. It was a relief when the Ghana II group was dropped off at a town along the way, and I carried that into our arrival at the Wenchi Secondary School that was to be our home for the next seven weeks. While the group moved in and Tim rested, I was shown our outdoor kitchen: a pile of ashes on the dirt floor under a patch of tin roofing. Before I could panic, a young woman named Julie materialized to guide me to the open-air market, where dinner ingredients to feed a dozen of us cost $3. She then showed me how to create on a charcoal cooker our first delicious meal of greens and tinned fish and tomatoes and rice.

That evening we were introduced to our two new Ghanaian counterparts, along with a French-Canadian teacher who lived with his wife across the field from our dormitory rooms. For the first time in these challenging first days of constantly negotiating to meet our group's basic needs on a restricted budget, our situation felt secure. I was reading Kurt Vonnegut's first novel, *Player Piano*, where in that sci-fi land everything was mechanized and hyper-programmed and clean. Vonnegut's world felt more foreign than this one.

The next day we were officially greeted by Wenchi's Chief, Nana Kusi Apea I, and his sister the Queen-Mother, Nana Afua Frema Tatuo II. They were the younger siblings of the recently elected Prime Minister, Dr. Kofi Abrefa Busia, so our Crossroads group's assignment to his ancestral village was both his prerogative and our honor. The fixed protocol for our ceremonial welcome was a triangular ritual where our English was converted to Twi by the Royal Linguist whose job was to translate and embellish. I would later learn that, not only did the Chief speak English, he had represented the Gold Coast at the coronation of Queen Elizabeth in 1953. As we sat before him to state the nature of our business in his jurisdiction, we were invited to sip from a goblet of palm wine. He then presented us with a pair of live chickens.

To pay our respects to the Queen-Mother, the girls and I were taken to a nearby building where Nana Frema greeted us, in English, wearing the uniform of a nurse-midwife. In her clinic there were four immaculate cubicles, in each a table with a hole cut into the center and a pan suspended beneath. It took us a moment to grasp that, here, a woman squats to deliver her baby. As the Queen-Mother watched us discover this, her laugh was so musical that I can still hear it.

As I walked back to rejoin Tim I thought maybe I could convince myself that, were I to be pregnant, there were less secure circumstances than to spend most of a first trimester in a place where the Queen-Mother was also a nurse-midwife.

But before I could describe the clinic to him, Tim asked me if I'd get an abortion if I were pregnant. He was working on our group's budget numbers and barely looked up as he told me he didn't want to live.

When I asked, "Why not?" he answered, "I'll never play tennis again."

We talked for two hours, until I felt that at least he could hear what I saw as the "illogic" in his fears about tennis, and how "egotistical" he was being. My wanting him to act like himself was because I wanted him well. I needed him not to have asked me if I'd get an abortion if I were pregnant.

After dinner we stopped by a party arranged by the regional manager of a social welfare service, and then because the housemistress's empty room had been opened for us that afternoon, we climbed into her bed and tucked in the mosquito netting around us. The town generator was switched off at night, and the darkness was so profound that when Tim began to violently shake I thought he was weeping. Instead, he'd been holding his breath until he no longer could.

I woke up one of our guys, and Charles and I picked him up from the floor – "Tim faked (I think) a faint" – and I got our flashlight so we could walk him down the road to the hospital, where the night watchman let us in.

From my diary:

There was a form to fill + temp 98 + blood 110/70 pressure + Tim just lying there. After about 30 mins the doctor arrived + he's a tall thin abrupt german or dutch – probably german – guy who's very businesslike + tapped around for pains etc. + said all beds filled in hospital + Tim needs rest + lots of rest + so he suggested going to the Côtés who are the CUSO people living near our dorms. He was to drive us here in the ambulance + backed it out of the garage into a mammy lorry – swore a bit in german (or dutch) and said "stupid people" (who?) + checked the ambulance which is brand new + it's almost ok + so we drove out here at 40 mph – jesus. The Côtés (Jean + Hélène) made a bed for Tim + Charles got some mattresses from the dorm for me + I gave Tim one of the sleeping pills + lay awake while he slept some. I didn't understand how to react but I feel sick myself + anxious that Tim do what the doctor said sleep 3 days take sleeping pills at night + 3 times a day. If he doesn't I don't think I can cope with him. he is the very weakness of his father in this moment + feels shame + says all of tonight was a fake.

The next morning Jean and Hélène made bacon and eggs for breakfast, and they said we were welcome to stay there for another few days before they set off on their summer vacation. From the narrow balcony at the top of the external staircase leading to their second-story apartment, I waved to our group as they set off to their first day at the worksite, with one of the boys delegated as our spokesman at the opening ceremonies. While keeping an eye on Tim I enjoyed the chance to speak French with Jean and Hélène, and to hear about their life as teachers at the Wenchi Secondary School in whose empty dormitories our volunteers were now housed. I also remember tucking the packet of sleeping pills into the pocket of my T-shirt to keep them handy but, more, to make sure Tim took them as prescribed.

Tim never slept that day, and at some point he roused himself to take a shower. When he nicked himself while shaving, and told me he'd done it on purpose, I saw it as a plea for more help, like his fake faint the night before. So I went back to the hospital to tell Dr. Beltman it was imperative that Tim sleep. I wanted him to change his mind and admit Tim to the hospital, but instead Dr. Beltman issued me three Phenobarbital and said I could come back for an injection if these also failed.

In the afternoon, one of our volunteers stopped by to describe the local version of a ribbon-cutting ceremony marking the start of our housing construction project in a neighboring village. Using the "Each One Teach One" method that the Peace Corps famously implemented around the world, our job was to motivate by example. If we cared enough to have come all the way from America and Canada to work alongside the people in this community, to better their lives, why wouldn't they also pick up the shovels that we had provided? Yes, we were a curious-looking group, but to these upcountry Ghanaians we foreigners looked like brothers and sisters, no matter that some of us were brown and some white. For most we would be the first white people they'd seen in person, as was evidently true for the toddler frightened to tears by my over-eager smile.

As I recall that day spent waiting for the sleeping medication to take effect, I have to believe that if one of the volunteers for whom we were responsible had exhibited the same series of symptoms as Tim, I would have recognized that it was my job to imagine a worst-case-scenario, and prevent it. The Legon University teaching hospital in Accra was modest by American standards, but – minus the untreated water that he'd been encouraged to drink by the quart – he'd felt well attended to. It didn't occur to me, not in Accra or even now in Wenchi, to make the executive decision to evacuate Tim back to the States.

Why not? Even though I'd effectively been in charge since our group arrived for orientation, I wasn't *solely* in charge. As leaders our designated authority was as a married couple, and I sensed it my duty not to undercut Tim's authority. In this postcolonial culture, in the aftermath of British rule – no matter that the Ashanti kingdom was matrilineal in structure – it was important to honor the men whose dignity was continually diminished by the racist norms of their British landlords. Without yet being introduced to African Literature, I knew this behavior from reading the imperial horror stories considered the masterpieces of British Literature. I also wanted our participants to know the Tim I knew. The man I married. The man whose message to the newlywed bride and groom on their rocky island ten miles off the Maine mainland had been:

> This new creation today is larger than you both, for the love and life that grow within it will add to the world outside, and those around you will add to that special union you two alone will share.

Later in the day we found the breadknife that our hosts had earlier noticed missing. I'd assumed it had been borrowed by our group and was locked inside the dormitory building along with the Tampax that I'd tried to access from my backpack when I got my period. I didn't tell Tim I wasn't pregnant after all because, all too matter-of-factly, he admitted to me that, that morning, he'd taken the knife and hidden it under his mattress all day, but then decided not to use it.

I interpreted this choice as a sign of Tim's own wish to recover. But when the Phenobarbital had provided him less than an hour's sleep and he was awake again at midnight, I got the night nurse to come out with the promised injection, which she administered by flashlight. Jean and Hélène went to bed, and while their kind hospitality gave us only one more night after this one before they were to leave for their vacation, as I watched Tim finally sink into a deep sleep, I convinced myself that the injection possessed the power to anesthetize him. I trusted that this enforced rest would restore him to full health, and I thought he did too.

Dr. Beltman's title is given as Medical Officer, Wenchi Methodist Hospital, and here is his entire report dated July 10, 1970:

> Patient was seen first on the 9/7/70: 2 a.m. He was depressed, made an impression of exhaustion and was suffering from sleeplessness. Physically nothing abnormal could be found. Cause of Death: (Suicide: cutting of the big vessels in the neck.)

The full autopsy report was written by Dr. Solomon Kwabena Baidoo at the Komfo Anokye Hospital Morgue in the Ashanti capital city of Kumasi, where Tim's body was brought from Wenchi in a coffin strapped to a flatbed truck:

HISTORY:
> A white American aged 28 years, tall, well-built, was alleged to have stabbed himself to death on the 10th of July, 1970, at Wenchi. He was said to be left-handed.

Articles Found at the Scene:

> A bread knife with blood stains and spurts of blood on the mirror hanging on the wall. His shirt was smeared with blood.

EXTERNAL EXAMINATION:

The body was very very pale. There were blood stains on the
left forearm and the hand, the right ear and the neck.
A bandage, blood soaked was tied around the neck covering
the wound. A fresh incised wound of the neck beginning
below the right angle of the jaw high up in the neck.
It proceeded to the left side, it was directed somewhat
downwards cutting the larynx and ending just by the middle
line. It was accompanied by multiple small superficial wounds.

The wound was deep on the right side about 2 cms. cutting the
skin, muscles and dividing the right jugular veins.
The wound was slanting downwards. The right carotid arteries
were intact but collapsed.

INTERNAL EXAMINATION:

The internal organs especially the lungs, heart and brain
were pale. The blood vessels were empty. The heart too was
empty of blood.

Trachea – slight amount of blood stains.
There were no abnormalities detected in the other systems.

CAUSE OF DEATH: Traumatic Shock due to
Cut throat (suicidal.)

After the injection at midnight, and once I was certain it had taken
effect, I lay down on the mattress on the floor next to his bed for my own
first real sleep in all these days. Jean told me later that at around 3 am he'd
found Tim standing in the hall and had brought him back to bed. It was just
before dawn that Jean heard Tim moaning and woke me – *"Viens! Viens!"* –
when he found Tim on the floor of the shower room. I grasped right away
that, in getting out of bed, Tim had to step over me as if I weren't there.

From the doorway I saw that Tim's torso was smeared with blood as if
with a child's finger paints, but I can't pretend to more of an impression
because I leapt on the excuse of seeking help by jumping on the back of
Jean's motorcycle as he sped away. It wasn't that Jean was asking me to

come with him to fetch the doctor, rather that, if I'd stayed, I'd have needed the power to try to save Tim's life. And what then? By fleeing, wasn't I also protecting us both from having to confront, face to face, what he'd done to himself? It may be partially true that I chose to spare us this, but primarily, I escaped. Clinging to Jean on the back of his motorcycle, I wanted him to keep driving. This is the flaw – in me – that cancels out Tim's. It's the love I still feel for him.

Tim was still alive when Dr. Beltman arrived at the house in the ambulance, giving the doctor a life to try to save. On the cement balcony where I waited, shivering in the heat, I watched the day's first light fully arrive, numb with dread. Without any real information about Tim's condition I already knew that for the rest of my own life I would be guilty of abandoning him.

When Dr. Beltman reemerged from the house he regarded me through the rectangular metal-rimmed glasses that I still always notice on European men because of him. "Your husband is died. Dead," he said, correcting his grammar.

During that decade of American assassinations our hearts had broken for three heroic young women in their black veils, but until Jackie and Ethel Kennedy and Coretta Scott King, my idea of a widow was my grandmother. On that balcony I accused myself of cowardice in not protecting Tim from himself in the first place, and then, failing that, for not holding his bloody head in my lap for the rest of his life.

I won't pretend I've never once asked myself "Why Me?" But the more compulsory question has always remained "Why *Him?*" When Tim was so talented, and deservedly rewarded for his diligence, *who was he* to prove capable of dying like this?

I could settle for any one of the hypothetical medical opinions I've been offered over the years. It's possible that the sudden high fever he had on the third morning after our arrival signaled an inflammation of the brain that might have been confirmed with a spinal tap during his overnight hospitalization in Accra. Or that once upcountry the Phenobarbital he was given in Wenchi – the "sleeping pill" – never should have been administered as a sedative since it can also cause profound agitation. Or that the routinely prescribed antimalarial drug Mefloquine was similarly associated with toxic psychosis, especially among foreigners.

Tim should probably not have been released from the hospital in Accra and should have been admitted to the hospital in Wenchi. And beyond these medical mistakes and the misfortune of Jean's not waking me when he encountered Tim awake several hours earlier than when he discovered him again, too late, there was another serious problem. On that entire continent there was nobody who knew Tim better than I did. But I knew next to nothing.

The first anniversary of his father's death was three days earlier, July 7, the day we arrived in Wenchi. I wasn't aware of the date's greater significance, but while we didn't speak about Lee I can assume Tim had him firmly in mind. After his hospital stay in Accra I remained focused on Tim's sense that he was getting better. I could downplay his lament that he would never again play tennis as a temporary consequence of his debilitating exhaustion. During our marriage I'd seen Tim rise to new challenges, not understanding that his insecurities were cosmic compared to mine. Since his fears were so strenuously concealed they were invisible to me, and because he was very, very good at what he was good at – at what he was already comfortable with – I didn't recognize his range as restricted. It felt way bigger than mine, but wasn't.

That I didn't want to look at Tim that morning has been true ever since, until now, when this is no longer the case. Now I *need* to have looked. I have finally come to understand this as a crucial part of my life, which went missing.

Between this building and our school dormitory was a large square grassy field that we were warned not to cut through because of the snakes. That morning, terrified as I am of them, I ran across it on the diagonal – on adrenalin – to tell the group what had happened. In a meeting with the Chief he reassured me that everything would be taken care of, and very soon – a necessity in this climate – a truck appeared, with a wooden box in its bed. Tim's body was to be transported back to Kumasi and held at the morgue until after the police autopsy that is required in the case of an "unnatural" death.

A ride was also provided for one of our volunteers to go to the cable office in the larger nearby town of Sunyani, to send word back to New York. The text composed by Doug said that Tim had "committed suicide result of depression following illness and imagined inability to lead."

From across that field I stood to watch the cinematic procession of the Chief and the council of Elders, all dressed in robes of black-on-black *Adinkra* cloth. They navigated the precarious external staircase and paused on the balcony before entering the apartment. I supposed they were officially tasked with expelling the evil spirits from those violated premises, and I felt relief on behalf of Hélène and Jean, our unsuspecting hosts whose lives had been permanently altered by these thirty hours that Tim had been their guest.

I was taken to the doctor's house on the hospital grounds, where I was interviewed by the police. Because they first had to rule out murder, to explain why the right side of Tim's neck was cut, I supplied the logic that my husband was left-handed – "So am I," I added – along with the testimony corroborated by Jean that he had wakened me just before dawn – *"Viens! Viens!"* – upon discovering Tim on the shower room floor.

I next received the three-man black-suited delegation that the Prime Minister had dispatched to express his condolences and to assess the extent of the scandal. I was informed that I must report the death to the American Embassy in Accra, and so, when the group returned at the end of the day, Joan and Dorothy helped me pack. Dorothy pressed my dress with an iron powered by live coals, but I left behind almost everything except Tim's abandoned journal and the pair of shirts that he and I had bought together at L.L. Bean on our way to the Monhegan Island wedding.

By my not telling Tim that I had gotten my period, late, he died without knowing if I was pregnant. I wrote in my journal:

> I couldn't have answered the question he asked me the other day – would I get an abortion? – and was glad it was settled for me. o god.

What I remember about that last evening with our group was Bud playing his bongos late into the night. Illuminated by our campfire's orange flames, they told me of the strength they'd seen in our marriage in our fourteen days together. I thanked them for the strength I'd witnessed, and relied on, in them. Of the volunteers it was Charles who either volunteered or was designated to fly with me to Accra the next morning to report Tim's death to the Embassy, whose help I'd earlier sought, ironically, for the visa extensions required for us to stay beyond the limit for tourists. In addition to the Ambassador's condescension I recalled that, by comparison to his Canadian counterpart, his office bore no evidence of the culture of the country to which he had been assigned.

I'd had no way to be in direct contact with my parents, but once in Accra I learned that the news of Tim's death had been relayed in a phone call from Dr. Robinson to my father. I later learned from him that my mother rushed to his office with his passport and an overnight bag containing one extra button-down shirt and a change of socks and underwear, and that at JFK airport my dad got the required yellow fever shot before boarding the first of his two eight-hour flights to Accra, fully expecting to fetch me home by return flight.

Instead, following my lead, he'd find himself patiently acquiescing to local protocol, specifically the maddening post-colonial triplicate paperwork that only once caused him to sputter, "I'm calling Bill Rogers!" We were in a taxi stalled by clogged traffic, but when I laughed so did he, realizing that, unlike his own Republican politics, mine expressly forbade association with Nixon's Secretary of State, no matter how good a guy he might be.

I hesitate to recall those next awful days as precious, but they were. Starting with my father's touchdown in Accra, the discrepancy between his Wall Street suit and the airport's succession of nonfunctioning monitors – each bearing a publicity photo of soul brother James Brown in place of flight information – instantly dissolved into my greater relief that he'd come in such haste, bearing such love.

From the perspective of today's technology where it's literally impossible to be incommunicado, the communication vacuum that was taken for granted in much of the world fifty years ago is hard to imagine. I could rely on my mother to gently deliver the news to Tim's mother, but without yet knowing that my father hadn't told my mother that the cable to the Crossroads office gave "committed suicide" as the cause of death, I didn't yet understand that a counter-narrative was already set in motion.

I sent word from Accra to Tim's Exeter faculty colleagues to ask them to create a memorial service at Phillips Church. I assumed this was what Tim would have wanted, although not even in the context of Lee's death exactly a year earlier – and never in the abstract – had Tim and I discussed our wishes in the event of our deaths. The only certainty seemed to be that the cemetery in Old Lyme was the place his mother would want for his burial place.

My father didn't second-guess my decisions on the ground in Ghana, no matter that I clearly lacked essential information. From the fact that cremation was Lee's choice I could reasonably guess that Tim would want cremation for himself too. I was told that in Ghana cremation was only customary for Hindus, so I contacted Victor Badoo, the head of Kumasi's Indian community, and made an appointment to meet. From within the labyrinth of paperwork regulations required by overlapping registries, this decision calmed me, whatever else it entailed.

On my travels five years earlier I'd been to India and visited the holy Hindu city of Benares, where I noted the exotic plumes of smoke rising from the distant hills. At the Ganges I'd watched bathers with open containers of ashes wade into the river to deposit them – I'd seen an old man brush his teeth with a stick dipped in the ashes cupped in his hand! – but still assumed cremation took place, as at home, in some kind of furnace. So I was startled when Victor Badoo told us that, even if modified for foreigners, cremation involved the building of a pyre of stacked logs to be ignited by the male next-of-kin. When he then said this could be arranged for the following afternoon, I asked my dad if he could consent to performing this role. Without hesitating, he said yes.

That evening I felt settled, but also unsettled. My discomfort was because, in India, in addition to many treasured encounters, I'd also had a series of scary isolated experiences. Sure, my friend Jean and I were two twenty-one-year-old American girls – and she was a blonde – but by that point in our travels we'd been halfway around the world already and not anywhere had we felt threatened. In New Delhi we'd scored tickets to hear Indira Gandhi's speech to open the session of Parliament, but when we arrived we were instead led off by two young men who took us to a small side room and shut the door. They "wanted to get to know us better" – which we evaded by improvising a getaway – while causing us to miss the speech. Another time was my own fault, when I accepted an offer to change money on the black market and was lured into the back room of a tiny shop where Jean was told to wait by the entrance. I'd never before had occasion to shout "Get your hands off me!" and, while it was almost comical, it wasn't funny. A third time we were on a train, and when it slowed to a stop we stuck our heads out the window to see where we were. When a dozen men started running toward us and jumped on the train, we only barely managed to lock the door of our compartment in time.

I hadn't told my parents about these incidents and, that night at our hotel in Kumasi, I didn't tell my dad then either. But it was necessary to acknowledge the attitudes I'd formed about Indian men. That afternoon I had thoroughly trusted Victor Badoo, and I still did, didn't I?

In asking myself this delicate question, while staring into the darkness I became aware of the transformative power of a thought becoming an insight. And within what felt like a fraction of a second, I knew the answer was that I wouldn't be in Ghana with Operation Crossroads Africa if I hadn't felt the obligation, and welcomed the opportunity, to address the persistent universal racism that included my own. I hadn't expected in Africa to confront the latent prejudice I hadn't let go of in the five years since my visit to India, but now was my chance. As soon as I saw this I realized that, in Victor Badoo's living room that afternoon, in willingly placing myself into his hands, I already had.

The next morning our Crossroads volunteers traveled to Kumasi, and I was relieved to hear that they were "deliriously happy" with the construction project and the people they worked with. Jean and Hélène came too, having postponed their vacation plans, and I was comforted by their presence.

I had bought a wreath and an armload of flowers that I carried through the gates of the Kumasi City Cemetery, uphill to its highest point, where a slab of earth had been laid with a rectangular wooden tower constructed like a log cabin. I wondered at the gold-painted coffin's pairs of rectangular porthole-like windows inexplicably inserted on each side, and while I'd neglected to ask how the coffin came to be provided, I saw how it rested on top of the pyre like a penthouse, with the midday sun glinting off the glass and the glittery paint creating a cartoonish effect, as if in sky-bound arrows of light.

We were met at the cremation site by Victor Badoo, whose white-robed priestly authority seemed absolute. The sleeves of my father's white Oxford shirt were rolled back, and my bare legs were exposed under the black and white striped skirt that, in the style of that time, was shorter than a café curtain.

A slight commotion occurred when a group of Americans arrived to join us. I'd seen the paragraph in the *Kumasi Star* where Tim was misidentified as "a Peace Corps Volunteer and a Hidu [sic] by religion," and evidently these spectators had too. From my bouquet I gave them each a wilting flower, and they joined the rest of us and the cemetery workers in placing them on the pyre. Across the top of the coffin I draped the new purple necktie that Tim had worn to perform his first wedding.

From my journal:

There was incense in the ground and a fire to the left from which the pyre was to be lit by Daddy – and so it was lit + kerosene poured on + flames leaping + flashes of heat giving sensations of incredible strength. I noticed everything all at once – the priest chanting, the colors, the incense + perfume smells, the blasts of heat, the sounds of the people there + conversations in all sorts of languages about things mundane + profound. I had no feeling of time and wasn't aware of my body except that I was standing as tall as I could for Tim's sake. When the flames took away one end of the casket + I realized Tim's body was indeed being burned – his head or his feet? – I felt capable of realizing + dealing only on the level of grief. But I sat + had conversations instead with Victor about how circular symbolism is + with Jean about whether he was ok. The end of the service part was lovely – the priest explained in english what he had been saying, how the five elements of the body were being returned to the five elements of nature because they are perishable but how the spirit of Tim is indestructible + can never perish. Then we repeated after him three times – om – shantih, triple peace of sympathy, control + giving.

It was the prayer for a triple peace in the body, the mind, and the spirit, for the past, the present, and the future. When the orange flames bulged into a mass of dense black smoke I leaned into that heat, fixed like a figurehead on the prow of a ship, with no capacity for peripheral vision. I recall trying not to breathe it in because of the kerosene smell, but how could I not? What other air was there?

> *Then Daddy and I placed the final logs on the fire. But still I was aloof from my own grief until Hélène said goodbye + we hugged each other + cried + then I could sob and did this, feeling my father on one side + a tree for support on the other until I could put myself entirely in his arms for a long long time of unselfconscious tears. I could hardly walk away from there + felt finally relaxed somehow. Went back to the hotel for tea + a bath + a chance to find out how we might get home – I hadn't thought of it all day. I was so relieved + so genuinely happy from the service – the feeling that we were all talking Tim's language + being together – all of us.*

It was in saying goodbye to Hélène that I finally released myself to the horror. My journal for the preceding days reveals my enforced success in *not* crying, but now, at last, I could, and did. We embraced, and wept. My father stood near, close enough for me to then be transferred from her arms to his, and it was finally now too that, entirely protected, I could absorb the assault. Sobbing in his arms, as unselfconscious as a child, I was fully comforted. The difference was that instead of being rocked to sleep like a baby, I reached a state of hyperconscious relaxation. It was as if I too had been freed by fire into that Sanskrit triple peace in the body, the mind, and the spirit. Or in the language of a Christian like Tim, into what Saint Paul termed the peace of God, which passeth all understanding.

It was too late in the day for a flight to Accra, but instead of waiting for daylight the way a Ghanaian would, it seemed like a good idea to ask the desk clerk to hire a driver to take us. When he didn't show up another was quickly recruited, but as we headed into that night we didn't yet know our driver had never been to Accra and didn't speak more than the few words of English he'd already used up.

There was no electricity in any of the towns and villages bisected by the road to the capital, and though there was really only one way to get there, our driver's unfamiliarity with the route meant that, after five hours, we were still less than a hundred miles from Kumasi. During these long hours in a dense darkness pierced only by the pair of headlights that had no peripheral vision, it was also as if my dad and I were encased in a cocoon suspended from a twig. We were destined to emerge, but what was waiting for us on the other side – in the First World – would make our being caterpillars, here, hard to ask family and friends to try to imagine. Would "you had to be there" be sufficient? Of course not. But what could accurately convey both the wrong and the right?

All this extra time in the car provided a chance for recapitulation before anticipating the rest of the journey. We talked about my dad's landing in Accra in a 747 and, the next day, the direct flight from Accra to Kumasi when the aisle was packed with crates of chickens that were dropped off in an unscheduled stop at Takoradi. I told him about the Chief's Royal Linguist and the dizzying roundabout ceremonial conversation required to establish our welcome – "Akwaaba!" – in Wenchi. I described the Queen-Mother's clinic, confiding my ignorance about childbirth under any circumstances, and my relief at not being pregnant. I admitted to being too intimidated by Dr. Beltman to ask the name of the drug administered in that supposed knockout injection. I knew this was a question I would be asked, to which I would now never have the answer.

My dad the corporate lawyer was a man whose secrets were so well guarded that, once, in a tennis game when he ran into the iron net support and injured his back, and was administered a painkiller of some sort, he later asked my mother if he'd said anything he shouldn't have said about the office. My mom was volatile enough for them both, the life of the party who could deliver the punchlines to her long jokes with a signature theatricality that didn't only depend on her J&B Scotch. Despite their very different temperaments, I don't think I ever walked into a room when I didn't interrupt an interesting conversation between them. My mother and I had our many weekday evenings together, but my father and I had rare chances to talk. We'd had more time together, here in Ghana, than we'd had since before I left home for college.

I couldn't resist noticing that, now that his one piece of career advice to me had been rendered moot – to choose something to go back to once the kids were in school – I'd been given the chance to ask him again. I'd instinctively made the decision to quit my teaching job, but it's possible that I could have been talked into sticking with it. I expressed the regret I felt in abandoning my students and Frank Kozaka, my principal – was I not tough enough after all? – while admitting that I'd want to leave Exeter even if I weren't required to give up our apartment.

My dad surprised me by encouraging me not to be afraid of not having a plan. We didn't have the words to express such radical thoughts as that, as a woman, I could craft my own destiny, but this weaker substitute was progress. It spared me from being a good girl for the rest of my life.

Out of a companionable silence during this epic journey to cover the relatively short distance between Kumasi and Accra, I asked my father – the only man in West Africa wearing Wingtip shoes – to tell me about the ritual bathing of Tim's body. This was the Hindu custom requiring his presence while prohibiting mine, and of all the culture shock that I'd subjected him to on a mission intended to rescue me, I worried that this may have exceeded his tolerance.

"He looked peaceful."

I told him I was glad to hear this because the autopsy report was so frightening. I thanked him for his gift, to me and to Tim.

"He was very pale and thin and, in spite of his size, he looked like a little boy."

I held my dad's hand for the rest of the ride, like a little girl.

"AND THEN WHAT?"

My brother Will rushed east from Colorado, a ski bum free to keep me company all summer if I needed him to hang around. Our childhood nicknames for each other were Lexine 'n Willard – sidckicks – and he was eager to reeducate me in all I'd missed out on by not being three years younger, like him. Will would gain traction later on by earning a second bachelor's degree in order to qualify for admission to law school. But back then he acted proud of his reputation as an underachieving undergraduate at Wharton, class of 1968, where – like his classmate Donald Trump – he couldn't be bothered to study. He barely qualified for graduation.

For the memorial service that I'd asked Tim's three Exeter colleagues to prepare, I'd made no specific requests. And while nobody who was a regular at Phillips Church or who had attended Tim's joyous ordination the previous fall would have been entirely startled, the gospel hymn "Oh Happy Day" was an uncomfortable choice. Similarly, to play the recording of Tim's voice from his school assembly talk earlier in the year was another way of deflecting the harsh reality of why we were there. What sense did it make to hear him recite his favorite Bible verse one last time, when the lesson of a seed falling to the ground and dying and bearing much fruit was supposed to be a figure of speech?

It was beyond ironic that, for my dad and me, at the Hindu cremation ritual that I'd inadvertently commissioned in Ghana, without our understanding a single word, its toxic blast of heat had enforced our embracing the horror of Tim's bleeding to death. Here at Exeter, there was no such reckoning, instead the fallback Christian belief in a time for everything under the sun, no matter how terrible.

I couldn't get out of there fast enough, and on the ride back to New York, with my parents flicking the lit stubs of their unfiltered cigarettes onto the highway, my dad at the wheel of his Pontiac and my mom in her partial swivel to engage the backseat passengers, I welcomed her seemingly spontaneous idea of a family trip to the Caribbean for Christmas week. We never took family trips because my father never took vacations, but in aiming to protect me from the hectic round of holiday parties as well as what would have been my fourth wedding anniversary, instead of debriefing the memorial service and revealing how lonely – how exiled – I felt, I was rewarded with the opposite, cozy, feeling of being brought home. I was glad to have one.

I met the next day with Dr. Robinson at the Crossroads office and, when I asked to return to complete our project, he initially agreed. He disappointed me a few days later, however, by deciding that it was "better for all concerned" – I know this is how my mother felt – for our group of student volunteers to "carry on as best they could" without me. Of course I was glad to hear they were managing all right on their own, but after being with Tim's family, whose deeply deflected grief required conversation about anything other than Tim's death, I wanted to be in Ghana with the ones whose experience overlapped with mine. I needed to be with the only other witnesses to the reality of it.

I didn't go back. Instead, I spent an entire day with my friend Jean, and we talked for twelve hours, from noon until midnight. During my years with Tim, she too had gotten married. As couples we had little in common – Malcolm Holzman was already a hotshot young architect – but the friendship that dated to kindergarten and saw us off to travel the world had been recalibrated. A year earlier, on the day of the moonshot, Jean suffered a near-miss medical disaster of a perforated colon resulting in peritonitis. She knew what it was to come back from that edge.

When I next returned to Exeter it was to empty the apartment, and my brother came along to help. Our mother had arranged for professional movers to put into long term storage in New York the hand-me-down furniture and unused kitchen gadgets and cartons of books that Tim and I had brought there by U-Haul less than a year earlier. I'd inherited the mahogany bed frame from our grandmother's guest room, where Willy and I were allowed to share it one Christmas Eve and kept each other awake all night long, impatiently waiting for morning. I hope it's not too unwelcome a spoiler-alert to divulge that this same bed later went to my daughter and now sleeps *her* daughter. On that day as it was being dismantled by the movers, lacking a fortune teller to supply a more upbeat vision, I believed I'd never see it again.

I couldn't say where Tim's secondhand upright piano came from, or where it went from there, but on one of those July days I can still picture sitting with his brother on the bare floor next to the piano, with him leaning into it for support. Our heart-to-heart ended with my telling him that, with Tim dead, he now had the "opportunity" – but it sounded like *obligation* – to make more of himself. I understood the burden it was to be the younger brother of an overachiever, but it clearly wasn't my place to try to motivate him, if that was my intent. I knew the youngest brother less well and would never have instructed him in this way, so I would like to believe that my remark was a forgivable expression of my anger at Tim. In any case, while I don't recall his response, I can't ever forget his eyes widening and narrowing.

I'd received a generous letter of condolence from Exeter's school principal, Richard Day, in which he said that Tim showed "tremendous promise" and achieved "an incalculable amount of good." He told me, "Tim always gave me a lift, a new insight, a new sense of direction, new enthusiasm for what I was doing." Dick asked to see me when I came to campus, and so, because his weak heart didn't allow him to climb the four flights to the apartment, we met at a picnic table in the side yard. My own complex relationship with the Academy would improve over time, but in that afternoon's encounter, beyond its genuine warmth, a cruel absurdity was apparent. I was qualified to teach at the Academy now that I was no longer a faculty wife.

In a letter from my own principal, Frank Kozaka, he said my students will be very sorry to lose me, and so was he, as a teacher and friend. He referred to the "inner core of toughness" that he'd mentioned in his letter of recommendation to Crossroads and hoped this would carry me forward. I continue to feel grateful to Frank for releasing me from my teaching contract without making me feel worse than I already did.

During that long month of August I didn't know what to do with myself, and nobody else seemed to either. It was both too soon to be asking what my plan was for the fall and too late for me to put one into place. Having forfeited my early passion for dance and concluded my immersion in the culture and language of Japan, I also wondered what else I should have studied instead of French. With a little more confidence I might have allowed myself to recognize as a clue the "A++" grade I got on a Psychology paper at Columbia, or been helped to see that my unhappy introduction to psychotherapy could be reversed with a different therapist. I was clearly drawn to investigate that territory, but it was so unfamiliar a concept to my parents that they were unable to provide the guidance I sought. This was illustrated when I suggested to my mother that she and I might benefit from counseling to work out the conflict generated between us by my emerging feminism, and she poignantly asked, "Would we have to be hospitalized?"

I had no destination in mind when I traded in the sporty silver Datsun two-seater that Tim and I drove to California and back, and came away with a new white Ford Econoline panel truck whose only virtue was that it could be outfitted like a tiny house. My friend Jean painted the interior with a sky-blue ceiling and gingham-curtained windows to decorate that space large enough to accommodate a platform for a single mattress and crates of books to store beneath. The van allowed me a partial independence, and when it wasn't conspicuously parked in the suburban driveway of the home I'd essentially left when I went off to college at seventeen, I had the equivalent of a base camp for exploring my new wilderness.

During the immediate weeks after Tim's death a number of the Exeter boys he'd taught or coached or advised asked to remain connected to him by way of me. They were younger by seven or eight years, but for those in the graduating class of 1970 who were either freshmen in college or deferring it for a year, the dynamic was sufficiently altered. I welcomed their friendship.

I'd mainly been familiar with those boys who didn't fulfill the Scholar/Athlete ideal, the dedicated Phillips Church "deacons" who earnestly grappled with the world's insoluble concerns, and the others who merely seemed burdened by a debilitating homesickness generated by the Academy's oppressive demands. The boys who had either sought out or been sought out by Tim were often suffering their first failure to succeed, and while the other faculty successfully ministered to the cream of the crop, I sympathized with these so-called misfits. As the saying went at the time, I could relate.

That respect was returned, for example, when early in this blurred time soon after Tim's death I was invited to visit an exquisite stone wall that one of these boys had been commissioned to construct. After admiring how each unique yellowy pinkish stone was fitted to the next like chips in a mosaic, we then sat beside it to enjoy the extraordinary miniature picnic he'd prepared for us to share. Such individualized delicacy reminded me of my time in Japan when people would untie the patterned kerchiefs wrapping their lacquered lunch boxes to reveal painstakingly artful floral-like bites, except that now this enticingly frugal offering was as if to honor my loss of appetite. A single ruffled radish. A brownie the size of a caramel. To anyone else it would have seemed silly to call this a feast, but to me it was the perfect emblem of the horror that was being acknowledged, which nevertheless mandated a celebration of life.

Another graduate's gap year was being dedicated to restoring the New Jersey farmhouse his parents had retreated to after his scapegoated father's ouster as university president during student protests. In one of the farm's outbuildings my new friend created darkroom magic of a quality I'd never witnessed (even though Tim and his two brothers each took up photography and home developing), and in an adjacent garage, with a younger brother who went to the local high school – not Exeter – the two were in the process of reconstructing, bolt by bolt, a first-generation Land Rover.

For me, their working farm's recovery world of participatory regeneration proved restorative, and I became immersed in the bonus task of his father's overstocked rows of vegetables to hoe and his mother's old Aga stove's variously heated surfaces and compartments for simultaneous cooking. The days felt purposeful, and the land itself consoled me. I can still vividly recall the overnight when I woke from a bloody nightmare and, too horrified to sleep, was guided up and down the dirt road in a pitch darkness infiltrated by trace phosphorescence. I couldn't grasp the science, not even the next morning when it was translated for me at breakfast, but I knew I'd experienced Mother Nature – as if for the pure purpose of alleviating my personal suffering – causing the roadside vegetation to dance for me with an eerily glittery brightly pale light. In my eagerness to be brought back to life I was so open to this revelation of nature's sublime beauty that I felt almost drugged. Like any new addict, I only wanted more.

One afternoon, as I was headed back to New York on the New Jersey Turnpike, my panel truck had a blowout. I managed to bring it under control, but although I figured out how to jack it up I was unable to loosen the lug nuts. So I was balancing my weight on the tire iron and jumping gently enough not to rock it too much. When help came it was some other's girl's alarmed father who told me he'd stopped to help me – hanging onto my jacked-up van on a banked curve of an exit ramp in the buffeting wind of speeding traffic – because he feared for my life.

During those August weeks I also discovered that it felt odd but not weird to be staying in my own old bedroom while my parents sailed off to France for their long-scheduled trip-of-a-lifetime. They'd been invited as the guests of a friend from childhood, the son of a mail carrier in their hometown of Sharon, Pennsylvania. George had made it big as a stockbroker in Pittsburgh, especially once he married the daughter of Richard K. Mellon and, as a wedding gift, was given the commission on selling a million dollars worth of Mellon's Gulf Oil stock. I urged them to stick with their plan no matter that I had no plan of my own.

I had a frequent spacey-headed feeling which doubtless meant, since an entire egg was too much for me to get down, that I was eating too little. But because I both was and wasn't seeking gratification, I was occasionally capable of being surprised and even delighted. The densely billowy white seersucker curtains in my bedroom as a teenager had been sewn for me by a friend of my mother's for whose children I'd babysat, and though they hung rather limply these dozen years later, it gave me pleasure to recall the gift they'd been at the time. I enjoyed remembering the college summer when I moved the ping-pong table out of the finished basement of that house and polished the hardwood floor so that, with a very large mirror propped against the wall as in a proper studio, I could teach modern dance to the girls whose mothers then asked for their own class, provided they wouldn't have to perform in the recital.

Now alone in my mother's fertile garden I fell in love with the tightly wound zinnias whose vibrant colors I'd never fully appreciated, as with the profuse velvety cascading pale pink roses, the flowers of the annual and the perennial both having the staying power to persist beyond late summer, into early fall. It was as if I was beginning to get the sensation back in my toes and fingers, even if the rest of me was still numb.

Every hour of each of these weeks seemed endless, but I focused my recovery on the 2 am arrival of our Crossroads group on August 26th, six and a half weeks after Tim's death. When I met their plane at JFK I could see that – for them – it may have been a good decision to "carry on as best they could," in Dr. Robinson's phrase. And while I treasure the two Ghanaian sculpted musical instruments that were the gifts they brought to me, I felt overwhelmed by my regret at what I'd been prevented from giving to them. Ever since, I've wanted to reclaim that missed opportunity with them, to live with the trauma of Tim's death there, where it happened.

By not returning right away I didn't realize how insufficiently alert I was to those beyond our group who were also impacted by Tim's suicide. I mean especially the Chief and Queen-Mother of Wenchi who had welcomed us on behalf of their elder brother the Prime Minister, Ghana's head of state, in whose ancestral village this violence had occurred. I would eventually correct for this mistake, but I'm ashamed to admit that it took me another thirty years, to the day, to revisit the scene of the crime.

The previous summer Tim and I had been too square for the "Woodstock" festival. But now, when his childhood friend, Barbara Sproul, invited me to borrow the cabin named "Wake Robin" that she rented in the Byrdcliffe Arts and Crafts Colony for which the town of Woodstock, New York was originally known, I went. "Wake Robin" was also just across the valley from the spacious farmhouse leased by Philip Roth, Barbara's partner for what would come to be most of that decade, and it would be there, in sharing the quiet rhythm of their life together, that I could begin to sense the new shape of my own.

Barbara knew Tim better than anyone, certainly better than I did, and I welcomed her calm descriptions of the frequent conversations she and

Tim had shared about the several suicide attempts Tim's father had made, and the one her own had succeeded at. "Tim didn't *get it* about suicide," she insisted to me, and while of course I certainly didn't get it either, her authority gave me permission to try understanding and accepting his death, more sympathetically, as a mystery. Whatever that meant!

I possessed no personal language for comprehending and embracing mystery the way Barbara and Tim did. She was a protégée of Joseph Campbell and had already assembled a collection of creation mythology. She too had studied at Union, and though she would never take up Christianity except as a scholar of it, she could help me see what Tim studied and believed. On my own parallel track I'd immersed myself as a student of French literature's passionately self-destructive Romantic poets, and tried to learn how to interpret their madness. Purely domestic in my own habits, I'd worked to appreciate – on the page – the abandonment of self that enabled their self-discoveries. With access to Tim's own studies in religion and philosophy I felt provoked to imagine possessing a greater intelligence than my own. Whatever *that* meant.

The Savage God: A Study of Suicide by A. Alvarez was published in Great Britain within months of Tim's death, and while nothing could have been more shocking for me to read, I read it twice. The book opened with the example of an "unusually sweet-tempered" schoolteacher:

> One day at the end of a lesson, he remarked mildly that anyone cutting his throat should always be careful to put his head in a sack first, otherwise he would leave a terrible mess. Everyone laughed. Then the one o'clock bell rang and the boys all trooped off to lunch. The physics master cycled straight home, put his head in a sack and cut his throat. There wasn't much mess. I was tremendously impressed.

Alvarez concluded this anecdote, "The master was greatly missed, since a good man was hard to find in that bleak shut-in community. But in all the hush and buzz of scandal that followed, it never occurred to me that he had done anything wrong."

The Prologue to *The Savage God* concerned the famous suicide of Alvarez's friend, the poet Sylvia Plath. I've seen a recent statement by Alvarez that he rebukes himself to this day for not recognizing that she was ready to kill herself. "I failed her. I was thirty years old and stupid," he says, and while I know what he means – I was twenty-six and stupid – the truth is, unlike Alvarez, who had by then made a failed attempt on his own life, I had no idea what it took to be smart enough.

Around that time I also read the novel *L' Amante anglaise* by Marguerite Duras, a stunning deciphering of the logic of madness in the form of a police interrogation of a confessed murderer. A haunting recognition by the accused has stayed with me ever since, when the protagonist understands, *"Je n'étais pas assez intelligente pour l'intelligence que j'avais ..."* – not smart enough, she means, for the clinical madness attributed to her – because I wonder whether Tim's not being intelligent enough for his own intelligence – his self-diagnosed disequilibrium – became another reason to kill himself. In the Duras novel the confessed murderer wished to be completely intelligent, but she realized that in the face of her own death one day her only consolation will be her knowledge that she wasn't intelligent enough for her own intelligence.

But that season's major publishing event was *Portnoy's Complaint*, and it was such a literary and commercial *tour de force* that Philip felt forced to seek refuge in the countryside from the strangers who accosted him – "Hey, Portnoy!" – on the streets in the city. In Woodstock, he and Barbara took long daily walks together, for which Philip kindly invited me to come along. On those walks and during the meals we regularly shared I felt adopted by him, like a rescue pet, and I fed on his jokes like a Continuing Ed student assigned to re-learn laughter.

During those Woodstock mornings in Barbara's "Wake Robin" cabin I devoured the four books that Philip had published by that time, and started in on his reading list of the American classics he was surprised to see I didn't know. At least I was already familiar with Flaubert's famous prescription for the writing life, from a letter he wrote on Christmas Day, 1876, nine years after *Madame Bovary*. Philip often quoted, "Be regular in your life and ordinary as a bourgeois, so that you may be violent and original in your work," advice Philip both practiced and preached so fervently that it felt like religion.

Beyond being childhood friends, Barbara and Tim were college lovers before becoming graduate students together both at Union and in a parallel program at Columbia. I'd been introduced to her by Tim in the completely white garden apartment in midtown Manhattan, the home from which Barbara commuted to college at Sarah Lawrence. Her older brother was killed in a car accident, and her parents had ruined each other with their vengeful divorce. Barbara's apartment was adjacent to her father's, where, when she turned twenty-one and he decided his life was over, he ended it.

Philip had declined to meet Tim, so he was curious to know why I hadn't had the same feeling about meeting Barbara. Over dinner on the screened porch of that Woodstock farmhouse I replied that it was because it was immediately clear that Barbara was in a different category from me. She was then still an undergraduate when she showed me the obscure varieties she'd already amassed of creation mythology – *creation mythology!* – for the collection that would later become her scholarly work *Primal Myths.* I told Philip there was no contest since I couldn't compete with that level of distinction – "Nor could Tim with you, incidentally!" – but Philip held his ground. I was glad at least that his admitted possessiveness of Barbara, relative to Tim, hadn't extended to me.

She was beginning her teaching career at Hunter College around then, and with the further example of Philip's writer-in-residence appointments at Penn and Princeton, I scrutinized my own academic credentials and concluded that my studies in French Literature were the definition of Lost in Translation. My life was missing a basic knowledge of my own culture, so no wonder I didn't feel grounded. This gross oversimplification prompted me to look into the doctoral program in American Studies at Yale, even if the soonest I could start was the following year.

I'd mainly had a job while Tim mainly went to school, so there was a small savings account for me to draw on. What enabled me to consider my prospects this abstractly – this boldly and/or this naively – was thanks to the last-minute meeting I'd had with Exeter's Comptroller, Colin Irving. His novelist son John Irving had written about Colin as a compassionate adoptive father figure, as Colin proved to be for me as well. He asked to hear what had happened to Tim in Ghana, and he concluded that Tim's death didn't entirely qualify for the suicide exclusion.

Then and there, he awarded me the $7,000 payout on a life insurance policy whose existence I hadn't known about. In those days this amount covered tuition money for two years, but I also quickly realized that, if I decided not to go back to school after all, it could support me twice longer. I could afford to figure things out.

As their guest in the steadying worlds that Barbara and Philip were creating together, I felt both sheltered and shielded. When they brought me along to gatherings, I was briefed. I was cautioned ahead of a literary *soirée* in New York to avoid a particularly acquisitive writer who "never sees where he ends and you begin" and always takes advantage. I felt protected. I felt safe.

When Philip read to Barbara sections of what would become his novel *The Professor of Desire*, she chided him affectionately, "Don't you people make *anything* up?" He laughed it off, but he remained irritated by the persistent speculations of literary critics analyzing the overlap between his fictions and the private life that was increasingly public.

So, yes, Barbara was the "Claire" of Philip's 1972 novella *The Breast* and in the later novel, *The Professor of Desire*. When Philip's "Philip" character, David Kepesh, describes the "Barbara" character – Claire – as "the most extraordinary ordinary person I've ever met," he is describing "prudent, patient, tender" Barbara. Although she left Philip over her own desire to have children eventually – and his determination not to – they remained closely connected ever after, until the night of Philip's death fifty years later, when Barbara was with him.

That is, it's only an ironic coincidence that *The Professor of Desire* is dedicated to Claire – Claire Bloom – whom Philip later married, disastrously. I only met Claire once, over lunch, but in a phone call soon after that wedding Philip's only – ominous – comment to me was, "Well, I did it."

The point is that nothing mattered more to the man I knew than to achieve the *oeuvres* Flaubert defined as *violent et original*. He did this time and again, and although Philip consecutively evaded the ultimate bourgeois creation of a conventional family life, with Barbara I saw him come close.

I suppose it looks inevitable that, during these early months when I watched Philip at work, I too discovered the urge to write. I had a story to tell, and while untrained in composition, I'd been immersed in the theatrical dances devised by Martha Graham, a dynamic choreographer whose themes were literary, in fact. Within the literal mechanics of choreography, the effect is realized by means of contiguous phrases of movement rising and falling on the contraction and release of a breath. I could see that Martha Graham's classic technique was organic the way good writing is alive when it moves across the page. I began to believe that from my own choreography in high school and college and beyond, it was possible that perhaps I already understood a few of the basics.

At the private school I attended in Dobbs Ferry, New York, I was impressed that my modern dance teacher, who was white, performed with the pioneering African-American dancer/choreographer Donald McKayle, in whose company Alvin Ailey also danced. From the first day of dance class at Wheaton, what I remember best is my classmate Denise Jefferson's horrified shock at the start of the standard warmup for the Martha Graham technique – "On the *floor?*" – that was the opposite of her own rigorous training in classical ballet. Denise and I became friends for life when I convinced her to come with me to a master class at the New England Conservatory taught by Donald McKayle. In him she saw a path forward, having been told by her teacher back in Chicago that a Black girl could have no future in ballet. After Wheaton Denise would find McKayle again in New York, as well as Alvin Ailey, who had formed his own company by then. When then Mr. Ailey started The Ailey School, he bestowed upon Denise the role of Director, a position she held for the next forty years, training ninety percent of the dancers for the world-renowned Alvin Ailey American Dance Theater.

Of course Philip's example meanwhile made clear that, no matter what I might know about dance, I still had everything to learn about writing. More concretely, I could observe in Philip's daily routine the value in spending twice as much time reading as writing. One weekend during those early months, I was visiting Barbara and Philip at the property he'd recently bought, shifting their base from Woodstock to Warren, Connecticut. It was on their couch by the fireplace that I read in the *New York Times Book Review* a featured review of a new biography of Virginia Woolf by her nephew, Quentin Bell. I'd had only the slightest knowledge of Virginia Woolf's writing from reading *To the Lighthouse,* too early, as an eighth-grade summer reading assignment, so this chance introduction was an epiphany. That afternoon I started with her first novel, *The Voyage Out,* and proceeded to read her straight through.

For the rest of his life I amused Philip by crediting him with teaching me how to read and, by extension, to write. Among his many actual students I knew I wasn't alone, just as I became only one of a legion of fans who would forever answer, when asked to name their favorite writer, "Virginia Woolf!" It was absurd for me to imagine myself a talent, but Philip encouraged me nonetheless. And while it was many months before I showed him my first effort – to which he awarded the title *The Child Widow* like a gold star – I'd already benefited from its therapeutic value by writing about the loss that defined me.

With Philip's validation I dedicated myself to his daily routine of alternating hours of writing with twice that many hours of reading. Though still assuming the way to repair my ruptured life was to go back to school and trade in my two degrees in French for one in the recently established field called American Studies, I was suddenly also able to imagine my new identity as an apprentice writer. Each night I found myself actually looking forward to the day ahead, which both helped get me to sleep and got me up in the morning. I felt alive, and was able to sense that a writer's life could be a way of *staying* alive. Could this be what they meant by vocation?

I'd seen Tim search out and claim his, but I always assumed I'd have, at most, a job. My father's homemaker wife, my mom, was one of those smart and ambitious women who lost her nerve before figuring out how to be happier, and then whose time ran out. This was back in the day when we college girls would randomly choose names for the kids we planned to have, all of them by the end of our twenties. We were ignorant of the irony that with the invention of each new appliance our post-war stay-at-home moms had increasingly less and less to do with their time. It was as if we thought the funnel cloud of change on the horizon wasn't spinning our way, as if we couldn't already feel its wind. The revolution was coming, but not quite soon enough.

In automatically changing my name to Tim's I'd only become aware of having lost my own identity when we got to California, where I realized nobody knew I'd once been someone else. After he died I felt guilty for having felt that way, and though I had symbolized the abrupt end of our marriage by immediately shifting my wedding band to my right hand, it wasn't until a writer friend of Philip's matter-of-factly wondered why I would continue to use Tim's name that I knew to take back my own.

After telling Tim's mother – who graciously interpreted it as my need for a *nom de plume* now that I was an aspiring writer – I submitted my application to Probate Court. This was the cumbersome protocol required at the time, in spite of the glaring discrepancy in there having been no equivalent formal judicial procedure for assuming Tim's name upon marriage. When I was granted an appearance before the Probate Judge, I felt what I took to be his disapproval. No matter that it was my father's name that I was asking permission to resume as my legal identity, his manner toward me seemed patronizing. I could see by my relatively recently acquired ambition to craft a new identity that I'd already come a long way from shrinking before Dr. Beltman's rigid demeanor in dismissing my urgent request for medical help for Tim, but I resented feeling disregarded.

When the Judge asked my name and I practically shouted, "*LeXa BuXton*," he surprised me by leaning down toward me from his bench to say, "I'd change it too. Which one are you changing?"

If Henry James could find *L'Education Sentimentale* "dreary" compared to *Madame Bovary,* so could I, no matter that Flaubert had written it. I wasn't altogether confident in telling the difference between irony and pessimism, nor was I always able to distinguish sentimentality from the subtlety that lay this side of it. But, as I was being taught by Philip, this too would turn out to be learnable.

I still value the lesson I learned from Philip on one of those peaceful afternoon walks back in Woodstock. After spending the day reading Rilke's *Letters to a Young Poet* for the first time, I thanked Philip for the recommendation. I was flattered by his taking my own education seriously, and told him I'd found Rilke's mentoring advice helpful.

Although Rilke's formal and somewhat stuffy language was a barrier to me who lacked Philip's ever sharp penetration, I felt I knew what Rilke meant when he advised the young poet:

> Ask yourself in the most silent hour of your night: must I write? Dig into yourself for a deep answer. And if this answer rings out in assent, if you meet this solemn question with a strong, simple 'I must,' then build your life in accordance with this necessity; your whole life, even into its humblest and most indifferent hour, must become a sign and witness to this impulse.

I told Philip I had been witnessing this in him without yet daring to propose the question to myself, but I was definitely on the lookout for some necessity to build my life around. I said Rilke spoke to me more directly with this:

> The quieter we are, the more patient and open we are in our sadness, the more deeply and serenely the new presence can enter us, and the more we can make it our own, the more it becomes our fate.

I honestly didn't feel very "patient" or "open" in my sadness, but I could appreciate that, with this new routine, my life was already becoming quieter. I was coming to believe it was possible to live according to Rilke's exhortation:

> Live the questions now. Perhaps then someday in the future, you will gradually, without even noticing it, live your way into the answer.

In the sometimes oppressive isolation of "Wake Robin" I'd been searching for answers and finding none to fit my questions about Tim's violent dying. But I gradually felt persuaded to let myself simply settle into the nourishment of a daily rhythm. Just by sleeping and eating better I was already restoring my own health, and I'd been able to gain back a little of my vanished weight. There were quiet dinners with Barbara and Philip at the farmhouse and frequent raucous dinner parties on the weekends with their New York friends who came up from the city to their own country houses. Philip's well-chronicled time in the Army yielded standup comedy routines that I found hilarious, such as the time when he entertained the table by mimicking the language of the fellow soldiers who inserted "fucking" between the syllables of most words. Like what? It can still make me laugh to remember him pointing to a casserole of baked eggplant and tomatoes and zucchini and saying "Like *rata*-fucking-*touille*."

Another gradual benefit was that, as I began to sleep better, the worst of my nightmares seemed to have subsided into mere bad dreams. If I could stop tormenting myself by dreaming in red, for instance, perhaps I could imagine learning to "Live the questions now." Now, with Rilke's help, if I could live my way into the answer – and maybe even recreate my fate! – I knew I could wait.

We three continued our walk along the familiar path and arrived at the little wooden bridge across a narrow stream. On this particular beautiful afternoon the air was still, as if poised, and though I know it's melodramatic to call this moment a crossing into literary consciousness, that's how it felt at the time.

In Rilke's definition of a good marriage "each partner appoints the other the guardian of his solitude, and thus they show each other the greatest possible respect." While this obviously wasn't the case with Tim or I'd have been clued into the depth of *his* solitude, I needed to believe in the possibility.

At the table by the window in "Wake Robin" I'd read this next passage so many times that I was able to quote it word for word:

> And this more human love [...] will be like that love which we are straining and toiling to prepare, the love which consists in this, that two lonely beings protect one another, border upon one another and greet one another.

In reciting this passage for Philip and Barbara, I believed in their having found "this more human love" with each other. And while acknowledging in myself an unrequited yearning for a bond of this dimension, I was also alert to the jolt of joy I was experiencing, despite my fears, in redefining myself.

Rilke's prescription for lonely beings provided an uplift so alluring that it was as if the toxic crematory smoke that infiltrated my lungs on a hilltop in Ghana could be forcefully expelled enough to become a vapor trail. Maybe I even looked up to the sky, expecting to see my breath escape, and evaporate.

And here's what I mean about what I really learned that day, as I stood there reciting Rilke's "two lonely beings protect one another, border upon one another and greet one another," still ignorant of – but not immune to – the essential, discernible borders between sentimentality and subtlety, between pessimism and irony.

Philip's purpose wasn't to contradict me when he stopped me with his deadpan gaze. But I felt myself being reeled back to reality when he gently asked, "And then what? Go bowling?"

HUMAN REMAINS

The ashes arrived in a flat package, neither square nor round, wrapped in brown paper and tied with knotted white butcher's string. It was mailed to me at my parents' home with no more of a return address than a mosaic of colorful foreign postage stamps. The customs form defined the contents as HUMAN REMAINS.

My mother and I received it from her regular postman at the kitchen door, and we let it sit on the Formica counter for a respectful minute or two before untying the string. The paper wasn't taped, so it fell right open to reveal the six-sided container. The design on the lid illustrated Wordsworth's ten thousand daffodils "tossing their heads in sprightly dance," the poem African children memorized in colonial schools no matter that not a single daffodil grew on the entire continent. It only made sense because the tin had once contained English biscuits of a brand evidently favored by Her Majesty the Queen, according to the superimposed royal seal of approval.

At the cremation site I'd been introduced to an old man sitting off to the side, who was hired to stay behind to tend the ashes overnight and for as long as it took until the fire extinguished itself. It was his job – his profession – to guard and gather the ashes, so I had to presume he knew what he was doing even though this shallow tin seemed too small for what it contained. I held it steady and shook it gently from side to side, and wished I hadn't when I realized the ashes also included pieces of bone.

As solemnly as we could my mom and I agreed that it simply was what it was, the whole thing was what it was, period. Of course it wasn't funny, not at all, but neither were we entirely able to *not* laugh.

From our hotel room on the overnight layover in Paris en route back to New York, my dad and I had our first chance to call home. Sitting on the edge of my twin bed, I felt pressured to say the right thing when my mother expressed how worried she'd been that I might have caught the contagious disease that had killed Tim. "No, I'm fine and I'll tell you more tomorrow," I deflected, needing to know why my dad hadn't shared the information he'd been given by the Crossroads office and why he didn't tell me he hadn't. His honest answer was that he simply couldn't. It wasn't clear if he meant that on the drive from his office to the airport he couldn't summon the courage, or that he refused to leave her behind to deal with it alone. Either way, I could identify all too well.

As we emerged into the terminal at JFK, my athletic mom ran to me like a sprinter and held me in her fierce grip. In the car she told us that Tim's mother and Aunt Lyd and his sister and a brother were coming for dinner, so I had my first assignment to tell the story in a way that could allow those who loved Tim to accept the *cause* of his death as well as the fact of his death.

Arriving back at the house I'd grown up in I felt welcomed in a way I recognized from the time when I got home from a rustic summer camp in New Hampshire and recovered, with all my senses, all at once, all that I loved about it. I kicked off my sandals and felt the carpeting with the soles of my feet. I took in the fresh arrangement of zinnias from my mother's garden, heard the ticking of the grandfather clock, and could almost already taste the fragrance of our dinner, cooking. To my right was the peach wallpapered dining room, its polished table set with silver and crystal, and to my left the sitting room's pastoral scene in the blue Toile couch and draperies centered on the wall opposite the fireplace. Not a single thing had been rearranged.

When Tim's family arrived we greeted each other with an exuberance suitable for such a once-in-a-lifetime event. But it also reminded me of the night before our wedding, when the joy of family reunion and the joining of two families was made somber by Tim. On that night, it was the ponderous toast he offered – not to me or my parents or his mother – to his absent father confined at the Bloomingdale Asylum. Now on this night of course it was Tim who was missing, and it was up to me to honor him while lovingly acknowledging his frailty.

Once we were gathered in our circle, I spoke. I suspect I chose to reverse the chronology in order to begin with the consolation of the cremation, working backwards to the cause of Tim's death, but it wasn't a conscious decision. And while I'm entirely responsible for burying the lede, I couldn't have imagined that for the rest of Tim's mother's very long life the breadknife would never be mentioned again. In reporting the events that night I sympathized with Helen's reflexive resort to denial. At the time I even found her stifled grief a kinder response than the muted blame my own mother conveyed to me later that night in her shock that Tim had done such a thing. To me.

The medical findings in the autopsy report surely exceeded the limits of normal curiosity, especially when what's missing from it is the only potentially helpful information: a chemical analysis of brain tissue and/or spinal fluid. Because it's impossible to see Tim killing himself with his father still alive, I'm unable to imagine having to show these disturbing documents to Lee. But I didn't volunteer to show them to Tim's mother either, and Helen never asked to see them.

I re-wrapped the biscuit tin and re-tied the string, and my mother and I sat on the porch overlooking her garden. Maybe I watched her eat one of her trademark sandwiches, cucumber and Bermuda onion on Pepperidge Farm thin-sliced white bread, but I'm confident that, since I had no appetite on a good day, I didn't join her for lunch. It had been eight weeks since Tim's death, and when I called Helen to tell her the ashes had finally arrived, she proposed driving to Old Lyme the next day since only the two of us and her sister Lydia, Tim's godmother, would be present for the burial. I described the biscuit tin container and apologized for it, but she wasn't upset. Without putting it into words, it was as if all the rules were already violated, so who cared whether the cemetery had policies about proper containers? This was how I felt too. Please just dig a hole and leave us alone to bury our dead.

So Helen and I drove together to Old Lyme, exiting the highway to pass by the classic Congregational Church where her sister Josephine's wedding and funeral took place forty-one years earlier. When Tim preached from that pulpit one Sunday after becoming ordained, he mentioned that the original church was established there in 1665 by its first minister, his ancestor Moses Noyes. The big white house next door to the church had been sold long ago, but the carriage barn remained in the family as a token of the illustrious heritage tarnished by the scandalous murder/suicide. I longed for that former hayloft where just five years earlier Tim and I would lie in bed together, listening to the trains' wailing horns, without any awareness of the shadow cast by disgrace.

Lydia drove down from Hill Top Farm, the property she was struggling to preserve. She drove the Lakeville school bus, and in the barn next to the cook's house she boarded the police chief's ponies along with her own aging horses. A Paris-trained "sculptress" whose bronze life-size fawn stood by the porch steps, she was a Civil Air Patrol pilot during World War II and became a flight instructor and dispatcher at a local airfield. It was rumored that she'd had a lover in France, a pilot shot down, but under the brim of her sun-bleached baseball cap, her own beauty had turned comfortably boyish. Here was a woman who could finish off a day of mowing with an hour of Cole Porter songs at the grand piano she'd rescued from the big house before renting it out. Lyd's buoyant good cheer was so motivating that she could even get me on horseback to canter along beside her as if I too loved riding.

The hole had been dug to the proper depth, so Helen had to kneel and lean forward to set down the biscuit tin. The only spoken words were hers, when she said, "With all he gave us, may we learn to give also."

I echoed the feeling but struggled with it because, yes, Tim was an inspiring teacher, and I knew how good he must have been in the classroom to have such devoted students, but I also knew how much more he still had to teach, and learn. What could Tim himself have intended as the lesson of his death? I preferred to conjure the expansive example he set with his bottomless love for Lee, and wanted Helen to have felt equally cherished by Tim. Of course I also wished he could have loved me that much, or at least enough to want to live more than he wanted to die. I wanted him to have told himself what he wrote to his father in that heartbreakingly parental letter to Lee at the Bloomingdale Asylum:

Please <u>never be afraid</u> in the next 40 years of your life, of being yourself – not a super man!! Love, Tim.

In the Duck River Cemetery Helen and Lydia and I filled Tim's small square grave and stood before it in silence, holding hands. My journal records that "Helen said 32 years ago today she was married to Lee – embarrassed that she told me. How sad it all is." On that thirty-second anniversary I imagined Helen as a girl marrying a man a half-generation older. There were two unmarried daughters who came between Josephine and Helen, so Helen's wedding on September 4th in 1938 was the next to come after Josie's high society wedding to Bert nine years earlier.

We were now standing between the stone for Helen's baby Kitty and the mother after whom Helen was named, the spine of the family laid to rest next to her own beloved first child. I described it in my journal as a "tragic day of tenseness and release though I couldn't speak of it out loud. release from punishment of myself but god how lonely. we couldn't have had a service because we needed to cry in privacy."

I moved to New Haven in October, three months after Tim's death, aiming to advance the hypothesis that after finishing my French studies I should reinvent myself in my own culture, with a doctorate from Yale in American Studies. Instead, I quickly realized that I was already achieving a certain equilibrium with this sustained opportunity to sit with my typewriter – my first, like Philip's, a blue portable Olivetti – at my plywood desktop on sawhorses in the spare bedroom of my apartment in the two-family house on a blue-collar block beyond the leafy zone where Yale's students and faculty lived. In devising the rhythm of a life alone I was developing a new definition of the kind of solitude – not Rilke's after all – that I not only welcomed but craved. I baked bread, for myself.

In automatically changing my name to Tim's I'd selected "earth-toned" bath towels monogrammed with my new initials. But I chose to leave them and everything else in storage, furnishing the apartment that I intended as temporary with primary-colored carpet remnants and Japanese-style floor cushions set around the low table that I put together with screw-on legs, and painted spring green. Most of my friends from the college class of '65 were meanwhile occupied with their infants and toddlers, a role I'd once anticipated for myself. But with that trajectory derailed, who was I now? It was as if I was being released, if not ejected, from the cohort of my peers. I could attach myself anywhere I wanted, it seemed, and so I did.

Though to some my choice of New Haven appeared related to the fact that Tim had grown up there, of his family just the stepmother whom his father had married only twenty months before his death actually lived there. A widow for the second time, Peggy was trying to decipher her own life. We formed a kinship.

In my early months in New Haven, while also remaining in frequent touch with Tim's mother in New York, I came to feel reinforced by the companionship of Lee's widow, whose own resilience had been less apparent to me during the chaotic span of their doomed marriage. When Lee died less than two weeks after his hospital release, the faux-family fell apart, as did the awkward step-sibling romance. By the time of Tim's death exactly one year later, Peggy had moved from their large house on the edge of East Rock Park into an apartment closer to downtown, where she found it possible to recalibrate by becoming a kindergarten teacher.

Not having spent enough time together to become close, with my move to New Haven after the deaths of our husbands we became friends. We now had in common the boomerang effect – "Who *was* that masked man?" – of our identically short marriages to the father-son duo we never really knew, and now never really would.

It pains me to acknowledge that I resisted my own mother's attempts to connect with me, rejecting her invitations with the excuse that I was too busy writing. I skipped Thanksgiving, letting her think that I couldn't handle it. It was therapeutic for me, in fact, that Peggy and I instead prepared a meal for two with none of the traditional elements – we ate lobster and chocolate mousse – but I know my mother was hurt by what she could only interpret, and experience, as my withdrawal from her.

Our politics were already divergent, and becoming more and more so. She was what used to be called a Rockefeller Republican while I was a fervent Kennedy Democrat, which I had proved with my first vote for RFK as Senator from New York. That election was the next November after his brother's assassination, and while my dad was a big fan of General Eisenhower, he was just eighteen months older than JFK and identified with his service as a naval officer in the Pacific. When President Kennedy was killed on my father's forty-eighth birthday, my dad stayed home from work to watch the funeral. I can't suppose he ever voted Democratic, and while we had our bitter arguments over Vietnam, I had less sympathy for my mother's Republicanism. It would be another year before *MS.* Magazine arrived on the scene and I became a charter subscriber, but I already regarded my stay-at-home mom as a casualty of the system that I was increasingly determined not to let drag me back down. I joked that the reason I didn't move back to New York was so that my mother couldn't marry me off to an IBM executive to compensate for my having married Tim. It wasn't altogether a joke for either of us, however.

I couldn't blame her for taking my rhetoric personally – it both was and wasn't – and I sincerely regretted the reopening of old wounds such as my shouting at her "Then *you* go!" when I had no desire to go to college (because I wasn't ready) and she absolutely needed me to (because she'd missed out). That collision was only one of our lost opportunities to wonder together What's Wrong With This Picture? During my high school years she'd made it clear that my blind allegiance to my absentee father was at her expense. When she accused "You're just like your father!" I took it as a compliment while knowing she meant it as an insult. I want to believe that, with the help of the same feminism that was driving us apart, she and I would surely have come to fully embrace each other's failings, given time. But we weren't.

The late-stage discovery of her ovarian cancer came in January, within six months of Tim's death, when she went to her doctor with an abdominal discomfort that led to tests and a biopsy and the decision after exploratory surgery to "sew her back up again" in that euphemistic way surgeons had for admitting defeat. Even at the time it seemed jarringly inept that her prognosis was as imprecise as "six months to two years," but it quickened the pace. That we had a long way to go was evident when I visited her in the recovery room and she woozily asked me how many times I'd taken LSD. I'm not sure she believed me when I told her I never had, or would, but I saw how deeply worried she was about me.

When she requested a new bathrobe for her hospital stay I picked out a jazzy zippered red and white herringbone-striped robe and hemmed it to fit. Her private room was in Columbia Presbyterian's Harkness Pavilion, where a journey to the solarium was rewarded with a Scenic Overlook across the Hudson to the prehistoric Palisades. And since smoking was permitted everywhere in those days, as we strolled the corridor she could hold a Lucky in one hand and push her IV pole with the other. Of course there's nothing like really bad news to change everything, but even under these radically altered circumstances I could have made it easier for both of us to relinquish the lingering hurt we each carried like stubborn mules with saddlebags on our backs.

"Alexa dearest," she wrote in July to say "thanks for coming – and staying" for "our 1st chance since <u>January</u>" to have the conversation she'd wished for and deserved:

> I had been trying to invite myself to New Haven for just such a chat but somehow each day that passed the opportunity seemed to go further away. Even when I was in the hospital I longed to have you visit alone but that never happened – in retrospect I guess it was by design! But now that some understanding has been reached I'm looking forward to – not an armed truce – but mutual respect. That doesn't sound too hard, does it? Just remember that my limitations are profound and numerous but I do mean well! I'm certain that we can have an enjoyable time together if we just stop looking for something to upset us. I don't think you try to make me angry any more than I do you, and what has happened has in reality been just plain silly and childish on both our parts. So – Right on and thanks for coming – and staying – it was fun – much love m.

I've mercifully let go of most of the hurtful particulars of those anguished six months she refers to, and while it's not literally true that I never visited her alone in the hospital, I can't dispute the alienation I both nurtured and neglected to address. That five of these seven sentences of hers contain a "but" represents for me the harsh series of reversals we achieved on the day she refers to. And while I'm not sure I felt "it was fun" the way she did, I've kept this precious evidence in my desk drawer ever since.

During that time when I commuted between New York and New Haven I regularly stopped off in Stamford to visit an old boyfriend and his wife. James Knowles was a bronze sculptor, and when Jimmy asked me to sit for a head I was intrigued to observe how similar his work was to the writing of a novel. A painstaking procedure is required for the eventual achievement of the finished product, and the process is the point.

In fact this gave me the premise for my first published novel, *Gus in Bronze*, which is about a dying woman pestered by her adolescent daughter into sitting for a head sculpted by the art teacher she has a crush on. The age of my protagonist, Augusta, was exactly halfway between my mother's and mine, so the family I invented had a life of its own. Nor did the fraught process of constructing my fictional head resemble my actual time with Jimmy and his wife Sue II, whose nourishing soups and crusty breads were motivating and sustaining. In those months when my mother's diagnosis eclipsed my efforts to live with the trauma of Tim's suicide, I found it unexpectedly healing simply to sit altogether still for hours at a time.

Although it was my intention to get my parents to purchase the bronze, when I took my mother to see it she said she couldn't. It made her too sad, she said, to look at that troubled face. In fact Jimmy had perfectly captured my fight-or-flight stare, with only a discreetly redeeming upward tilt of the chin. I tried to point out to her that – "Chin Up!" – my gaze was hopeful, but she wasn't convinced. Yes, I could acknowledge that my expression was severe, even stark, but I was flattered by it. Jimmy's head made me look like my hero, Virginia Woolf. And to this day it still does.

Later that spring, my mother had an idea. She'd always wanted to travel and almost never got to, unlike me, and while her chemo regimen would dictate the itinerary, she wanted me to take her to France. She insisted that I not revise my preexisting offer to help construct a trio of houses on an island in Greece – heavy lifting, in a good way – and so I went on ahead. I'd been to Greece with Jean and her parents on The Grand Tour, but this rustic alternative consisted of prying rocks from the earth and piling them up to make walls and even the built-in furniture, the beds and couches and tables, that we then plastered and whitewashed. A close friend of Tim's and two other college classmates and their girlfriends were living in a rented house that was a strenuous hike from the site. It was hard work, and every evening we relaxed, exhausted, sharing a communal meal and the retsina wine that I came to detest but which functioned as a nightly knockout.

So when I arrived in Paris a day ahead of my mother I wasn't surprised that I needed to sleep for twelve solid hours, nor that I took advantage of her jet lag with more sleep. The following morning I noticed the rash that I hid from her with a turtleneck and opaque tights. But by the time our TGV pulled into Carcassonne that evening, it was obvious to us both that I was the one, not her, who needed medical help.

A doctor was summoned to our hotel room and I was diagnosed with *la roséole* (not *la rubéole*, the childhood measles my mother verified my having had). I'd never heard of this *"sixième maladie,"* and while I was assured that it was only a benign childhood disease, I worried that it was contagious and told the doctor of my mother's compromised immune system. He said not to worry, confining me to bed with a regimen of greasy suppositories. The next morning, from our hotel room within that historic fortress site, my mom waved to me as she gamely went by on her guided tour of the battlements.

I'd been sufficiently apprehensive about my responsibility for her care during this reprieve between chemo sessions to have inadvertently blunted her triumphant arrival in Paris with my inquiries at the airport into the strike announced for our departure day. She interpreted my anxiety as my wanting to get the trip over with before it began, no matter that, as I tried to explain, in France a threatened strike is serious. In Carcassonne she now had the chance to remind me that, in the context of her fatal illness, my whatever-it-was was a prescription for me to relax and enjoy our time alone together. That I'd somehow contracted a childhood disease underscored her point that this mother-daughter trip was a long-deferred first adventure. I wished with all my heart to have the power to reverse this sad truth, and start over.

As we then confidently made our way from one country inn destination to the next, she took pride in my fluency and pleasure in the navigational ease that it enabled. And since our visit overlapped with asparagus season, we daily indulged in those velvety white spears cascaded with *sauce mousseline*. I know she would have wanted to grow this more exotic variety at home, if not for the foreshortening of her own growing season.

My upbeat brother again paused his life in Colorado and rushed east to enliven our mother, just as he had for me during those fragile weeks after Tim's death when he gave me the simple reassurance of his steadily entertaining companionship. He had gotten a job as a middle school librarian in the Aspen Public Schools, where the principal and Will belonged to the risk-defiant ski troupe that called themselves "The Fliers." Now he was legitimately on summer vacation, and while I'm sure our parents wondered what they'd done wrong to raise two children who had no real prospects, we focused on the future staring us in the face, bridging our blatant differences by overcompensating.

In our dad's stunned disbelief, he couldn't handle hearing talk of her dying – so would get up and leave the room – assigning us to become familiar with her repeated declaration "I'm not afraid to die." In fact, none of the four of us could fully absorb her fatal diagnosis, despite the fact that her lively younger brother's pancreatic cancer had so recently and rapidly swept him away. For our dad it simply wasn't the plan for her to die first, not when his workaholic life was such a trustworthy killer.

In addition to being undeniably blunt, she was reliably stubborn. When President Jimmy Carter's oil embargo threatened the daily commute for radiation with standstill lines at the pumps, our generous neighbors systematically substituted our cars for theirs. Even so, her preferred route into Manhattan was calculated to evade the 10-cent toll at the Henry Hudson Bridge, and she methodically collected all those unspent dimes in a big glass jar destined to succeed her. In her cranky frugality she remained the proud daughter of a small-town bank president who managed not to let it go under in the Depression.

Now that her volunteer work was suspended, I finally came to recognize and honor its meaning and purpose, for her as well as for me. In her devotion to helping those referred to as "the disadvantaged" – their handicaps too often seen by the more fortunate as self-imposed – her aims were consistent. She supported educational outreach by the local Planned Parenthood clinic but also supplied maternity clothes and baby blankets for the St. Faith's Home for Unwed Mothers. Yes, she served on committees to create fancy fundraising events for charities, but she worked toward justice. She set the example for me.

She understood my desire to travel for what it was: to see what there was to learn from the unfamiliar. The poignant image of her as a young woman – my age – imagining the destinations of the passengers crisscrossing Grand Central Station was both a cautionary tale and motivation. I couldn't recognize at the time that she valued upward mobility, but she did. She wanted it for herself, and for me.

I began to collect images of her, a vagabond's portable scrapbook to store in my mind. I often wish I had the actual photos that her illness didn't allow me to capture with a camera, but I can still see her stubbing out her Luckies in a pearly pink seashell ashtray on the sunny back porch overlooking her garden. Harvesting the last of her zinnias. Boiling the final batch of the tangy red currant jelly she favored for glazing her toast. Inspecting the evergreen boxwood hedging that she'd nurtured from clippings discreetly stolen from Monticello – which the accommodating groundskeeper proudly confided as having originally come from England – and which with proper grooming could be counted on to endure into the next century.

On her sitting room couch she sat with her legs tucked under her, like a bird on her nest, where I could find her every day after school in case I was willing to talk. She claimed, "I'll never understand you," but she always made the attempt.

I had already let go of my vague plan for graduate school in favor of what I experienced as the healing properties of the writing life. So in my move from New Haven to Amherst, while I appeared to be trading in the outskirts of one academic community for the fringes of its Five College counterpart, the greater difference was that I was making plain what was still to many an incomprehensible romantic relationship. While settling into a trustworthy writing routine I was also enjoying my cautiously tender romance with one of those "Exeter boys" I'd come to know, and come to love, during these several years since we'd briefly overlapped there. What he and I had in common, beyond Tim, was that we were equally in search of identity, which permitted both of us to modify the rules of coupling. Our age difference of more than seven years gave me an automatic authority in the relationship, and this allowed me to let down my guard. His reward was in escaping the random chaos of college dating, and while we were mutually dependent – but in a healthy way – in this parallel coming-of-age we devised a sweet passion that I found deeply consoling. Without a blueprint we were freer to improvise, and though we would later separate, in this unconventional romantic apprenticeship I felt both independent and committed.

My mother tried her best – to try her best – to find a way to accommodate it, but I think she simply couldn't grasp how I could act so immune to shame. During that summer and fall her solution was to pretend that my "young man" and I would be getting married just like any normal couple, and I really couldn't blame her, from within the confines of her illness, for wanting to predict my future.

"No, Mom, that's not going to happen," I tried as gently as possible to inform her, and while I'd like to think there was good news for her in this because it allowed her to fantasize that one day my prince would come and we'd get married in a heartbeat and have a daughter and a son and a beautiful house and a garden with an asparagus bed – *just like her* – I'll never know if it actually did.

Needless to say, a version of this happily-ever-after dream had been mine too, once upon a time, but I had become an adamant convert from faith to cynicism. There was *No Way* I'd ever say "I will" again, *No Way* I'd ever buy into *that* again, no matter *who* came along! So no wonder she didn't press the issue.

My mother had been as eager as Lee for me to provide a grandchild, but with her "six months to two years" clock running out, this was one more thing she was losing out on. When I mentioned to my gynecologist that my mother seemed to have achieved an uncharacteristic calm – without giving up, she was relinquishing – my doctor shared her unscientific theory that her patients diagnosed with cancer very often appeared to undergo a chemical change, a compensatory mood shift to enable their coping. In my mother's case her suffering seemed eased by being relieved of the fighter's intrinsic need to throw a punch. Instead of battling her disease she confronted it with a more considered intelligence, which prevented her from merely flailing against it, the way she'd always seemed to live her life. Never passive, it wasn't an option for her to quit, but neither was she capable of fooling herself. After a lifetime of feeling thwarted, my mother was coping! This was her last, and best, achievement. And while I hated her having to suffer the intensifying agonies of the spread of her cancer, I wanted her to live on and on.

One afternoon, from her perch on the couch she concluded that the slipper chairs by the fireplace needed to be re-slipcovered. She'd already had a pair of etched antique glass vases made into lamps for those side tables, and although the Christmas holidays were approaching, she persuaded someone to accommodate the pressure of her own accelerated schedule. I agreed that the chairs needed an upgrade, if not necessarily at that particular moment in time, because I could see what she was envisioning. She wanted the chairs to look good when the house would be full of family and friends and neighbors after her funeral. She knew it wouldn't be long now.

My sudden switch from calling them "Mom" and "Dad" to "Mother" and "Daddy" still nags at me all this time later. It was a mere copycat college girl affectation, a phase, but the shift also had the power to make them seem, and likely make Mom feel, less than equally loved. Though she never let me know if she felt hurt by this, it's one more thing I wish hadn't happened, and for which I still want to have apologized.

"How sharper than a serpent's tooth it is to have a thankless child!" was her acknowledgement that she too had given her mother a hard time. By making my non-compliant behavior the payback for her own, she wasn't comparing me to Lear's state-of-the-art abominable daughters so much as forcing me to identify with her. I had a hard time believing that she'd ever made life difficult for her sweet mother when in my opinion her "Mama" was perfect. But this turned out to be my mother's way of proving that nobody is perfect. Which drew her lesson back to an admission of simple gratitude for the people who love us.

On my twenty-first birthday in January of my senior year in college she sent me a telegram:

HOW DO I LOVE THEE LET ME COUNT THE WAYS. THE 21 YEARS
YOU HAVE BEEN ALL THINGS PARENTS COULD HOPE FOR: WISE,
CREATIVE, LOVELY TO LOOK AT, AND MOST IMPORTANT OF ALL
KIND. I LOOK BACK ON THESE YEARS WITH GRATITUDE AND LOVE.
I THANK YOU FOR JUST BEING YOU.
MOTHER

Her signing it with my pretentious MOTHER instead of the good old
MOM that I'd abandoned so unkindly was to let me know that I could test
her all I wanted and still be entirely loved.

I preserved the telegram, unable at the time to imagine that one day I
would have the opportunity to frame it for my own daughter's twenty-first
birthday. But I did. I did. And I felt – and felt and felt – the force of that
continuum. My mother already lived on in the altogether literal form of
my daughter's given name, Elizabeth, and I dearly want to hope, so I do,
that within the dailiness of what has turned out to be the unexpectedly
fortunate life that I've had, and managed to hold onto, and cherish, I am
always seeking, and finding, a way to be deserving of such extravagant love.

In her hospital room we took round-the-clock turns in the vinyl lounge
chair next to her bed, and it was my father who accompanied her through
that Christmas Eve and into the early morning. Had she and I said our final
goodbyes that evening, or merely wished each other goodnight? In those
last few days there was what turned out to be a phantom hope that she
could be brought home, if only for Christmas Day, and while we'd quickly
set up a tree, in case, the plan was withdrawn.

Instead, her death arrived that Christmas morning. Each of those
December days had been counted out on the hand-sewn Advent calendar
we'd brought from home to her hospital room at her request. The colored
felt ornaments are a miscellany of holiday symbols to decorate the tree,
day by day, and during those weeks she had worked her way through them
– the gingerbread boy, the wreath, the candle, the mitten, the camel, the
party hat, the poinsettia – as her strength diminished. On the morning she
died, the only ornament left was the sequined star for the top of the tree.

The funeral was in the little stone church where Tim and I were married
on another late December day just a few years earlier, in another lifetime.

A number of these same people were present then too, but on this day – this is who she was – the overflow crowd overflowed the overflow room.

We'd lived in each of the three towns of Hastings, Dobbs Ferry, and Irvington that were home to all the men like my dad who commuted on trains that ran along the Hudson River to Grand Central Station. From their offices at the top of the pyramid they ran the worlds of high finance, law, medicine, commerce, education, sports, and entertainment. But in these three communities there also lived the men *and* women who ran our smaller worlds, and the local counterparts of those professions were also in attendance: the banker, the cop, the pediatrician, the shopkeeper, the teacher, the golf pro, the grocery clerk, the hairdresser, the restaurant owner, the landscaper, the librarian. Afterwards, our house was filled beyond capacity too, and along with the bouquets of flowers on every available surface, I know she would have been happy to see her guests sitting in that pair of freshly re-slipcovered chairs.

Oh how I wish she hadn't had to pressure me to embrace what so many others valued in her! But at least I became able to fully recognize her gifts, in time to tell her. My large inheritance from my mother is this loving pride that has increased in value over time, like a trust fund.

"NOT NOW!"

With my mother's death came the realization that, at twenty-nine, I was the age she had been at my birth. I knew her life was forever defined by her father's decision to send her to the two-year "finishing school" her two older sisters attended instead of to Smith College, where she'd applied on her own, but I hadn't wondered what else she made of those years. In marrying my father when she was twenty-six and a half, wouldn't she have been considered old? How could it be that when I got married at twenty-two she didn't tell me I was too *young*? By the time I got to be the age she was as a bride, I was already widowed.

When I dropped my vague plan to go back to school in American Studies, I found it a relief to let go of that construct. Instead, I could devote myself to my writing with an increased intensity. About my first attempt, Philip had written to me in a letter dated January of 1972:

> I think it's a very sweet and charming and delicate book — and skillful. You walk a very thin line sometimes, but amazingly swing back from the mawkish and hold to an emotion that I can't name, but that's okay. The humor is soft and right — probably there's room for more pain, in the book, but as it is I like it a great deal. Except for the title. Too many words, too little said. I would prefer THE CHILD WIDOW. That says something about the subject herself, and plays of course on The Child Bride: and takes an attitude toward the experience itself.
>
> I think you're a natural writer and you ought to stay at it seriously. If you want to try an agent, and see if he thinks it's publishable, I know

a good one I'll recommend. Frankly I don't know what a publisher would make of it. They ain't overly smart, you know. But the agent I have in mind is, and he might be a help. You think about it.

But in the meantime you've done an impressive piece of work and should be pleased.

I *was* pleased. And when nobody turned out to be "smart" enough to like it the way Philip did, I wrote another novel that he also read but liked less well, which also went nowhere. I gamely considered these two as my "practice" novels and began a third. I didn't need to worry this time whether "probably there's room for more pain, in the book," as Philip had wondered about *The Child Widow*. The novel that became *Gus in Bronze* was fueled by such available emotion that it was all I could do to contain it.

I was Barbara and Philip's guest one weekend at the Connecticut farmhouse when they asked if I would like to live there while they traveled. Barbara already chaired Hunter College's Religion Department and was involved in the work of Amnesty International, whose advocacy for imprisoned dissidents coincided with Philip's public support for the suppressed work of the censored Eastern European writers he championed. From Czechoslovakia they went to Cambodia to Angkor Wat, the temple complex larger than the city of Paris, whose construction required millions of sandstone blocks that were carved with intricate bas-relief friezes. The restoration of Angkor Wat was discontinued during the Khmer Rouge era, but in this interval it was still possible (if discouraged by conservators) to make the souvenir rubbings that could be rolled into tubes for safe transport. The scroll of the life-sized helmeted archer-warrior that they chose for me has hung by a doorway, like a temple guardian, in each of my homes.

Philip's studio was in an adjacent building, and he allowed me the use of it. They were gone long enough for me to settle into that ideal daily rhythm of writing and reading and walking the manicured trails that crisscrossed open fields to enter the woods beyond. At Philip's desk I focused intently, depriving myself of peripheral vision to keep from being distracted by the masterpieces that crowded his bookshelves. My solitude was purposefully *solitary*, without the interference of Rilke's definition of "two lonely beings" creating "this more human love" to make me long for more than what I had.

I kept Rilke's words in mind, however, as a way to keep walking the "very thin line" between "the mawkish" and what Philip called "an emotion that I can't name, but that's okay." Even in this grief-infused story of the approaching death of a young mother, I still wanted to manage to write the "soft and right" humor that Philip had appreciated in *The Child Widow*. In the silence of his studio, I could hear the voices of my emerging characters, and see them as family. In that simple gray clapboard building set apart from the house and camouflaged by stone walls, when I summoned my muse, and she came, I understood she was related to Philip's. And if this was true, she also belonged to the community of muses attached to each of the authors of all the books that lined these walls.

I wasn't alone after all.

Still, the approaching fifth summer after Tim's death made me restless. And while I contemplated a reckoning return to Ghana, when I learned about the recently created Crossroads program for high school student volunteers in the Caribbean, I opted for that. I saw it as a way to mark the anniversary by retrieving my unfulfilled commitment. A PBS documentary called *Roseland* produced by Bill Moyers showed the violence of white adults against a group of young black children whose families had moved into that "Community of Harmony" in Queens. This was 1975 in New York City, not a decade earlier in Selma, and I was motivated by my own shock and horror to reinvest in the Crossroads mission. With the death in 1972 of the program's founder, Dr. Robinson, the new executive director was Jerome Vogel, at whose African art-filled apartment Tim and I had been hosted with the other prospective group leaders. It was Jerry who flew in to support our group in Wenchi, and when I wrote now to ask about my reapplying he answered, "We don't consider you our worst risk. I can't think of how to put it tactfully, but I have no doubts of your ability to get through any and all forms of difficulty."

I had spent a lot of time with my father in his first year after my mother's death, and while I wasn't surprised by his being "fixed up" with what seemed like an eager lineup of available women, he never bothered to describe them. So I was glad when he now indicated that he'd found someone with whom he'd begun a relationship. I wanted to meet her, but he was characteristically cautious. It then took him several more months to introduce us over dinner, but the encounter proved simpler than he seemed to have anticipated: I was charmed!

I was impressed to learn that, not having finished college, Sue had entered the innovative degree program at Columbia that was developed as a second chance for those, like my mother and her, who had missed out. I wanted her to like me as much as I liked her, so I appreciated the chance to display my fluency in the fine French restaurant they'd chosen. I learned that Sue had a daughter, and that, entirely coincidentally, her father was the very nice gentleman I'd heard about when my brother was hired as his driver one summer to convey him back and forth between an office in the city and his home in the town next to ours.

I met Sue only that once, though, because as she and my dad began to plan their future together, Sue's daughter intervened on her ex-husband's behalf to ask if – now that the "bimbo" for whom he'd left Sue had left *him* – Sue would take him back. My father told me this on the June afternoon before I was set to leave from New York for my Crossroads summer. He acknowledged that he felt threatened by the possibility that Sue could agree to reconcile, and I told him what I thought of her ex-husband using their daughter as an intermediary. I urged him to give Sue a chance to reject her ex-husband's arrogant request. I asked, "You love each other, don't you?"

But while replying yes, he admitted helplessly that this was precisely the problem for a man unaccustomed to being at the mercy of his own emotions. "I need to find a widow," he decided – for his own protection, he meant – and although he also casually mentioned an invitation to lunch the next day with a widowed friend of the next-door neighbors, I reminded him that in Ghana I'd seen his ability to cope with the radically unexpected. I told him how much I respected Sue, and by the end of our long conversation I believed I'd convinced him to have faith in her. And to trust himself.

I left the next morning for Antigua and the full-time Crossroads challenge of "building bridges of friendship" both within our group and with the local community. The island advertised itself to tourists as having 365 beaches, one for every day of the year, but my group of volunteers and I would be housed in a village in the interior. On our flight from New York I sat across the aisle from a handsome man who introduced himself as Lord

Short Shirt. He was Antigua's Calypso King returning home for Carnival to defend his title. From the pocket of his tropical print shirt he presented me with the cassette tape that would become our summer's soundtrack.

In my first leader's report I would write: "What do two sixteen-year-olds (one a Black male from Oakland; one a white female from a fashionable zip code in New York City) have in common?" "How does the Black American girl react to being asked if she and the tanned white American are sisters?" "What is it like to be the minority race at home and the majority for the summer? Or for the white participants, what is it like, for once, to be a minority?" This was our Crossroads assignment, and I welcomed it.

We worked for the Ministry for Community Development in 12-hour days, six days a week. Like a traveling circus we'd roll into a village and, from the bed of our lorry, roll out our donated equipment for sports or drama improv or arts & crafts. Two afternoons a week we devised book projects in the main town's children's library, and two mornings a week at a calm beach we offered beginner swimming lessons to a busload of kids and, gradually, their parents and grandparents too. One morning, an elderly man indicated to me that he wanted to learn to swim. We waded in, holding hands, and I had the honor of holding him in my arms, supporting his horizontal body while he touched his face to that sparkling aquamarine sea for the first time in his very long life.

At the end of each day, for our shared cooking chores I'd asked each volunteer to bring an index card with a recipe from home. A boy from Florida brought the simple recipe for Key Lime Pie, and it quickly became everybody's favorite, including mine, because its chief ingredients of tinned evaporated milk and the pale juice of tiny tropical limes were so readily available. Our strict food budget proved both adequate and adequately managed by me in this place that was dependent in the off-season, except for fresh fish, upon weekly shipments of frozen meat from South America and fresh produce grown on the larger neighboring Caribbean islands.

It was an adjustment for me to rarely have time alone, but our communal household was happy, if noisy, and by the end of the day it was possible to hear the sounds the night makes when it's possible to listen. Every morning the local roosters bossed us about with their crowing, but we were settling into a rhythm.

In walking the dirt road to and from Bendals Village I walked slowly in the heat, accommodating my pace to the climate, which then permitted the friendly greetings considered standard by the other pedestrians. The habit of saying Good morning, Good afternoon, or Good evening became my own rule, and however new this experience was, it soon felt entirely natural not to rush. I let my North American values and the frenzied pace of our hyper-mechanized lives drain like rainwater into the absorbent sand underfoot, and relaxed.

But just then my father's letter arrived. While the nearly transparent airmail stationary rattled in my hands there was no misinterpreting the news. Over lunch that next day, the day of my departure for Antigua, his matchmaking neighbors had found him a widow. The purpose of his letter was to announce that he would marry her immediately after my return.

Since there was no reference to Sue I supplied her distress, amplifying my own. I felt like a parent whose kid wasn't responsible enough to have been left alone, and who wrecked the house. I was angry, at myself and at him.

In his letter he blithely asked me to phone home that Sunday evening so I could "meet" the woman he himself had just met. He clearly had no idea that from Bendals Village, whose electricity was inconsistent, an overseas call involved transport to a larger town to queue up at the telegraph office during its limited hours of operation. I took satisfaction in picturing them waiting by the silent phone that night. The following morning I rode a bus to make the call and was able to get through to him at his office. We spoke only briefly, but it was long enough for me to find his sudden happiness suspect. I felt betrayed, as if I were Sue.

The rest of my summer unfolded with a reassuring regularity. Of course I often thought of Tim, trying to picture him there with me, and couldn't. I was completely comfortable in the summer heat this near to the Equator, even while keeping up with these high school kids and the children they powered into action like wind-up toys when we pulled into their villages in our lorry loaded with sports equipment. Unlike the college-age volunteers in Ghana who were only a few years younger than Tim and me at that time, I was by now sufficiently older than these volunteers, even twice as old, at thirty-one, as the youngest of them. Although my role here as a Crossroads leader was less demanding, I couldn't see Tim being reeled in like I was, like the freshly caught fish we had to learn to prepare for our dinner.

Every Sunday, on our day off, the Ministry of Tourism insisted on bringing us to one of Antigua's famous resorts, where we were the only guests during this season when the island wasn't obliged to cater to vacationers. The beaches were indeed beyond anything most of us had ever experienced, and while it would have been a novelty for Tim too to swim at ease in these pale blue waters where a rainbow parrotfish could be viewed from the surface, floating like us, I pictured him only wanting to play tennis on those first-rate courts, and not having anyone good enough to challenge him.

Most of the Crossroads kids had raised the modest fee for participation with bake sales and car washes, and all our supplies were donated by small business owners who knew they had the power to change lives. When we showed up in a village in the bed of a lorry and turned an open space into a baseball diamond, we displayed the beneficial meaning of American power.

My job was merely to keep up the momentum, which meant inventing solutions whenever the truck was late or didn't show up to carry our circus-like troupe to meet the excited local kids who saw us, Black and white equally, as foreigners. (Who saw us, equally, as freaks.) Our group's purpose was to demonstrate the virtues of our being a mongrel breed, unlike the fully-white winter people they'd seen get off the cruise ships. The difference was that we were there to meet them and to learn about their culture, beginning on the flight down when Lord Short Shirt became our own claim to fame. And except for the fact that indulging in the local rum would get our volunteers expelled, we weren't considered unduly suspicious.

As it turned out, the group's only medical problem was the sexually transmitted disease that one of the girls took home to the Long Island town of Port Washington where my father's new wife-to-be lived.

Will and I met Betty's son and two daughters the night before the wedding. They were thrilled by their mother's surprise remarriage – "Thank you," her son actually said to me – with the big advantage over us of their father's death not having been recent. And while our dad was as giddy as their mother, I wasn't convinced. He called her "Betty" rather than the "Betty-

Mae" she was clearly known as by everyone else, and I felt she should object to his shortening the name she'd been given back in Dayton, Ohio. I also thought "Betty-Mae" suited her better. With her blonde curls she was pretty, but in too girlish a way for a woman in her sixties.

I'd been alerted to the decision that her kids and Will and I would "give them away," which meant flanking them at the altar of Betty's church. The wedding reception was held at the waterfront home of her cousins by marriage, who had clearly taken an instant liking to my dad. I wanted to be as glad for him as he surely wished me to be, but I couldn't. It was already made clear that he would be giving up our house and moving 100% into her world. That his gung-ho enthusiasm reeked of overnight conversion made me an unbeliever.

Tense from the start, it got worse four months later, on Christmas night, when my dad was officially inducted – as an "outlaw" – into his new extended family. Their raucous welcome wasn't his fault, but as I grew increasingly overwhelmed by his new wife's boisterous clan, I blamed him for my having waited all day for an acknowledgement that this first Christmas with Betty was also the anniversary of his first wife's death. Even while knowing that his linear mindset defined him – that he couldn't tolerate ambiguity, as he'd demonstrated in exchanging a divorcée for a widow – I was still shocked, and hurt, by his inability, or unwillingness, to honor my poor mother's memory. Poor Me, was the real feeling.

I resented and mourned the loss of the easy intimacy that my father and I had developed as survivors after the deaths of our spouses. Our hard-won partnership was a monument to fatherly love forged in the furnace ignited on that hilltop in Ghana. If that bond between us couldn't be shared by my mother, it certainly couldn't be extended to include the newcomer who had snagged him on the rebound. Even though my widowed new stepmother technically qualified as one of us, I didn't give her that benefit of the doubt. I could see that her acute possessiveness was a measure of her love for him, but a stubborn, irrational, childish part of me never stopped wanting him to have married Sue instead. I didn't want him to have disappointed me so, by being all too human.

When I finished writing *Gus in Bronze* I showed my manuscript to Don Cutler, whom I had met in the months before my mom's death. Don happened to have escaped from the same downwardly mobile region of Western Pennsylvania as my parents, and my mother and he were very fond of each other. Don was at her hospital bedside in his role as the new minister at her church when I learned that, in his other full-time job, he'd been an editor and had recently become a literary agent. He agreed to represent my novel and submitted it to Nancy Nicholas, an editor recommended by Philip.

While *Gus* was under consideration, I once again turned my attention to the Crossroads Caribbean program. I still didn't have the emotional energy for Ghana, and I didn't have an idea for a new novel because I needed a break. Though it had been six years since my interrupted career in the classroom, it was a form of teaching to preside over the Crossroads learning experience of authentic cultural exchange. In Boston that spring a Yale-educated African American attorney was on his way to a meeting at City Hall when he was attacked by a mob of white high school students protesting the bussing of Black schoolchildren into white neighborhoods. When one of them them thrust the point of a flagpole at Ted Landsmark's face, a *Boston Herald* photographer recorded the image that shook white America, the way Bill Moyers's *Roseland* documentary did the summer before. Dr. Robinson's work to educate America about race was ongoing.

The island of Sint Eustatius is only two miles by four, but the Netherlands Antilles outpost nicknamed Statia was once a thriving center of commerce because its protected harbor could accommodate two hundred merchant ships at once. Almost all the weapons for the American Revolution were smuggled through its port, until Britain retaliated by destroying this brazenly lucrative resource for the colony's rebels. In July of 1976 the American Bicentennial would be celebrated there with the freshly coined tourist slogan "America's Childhood Friend." Our summer assignment was to help the Sint Eustatius Historical Foundation shore up a self-respecting island that, for its support of the Colonies during the American Revolution, had been punished by British warships dispatched to batter the fortified trading post until it fell into the sea.

I'd been promised a definitive reply from the publisher before leaving New York, but the happy news instead arrived one day late by the quaint means of a telegram delivered by a boy on a bicycle. We'd arrived the day before and were brought in the dark to the far end of the island for that first night in a hotel still under construction. I was awake, but barely, when the boy tiptoed into my room and placed the telegram by my pillow.

When I saw that *YES* I slipped on my bathing suit and went outside, past the closed doors of the rooms the others had been assigned, and raced to the nearby beach. I dove in and swam out as far as my deeply invigorated breath would take me. My triumph seemed even larger than the validation every young writer feels with the promise of a first publication, because I'd evidently succeeded in taking on death as my subject without any pretense of a happy ending. That I was now able to claim writing *as my life* was the beginning of my own life-after-death.

As I flipped onto my back to let out a shout of joy I realized that I was being carried farther out, and that the way back in could be impossible. The beach was empty, and except for us, the unfinished hotel was unoccupied. In our orientation meeting the night before we weren't told it was unsafe to swim here, as if the disparate natures of the North Atlantic and the Caribbean Sea went without saying. I knew this from Antigua. Worse, I had failed to learn this lesson from Tim when, exactly six summers earlier on our first day in Accra, he automatically dove into the misleadingly treacherous Gulf of Guinea with the same trusting abandon. Though he was a very strong swimmer, his panic initiated what he then perceived as a succession of debilitating threats to his life over the next ten days, composing a mournful prelude to his taking it away for good.

The water took me with it. I was beyond the line of waves breaking against the shore but wasn't being pulled in by the tide. I felt the current and watched it bring me away from the hotel.

In that instant I decided, "NOT NOW."

It wasn't simply *"NO!"* It was *"NOT NOW!"* It was "I can't have survived my husband's suicide and my mother's death from cancer only to forfeit my own just-won future to a goddamn riptide!" It was a refusal. I heard my own voice, aloud, refusing to allow it. Not when I'd just been told in a telegram that I was a survivor.

So I acted like one, the same way I'd accommodated those deaths, by supplanting my grief with a grim determination to claim my default life however possible. Though I'd never before had to employ the recommended lifesaving technique of swimming parallel to the shore, I managed to summon, and trust, my ultra-calm temperament – whether intrinsic, or developed by difficult trial and error, or both – to outlast the immediate challenge. I regulated my breath and held my face out of the water in a sidestroke that allowed me to keep my bearings. And it worked.

By the time I reached the shore the kids whose own safety I was responsible for were drifting down to the beach. Emerging from the sucking undertow, I gasped out my warning. None of them went near the water, the girls content to spread out their towels to sunbathe while the boys played touch football with a coconut.

So in that first hour of that first morning on the island, I'd spent my entire adrenaline supply. Unlike Tim, a far superior athlete, I was determined to rebound instead of becoming so weakened that further decline could only seem inevitable, the way it did for him. I caught my breath. In my newfound joy, how could I allow myself to be undermined by the horror of my own choking sorrow? When I stood up to lead the way back up the path to see what our hosts might have set out for our breakfast, I realized to my surprise that my legs could still carry me.

Later that day we moved into our designated house on the other side of the island, where the sea was pale enough to reveal a sandy bottom and treasures including 17th-century beach glass, trading beads, and chips of the Delftware that once dressed the sea captains' dining tables, all washed ashore from the virgin shipwrecks that attracted contemporary underwater explorers. That afternoon we swam there where the Caribbean Sea cooled the sand that was hot underfoot, a tan and gray tweed resulting from a volcanic eruption.

We would learn this dramatic story and others in our work for the Sint Eustatius Historical Foundation, which assigned us to a variety of archaeological efforts including assisting on an official "pre-Columbian" dig; restoring the overgrown site of a *mikvah*, the purifying ritual bath signaling the early presence of a significant Jewish population; and cataloging the library's oral history collection. At the library a crew of kids would prove curious to learn about their own island, and our supply of tools would include enough for local teenagers to join us at our worksites. Statia's anticipated future as a tourist site was proclaimed by the avenue of oleanders we planted by the new pier.

Our bungalow was across a dirt lane from a neighbor whose yard featured a washing machine that she filled from a cistern and drained into a gutter. Her children and the other kids from the neighborhood circled the house to watch us, as if our windows were television screens and we were a sit-com. In pairs we rotated shopping and cooking chores, and after our workday and a swim we often entertained the teenaged counterparts with dance parties. Beyond our common living space and a cement porch, our house included two small bedrooms, girl and boy, where our thin mattresses were arranged on the floor in pinwheels, as in a rescue shelter.

I didn't even know how to say the name of my publisher – do you pronounce all the consonants, or is it *Noff?* – when I wrote home to announce it. The imposed need to start over, widowed, had yielded a glimmer of the liberation I'd sought and won. I had a new answer to the old question of what to be when I grew up.

Tim's mother wrote back immediately to say how glad she was for me. I knew Helen was relieved, too, that though I'd embarked on my writing journey with a work of fiction called *The Child Widow* – exploring the loss that continued to define, and defy, me – the publishable novel, *Gus in Bronze*, was "inspired by" my mother's death rather than her son's. It was in this letter that Helen reported her distress over the just-published excerpt in the *Atlantic Monthly* from the forthcoming biography of Harry Crosby.

Immediately upon my return I read *Black Sun* twice, the first time for Wolff's account of the deaths, the second time for the lives. Of course I was most curious about Josephine, but since she was treated as a minor character and her bridegroom was given scant mention, I was like all the other readers who made the book a sensation. I was a *voyeur* peering into the windows of the vanished world my mother-in-law had grown up in, and I was fascinated, not only by what Wolff wrote but by the collateral reading referenced in his bibliography.

By following these leads I learned that Harry and his wife Caresse were notorious partiers, but as writers they ran with the best of their generation. What they published was judged to be better than what they wrote, and in their serious dedication to craft they created a series of books that became immediate collectors' items. The Black Sun Press editions were stunningly meticulous examples of how to print words so they leap off the page and balance, suspended, like dancers. Each book's artful design was tailored to the particular body of poetry or prose, like a bespoke suit exquisitely fabricated. Although they also published their own, lesser, work, their reputation was based on the authors whose books are still in print almost a century later.

Harry's diaries were posthumously published under the title *Shadows of the Sun* and are fastidious inventories of his routine use of the drugs and alcohol meant to set him free from Boston's overregulation. "Am apologized for, for my appearance. Annoyed. Nevertheless donned a stiff-bosomed shirt to please my mother, but on returning to the hotel it went out the window cuff links and all." His mother's wishes were more lovingly ignored than those of his father, whose rebukes were either challenged – "I cannot seem to and I do not want to stop being extravagant." – or else flatly refused.

In a letter to them Harry wrote, "Mamma says she fears disaster 'what is your life leading you to' I am sure that it is arrowing me into the Finality and Fire of Sun by means of Catapults and Explosions Gold and Sorceresses and Tornadoes I believe in giving my life new and violent associations." (Which put me in mind of Philip's comment after my reciting Rilke's melodramatic definition of love: "And then what? Go bowling?")

That Harry was reading Zarathustra's "die at the right time" just when he discovered Josephine got my attention. Tim's Princeton honors thesis explored the dichotomy between what Nietzsche termed the Apollonian (harmony, progress, clarity, logic) and the Dionysian (disorder, intoxication, emotion, ecstasy). It also recalled for me the disconnect of Tim's first Christmas with my family, when he wore an oversized button bearing Nietzsche's radically mustachioed image and the slogan "Thus Spake Zarathustra." Tim wore the button pinned to his green lambswool sweater all day, against the background music of our Bing Crosby album of holiday favorites.

Harry's wife's impression of her husband was that "he seemed to be more expression and mood than man – and yet he was the most vivid personality that I have ever known, electric with rebellion." I was startled to learn that Caresse Crosby outlived Harry by sixty-one years and died, at age seventy-eight, the same year as Tim.

Caresse's story is best told by her, in her memoir *The Passionate Years* first published in 1953 and reissued twenty-five years later in an Ecco Press series called "Neglected Books of the 20th Century." The eccentric tone is set with her first sentence: "I will never forget the day I was born – born to myself, that is."

While establishing her pedigree as a *Mayflower* descendant of Governor Bradford of Massachusetts – her "great-great-great-great-grandfather" – the New Yorker Mary ("Polly") Phelps Jacob more willingly identified with another ancestor, Robert Fulton. "I can't say that the brassiere will ever take as great a place in history as the steamboat, but I did invent it, and perpetual motion has always been just around the corner."

She was referring to having fashioned her prototype brassiere by instructing her maid to sew together two silk handkerchiefs with a bit of pink ribbon, as an alternative to the binding boned corsets inhibiting freedom of movement at her debutante balls. Her practical solution was immediately met by requests from other girls to provide them with their own, and when a stranger sent her a dollar to purchase one, Polly saw the sense in acquiring a patent for her design, which was granted in 1914 when she was twenty-three. She sold the patented design for her "Backless Brassiere" to the Warner Brothers Corset Company for the "magnificent" sum of $1500, and though she regretted the sale when the company quickly earned fifteen million, she noted with good humor that the friend of hers who brokered the deal had succeeded in marrying the boss's daughter.

Caresse was an independent spirit possessing an intrinsically entrepreneurial ability to merge rebellion with practicality. It was in the year following her successful business venture that Polly married Richard Rogers Peabody, who descended from another Massachusetts Governor and was, along with Harry Crosby, another godson of "Uncle Jack" Morgan. She later commented, "My two marriages had related me, often twice, to most of Boston," and indeed Uncle Jack had paid for the births of her two children as well as later funding Harry's expatriate exploits. It was also evident that, with her two marriages, Polly/Caresse twice scandalized most of Boston as well.

She had funded Dick Peabody's business failures before he joined the war effort, after which he returned to his parents' household, where Polly had meanwhile lived and which she experienced as "a strange muted life, uneventful and unjoyful." More damaging for their marriage was that, "Whisky was so plentiful, jobs were so few, and he had not accepted the reality of marriage. (I have never had a husband who did.)"

Upon Harry Crosby's return to Boston after the war, his mother asked Polly Peabody to chaperone a July 4 picnic and amusement park outing for her son and a few friends. Within two hours Harry fell in love with Polly (which he confessed to her in the Tunnel of Love) and, within two weeks, he convinced her to have sex with him. In demanding that she divorce Dick Peabody, Harry proposed, "if worse should come to worse and you couldn't get a divorce," he would kill her and then kill himself "so that we can go right to Heaven together – and we can die in each other's arms and I'll take the blame so you won't have to, Dear."

When her divorce was granted in 1922 Harry and Polly had a municipal ceremony in New York and two days later escaped to Paris to launch their Lost Generation life together. She wrote, "We built a gossamer bridge from war to war, as unreal as it was fragile, a passionate *passerelle* between a rejected past and an impossible future. Perhaps no such span of years (only two whizzing decades) have ever so amazed and disturbed a generation. Harry Crosby and I briefed the pattern of our times and, unknowingly, we drew the most surrealistic picture of them all."

After Harry abruptly quit the job provided by his Uncle Jack at the Paris branch of the Morgan Bank they both dedicated themselves to writing poetry, and it was with the publication of her first book, *Crosses of Gold*, that "Polly" became "Caresse." When Harry wrote home to announce "the birth" of his wife the reaction was predictable – a cousin thought the name was like "undressing in public" – but this initiation to the printed page in fact led to the creation of their own Editions Narcisse. Their next venture, the Black Sun Press, published beautifully crafted limited editions of the work of the best writers of that uniquely productive generation.

In the autumn before his death, Harry noted in his journal, "The Black Sun Press is editing six books all at the same time (MacLeish's Einstein, the Proust letters to WVRB, the Escaped Cock D.H. Lawrence, Jolas' Astropolis, Lymington's Iscariot and the Liaisons Dangereuses in two volumes) which makes things too complicated and much too much work for Caresse." (The abbreviated WVRB refers to Walter Van Rensselaer Berry, his father's expatriate cousin, the handsome and erudite longtime companion of Edith Wharton, who disdained Harry.)

Caresse carried the Black Sun Press forward for another two decades beyond Harry's death, adding many authors to an already distinguished list. For a few years she also published a popular paperback line called Crosby Continental Editions, including books by Ernest Hemingway, William Faulkner, and Dorothy Parker. The best endorsement was provided in a blurb by Jean Cocteau: "The *Crosby Continental Collection* fits easily in the pocket, can be carried everywhere, ready to give life and hope – in fact, the opposite of a revolver."

Letters between Harry's parents and his mother's influential brother-in-law reveal the help "Uncle Jack" Morgan gave in arranging a contact in Paris to look out for Harry as he set out for the war in France. "He is a good boy, and I think you will like him," Morgan wrote, describing his nephew as "pretty young, and, while perfectly sensible, may very much wish and need a little help sometime or other."

On the day Harry died he was expected for tea, along with his mother and Caresse, at Morgan's Madison Avenue mansion. In confirming the appointment, Morgan wrote to Henrietta, "I should love to see you at 231 on Tuesday afternoon, the 10th, at 5 o'clock. I hope you will come prepared to tell me the title of Harry's new book."

This book of poems called *Transit of Venus* was dedicated to Josephine and was regarded as superior to Harry's earlier work, as T.S. Eliot indicated in his Introduction to the volume. Harry was to deliver a copy that afternoon to the graciously loving uncle who was "much interested," so it was of immediate concern when Harry failed to appear. But it wasn't until later that evening, when he didn't join his wife and mother for dinner or the Broadway play they planned to attend, that they realized how unusual this was, even for their always unpredictable Harry.

In the chaotic aftermath of the murder/suicide Caresse boarded a ship for France with Harry's determined mother, who remained a sustaining presence for Harry's widow. Harry's father returned alone to Boston, never to recover from the shame. As Caresse had correctly perceived it, Boston Society presided over an overlapping series of connections that provided both stability and constraint. As a means of compensating for a large and tragic failure to conform to commonly held expectations, it seemed almost sensible that the automatic first response was denial.

The important and enduring exception to this reflexive escape to denial remains that Polly's seemingly doomed first husband, Dick Peabody, not only turned his own life around but published a book about his alcoholism. "When you need a drink you need a friend," he counseled, urging his readers to "Come talk to me then, we will talk it out at any time, day or night."

The innovative theories and practices contained in Peabody's *The Common Sense of Drinking* are why it is regarded as the precursor text for the movement called Alcoholics Anonymous.

"GET TO YOUR DESK BEFORE YOU DO"

Helen had moved from New York to The Farm, where she built, on land that had once been a golf tee on the family course, a prefab house she called "Tee Top." With my new book contract my own ticket to ride, I too was on the move. I'd already liberated myself by holding a yard sale to offload the still remaining unused wedding presents, and once again I packed a U-Haul with all I needed.

My move from Amherst to Boston returned me to the world of the New England Conservatory, where I'd once studied and imagined a future. In a dance studio in my new neighborhood I found teachers to coax out my dormant skills, and while those early professional aspirations were clearly gone for good, I enjoyed submitting to the familiar discipline of those ninety-minute classes.

It was a twelve-block hike across the city from my street to Commonwealth Avenue in the heart of the Back Bay, where the Rotch daughters and Bert Bigelow and Harry Crosby had lived. In early January the intricate architecture of those attached mansions made the grand impression their architects intended, and I knew from *Black Sun* that some of these homes, including the Crosby family's, contained a ballroom. Behind these bow-front windows were parlors or paneled libraries with landscape paintings or portraits illuminated by discreet fixtures attached to their ornate frames. The fine furniture, as in a museum of decorative arts, was unoccupied. One of the most distinguished of these buildings had become the Boston Center for Adult Education, where I'd signed up for a Victorian Literature class called "Upstairs, Downstairs" on the mistaken assumption that it was somehow connected to the popular PBS series.

While I considered my apprenticeship completed and had thought about reclaiming my home town, I wasn't yet confident that I could afford an air-conditioned apartment in a doormanned building in Manhattan. In Boston I found a two-room floor-through in a newly renovated townhouse in what was then its pre-gentrified South End neighborhood. My landlord cautioned me against getting out of my car without first checking to see who was on the sidewalk, but the rent was $180 a month.

When my father came to check it out, his taxi driver told him, "Oh, sir, you don't want to go there."

I argued, "I'm a *writer*, Dad!" and he had to agree that, with a novel in production, this was no longer a made-up definition. In the New York publishing world, I'd learned that Alfred A. Knopf was everyone's idea of how to make literature important-looking. The book jackets were standout and, in my case, when the first proposed illustration by the premiere cover designer was rejected, a photograph of the bronze "Portrait of Inge" by Giacomo Manzù, from the collection of the mother of a Knopf editor, was deftly substituted. I was dazzled. My first book's jacket was a work of art!

And I'd been hired to write *Still Waters*, the companion book for a PBS "Nova" film about a beaver pond at the Quabbin Reservoir, the source of Boston's drinking water. True, it made little logistical sense for me to be traveling nearly all the way back to Amherst in order to observe a world I hadn't explored when it was convenient, but *Still Waters* represented the rapturous feeling of the independence I'd earned, the hard way.

I will always wonder what next novel I might have written instead. While *Still Waters* vibrates with my fresh discovery of the natural world, its real power source was my newfound faith in myself. I was an amateur in the wild, but I could wake up and go to work like any normal person. It was possible, even realistic, to follow my new friend Herb Gardner's smart advice to writers to "get to your desk before you do."

My first day in the field was an overview from a single-prop plane going sixty-five miles an hour a hundred feet off the ground. It was a dim January morning, and while the naturalist filmmakers got their footage I searched for signs of life in the acres of water created by the beavers who had dammed the brook twenty years earlier, flooding the forest floor to a depth of five or six feet to mostly cover their underwater lodges. I could see from above that the snow was melted around the vents that allow air in and gasses out, but my colleagues assured me that this stilled water accommodated many other life forms sustaining the simple and complex relationships out of which each depends on the other for food and shelter and reproduction. Of this first impression I wrote, "And all of this is realized as a by-product of the beaver's own agenda. What the beaver does, alone with man among mammals, is habitually, radically, alter its environment to suit the needs of its lifestyle. What audacity, what common sense."

In my own altered environment I could feel my own life opening up. By having restricted myself to the safety of a romantic relationship where Tim was both present and absent, I'd deflected the vexing come-ons of men who claimed they were attracted to my vulnerability as a young widow – quote unquote – and now began to allow myself a cautious interest in meeting certain friends of friends. When I met with my literary agent in New York and Don gave me the phone number of his "other Boston novelist" I listened to his detailed sales pitch for James Carroll's work-in-progress and heard about the first novel, *Madonna Red*, that Jim had published that summer while I was planting oleanders in Sint Eustatius. I may have thought about calling, but didn't.

A few days later I returned home to a ringing telephone to discover that our shared agent had also supplied my number to Jim. To his invitation to lunch I proposed something as vague as "How about a week from Thursday?" But as we kept talking I shrugged off my coat, and my ambivalence. I have no memory of what we talked about, for an hour, until the conversation ended with my revising my answer to "How about tomorrow?"

The next day I rushed back after a dance class but wasn't quite ready when the doorbell rang, lacking the necessary minute to rewind my long hair back into its twist. This was necessary in order to compensate for one side being significantly shorter, due to my having bolted halfway through my haircut a few weeks earlier, back in Amherst, when the town barber didn't just trim off the dead ends as I'd requested. I hadn't failed to note Jim's green eyes, nor the Frye boots that were a political fashion statement.

Out of chicken curry leftovers I'd made soup, so we sat at a table in my sunny window and talked for another few hours. Eventually, I needed to leave for the "Upstairs, Downstairs" class. "I'll walk you there," Jim offered. And, sure enough, once we arrived I decided to skip class.

We went instead to a bar at the top of The Pru, a skyscraper built by Prudential Insurance, where happy hour drinks were conveniently two for the price of one. After another couple hours of such absorbing conversation that I recall nothing other than leaning into it like a car on a steep curve, I told him that *now* I really had to move along. I had a date I was meeting in balcony seats at Symphony Hall for the Wednesday night open rehearsal. "I'll walk you there," Jim offered again.

This next reflexive decision of mine wasn't the first instance of impulsive disregard for good manners during this period of my life, but it was beyond rude. I nevertheless told Jim that if he wanted to come inside with me I would go find my date and tell him I wouldn't be sitting with him after all. Which I did. Jim told me later that as he waited at the bottom of that marble staircase he'd wondered whether I'd reappear and, if I did, how soon it would be before I abandoned him for another man. I couldn't account for my recklessness other than by not wanting to interrupt whatever it was that was happening. And although I was a newcomer to Boston and this was my first experience of the majesty of Symphony Hall, we left at Intermission.

After a few more days of acting like teenagers we took the ferry to Nantucket for a "get-acquainted" weekend, clinging to each other to walk the cobblestone streets made slippery by the extra-large flakes of a very steady snowfall. It seemed like no accident that we then got stranded there when the harbor froze so solidly – for the first time in a hundred years, the *Globe* reported with its Page One aerial photo – that an icebreaker was required to create a channel so the ferry could get back to the mainland.

By then we were way overdue in reckoning with the fact that we had yet to read each other's novels, so we settled onto opposite couches in Jim's apartment and passed the test in tandem, reading through the night to finish almost at the same moment – cue the trumpet fanfare – with real relief that, after our otherwise promising start, one of us wasn't obliged to call it off.

And that was our courtship.

We drove to New York a week or so later, and for those entire four hours Jim recited the intricate plot of his new novel. *Mortal Friends* was a narrative so wrenched by violence in Ireland and America that I felt compelled to ask, sincerely, "But how do you know so much about evil?" He made me smile too, though, when on our way to his first meeting with my father and stepmother he bought a red cotton knit necktie, for Valentine's Day, from a street vendor on 42nd Street.

My brother was also visiting from Colorado, where he'd been working in Durango as a Public Defender – the opposite of our dad's corporate work at Cravath – which meant everybody got introduced all at once. Dad and Betty had been together for two years, but only now could I understand and accept, belatedly, the abruptness of their immediate decision to get married. My father's open and uncomplicated regard for Jim was apparent that night, and the old father-son tensions dissolved when Will regaled us at the dinner table with a description of his first meeting with his first client. "I'm your defense attorney, so you're not supposed to tell me that," he'd informed the biker who admitted unapologetically – "Hell yes!" – to killing his girlfriend for violating some aspect of Hells Angels code.

Jim and I then connected the next day with my dear friend Barbara and her new partner and eventual husband, Herb Gardner. *He* was the one who took Jim aside with the blunt warning, "You'd better take good care of her." Or else.

We returned to Boston and went back to work. For Jim this meant writing a next draft of *Mortal Friends* in record time, while I spent long days at a lab in Cambridge, where the filmmakers kept tanks of pond water so they could photograph a bounty of microscopic simple-celled miniature things I'd never heard of.

As I looked under the microscope through the transparent casing of a species of water flea called *Daphnia* they looked to me like tiny beanbags filled with bright-green jitterbugging daughters. I was equally charmed to observe the filamentous algae *Spirogyra* which has within each cell a vivid green spiral and at the center "a milky iridescence, the opalescent nucleus." I observed that "The *Spirogyra* are both uniquely lovely when seen through a microscope and one of the commonest of the green algae."

I learned about "the dangling-rooted duckweed that divides to produce up to 84,000 plants per square meter" and "photosynthesizes cleverly, arranging its chloroplasts vertically in strong light and horizontally in weak light. We can think of the duckweed, keeping in mind that chlorophyll is the pond's hemoglobin, as a capillary-rich pulsing circulatory system, or a blood bank." At the microscope I became mesmerized by the development of "ripening infinitesimal fruits and cannibalistic insect minutiae" in these isolation-chamber tanks. So who can blame me for overwriting?

Imagine my joy when winter finally began its turn toward spring and "the sun is no longer a metal disk in the sky but a maker of puddles." At the pond I saw the "crystal beads of ice on the branches melt into tears and weep themselves out of existence. There are trickles everywhere, drawn by gravity down to the pond. The frost heaves itself up and out of the soil as if magnetized by the sun that melts it." The trees that absorb all this groundwater didn't appear so, but they stood ready to be activated. ("If activation is the word. It might more likely be detonation.")

As winter ended the sun was "melting the ice down into sheet cakes and down again into cubes, releasing the nutrients that will be kept from being swept downstream by the beaver dam. A billion overwintering eggs, or more or less, will one of these days be set off by the sun. The single-cell plant life likewise. Winter is receding and at the same time yielding to spring, acceding to succession."

I'd taken entry-level Biology twice, in school and again in college, both times to fulfill the science requirement in order to return my attention to literature. So I was in over my head here, and nevertheless feeling both an earned vigor and an unwarranted sense of security. This project required, and had, my full attention. But so did Jim, whose many charms were equally visible and invisible.

It was early one morning, still only within a month or so of our meeting, when Jim said he thought we ought to move in together. His apartment was on a point of land north of the city with a fine view looking back toward the Boston skyline, but it was too far away. It wasn't big enough either, although this wasn't what I meant when I answered, "Well, in that case I'd want to keep my own place." This required Jim to say that, in that case, then so would he, which made no sense.

We were standing on either side of the new mattress and box spring that I'd acquired for my transition to Boston, regarding each other across it and trying to gauge what was happening and/or not happening.

I was aware of not wanting Jim to feel like he'd misread me when I clarified, "That is, I wouldn't want to live with you. But I would marry you."

He asked, "You would?"

"I would."

"You will?"

"I will."

So that was that.

I nevertheless wrote this sentence: "Mating is for human beings a long-postponed, deliberate act undertaken thoughtfully, responsibly, and with often elaborate premeditation."

I was learning so much about reproduction for my *Still Waters* chapter called "Mates" that it became an almost nauseating task to stitch the material into a wearable garment. I'll spare you my exhaustive (and exhausting) detail about copulation rituals among the mammals inhabiting the perimeter of the beaver pond – not to mention the bullfrogs, snails, newts, bass, dragonflies, redwing blackbirds, hawks, heron, ruffled grouse, and wood-duck – in order to quote myself with the simple observation that "There are two points to be made: the first is that none of the rest of nature mates exactly as human beings do, and the second is that it's not the exact opposite either."

For instance, the beaver is known to mate for life and share in the birthing and care of the young. It may be merely the largest rodent in North America, but a million years ago in the Pleistocene era beaver ancestors, the Castoroides, were giants weighing seven hundred pounds.

I'd learned from Barbara's *Primal Myths: Creating the World* that in Cherokee creation mythology the Great Spirit deputized beavers to dive to the bottom of the sea for the soil with which to build the landmasses. In my research, with reports of a beaver dam in New Hampshire that stretched for four thousand feet to create a lake around which forty lodges were built, I can imagine that beavers created the earth the way the Cherokee have it. I can write, "As a theory it even beats, in my opinion, almost, science."

The technique of observation for naturalist filmmakers is to go into the field, set up, sit, and wait, so that when something happens they're there to capture it. This practiced routine coincided with my own habits as a "creative" writer, and while I often think of my *Still Waters* assignment as an academic fellowship, my filmmaker colleagues would probably say *"there you go again"* with my imperfect comparisons.

But once full spring arrived at the pond it was a lot to keep up with. I read and wrote about reproduction as if it didn't shock me to suddenly know that the female bullfrog will lay, at night, in a mass on the surface film among vegetation, in a one-by-two foot area, ten to twenty thousand eggs! I'm gullible, I admit, but compared to human beings needing to replace ourselves one and a half times to ensure our survival, it was hard for me to believe in the need for such an oversupply of frog eggs.

I preferred watching dragonfly pairs maneuver in tandem, all four wings in synch and genitals interlocked while the female collects the sperm from the male to fertilize the eggs she injects below the water surface. At the end of February I'd seen red-winged blackbird males arrive north to claim their nesting territories around the edge of the pond, the female arriving two weeks later to select her site, accepting the male with it. It was fun to study these varieties of female behavior, noting the achievement of coupling according to set procedures. As opposed to my own.

The carnival pace of my personal life seemed equally demanding as we charged ahead with the wedding plans I'd set in motion somewhat inadvertently. If we'd thought to call a Time Out perhaps we might have seen to take a slower or more conventional approach, but we didn't. We had in common both our current lives as writers and the distinctly different but similar fact of our former lives, where vows had been made and broken, out of which we'd each crafted new identities. If Jim was a former Catholic priest, maybe that made me a former widow. I felt reclassified.

The realtor we consulted advised us to buy rather than rent, so we further tested our beginner's luck by putting an offer on a miniature townhouse on an affordable street in the Beacon Hill neighborhood whose property values would quickly quadruple. Securing this upgrade from my place on the other side of the tracks (where one day's sidewalk litter included a decapitated pigeon and a used Kotex) became a challenge when, on the drive downtown for our interview at the bank, I dropped my burning cigarette on the floorboard and released my seatbelt in order to retrieve it, just as Jim braked hard. That my head cracked the windshield would require us to rush from our meeting to the emergency room to see if I had a concussion.

First, though, after the banker granted his approval but before letting us go, he opened his folded hands to the two of us and said, "Can I ask you a question? What is it that writers *do* exactly? I've always wondered."

I had no honest answer to this good question, not when my writing life no longer consisted of peaceably solitary hours in meditative pursuit of the fictions that came to me more naturally than naturalism. But I'd already grasped the fundamentals of how to devote this secondhand life of mine to the writing craft, whose value resided in its clear ability to capture my complete attention. In search of the imagination's power to enliven – in my case, to heal – what writers *do* is to stalk intuition, a task bound to produce mixed results. When I ask myself if, had I known that despite my promising start I would only succeed in getting my work published less than half the time – not a banker's odds – might I have reconsidered? Not a chance.

We were on our way into our premarital meeting with the rector of the Episcopal church down the street from the townhouse we were now buying when Jim mentioned, "By the way, the rector might have a problem with me." Jim meant that he had been a high-profile dissident priest and, even though it had been three years since he'd left the priesthood, conservative Episcopal clergy might be wary of offending Boston's powerful Cardinal.

So I was prepared for Father Collingwood to raise a problem, which he did, but with me. Didn't I know that in "our church" I'd need special permission to marry because I'd been married before? On our paperwork I'd checked the "Episcopalian" box, but I was surprised to learn there were rules I wasn't aware of. When I timidly asked if this was still true in the case of a death, he sat back in his chair and straightened his arms, turning his clasped hands inside out as he exclaimed, "Oh, he's *dead*! No problem!"

Among the few friends we invited to our wedding were Barbara and Herb, in addition to the immediate families we mostly hadn't yet met. Jim looked handsomely festive in a pink Oxford shirt with a navy blazer and white trousers, and I wore the turquoise "Mexican wedding dress" I'd bought in a hotel gift shop in Cancun on the nonrefundable winter getaway we redefined as a "prenuptial honeymoon" after fixing our May date. Our own improvised plans happened to coincide with an elegant anniversary event in the Public Garden, a jeweled link in the city's Emerald Necklace, which was right across the street from the Hampshire House whose wood-paneled library room was where we held our lunch after the ceremony. Our wedding party adjourned to stroll along the edge of the spectacle pond under the spring-green willows while the Swan Boats glided by bearing handsome people posed in Victorian dress. It seemed fitting, then, to parade several blocks to the brick building soon to be ours.

Helen was with us that day, the blessing of her presence giving my skeptical new mother-in-law a reason to think better of me. In fact Jim and Helen were already fond of each other, and she would continue to play a role in our family life, celebrating our books and welcoming our children. Since Helen was young when her big sister and Bert settled into their new home, if she had visited them there it's unlikely that she would have remembered its location. I was unfamiliar with Beacon Hill, so their address wouldn't have registered with me either. I had yet to see the *Josephine Rotch Bigelow* book, and hadn't examined the candids and formal portraits brimming with her distinctive energy, or studied the book's last four pages consisting of photographs of the carefully arranged empty rooms that Josie and Bert had occupied together from October until December.

Beacon Hill was economically diverse in those days, and our immediate neighbors were a true mix of people served by seven cozy bookstores (since replaced by seven banks) and a variety of mom-and-pop shops. We felt at home, and while Jim knew the city's history well enough to write about the ancient roots of the contemporary battles between the Brahmin and the Irish, my own writing focus was already split between finishing my year at the pond and beginning a new novel. I was too busy to pursue the story behind the story that was literally right there in front of me.

When I investigate those photographs again now I note the scallop-edged flowered print draperies, the books stacked on side tables next to comfortable armchairs by the fireplace, the upright piano, the traditional sideboard adorned with a Brahmin bride's proper silver tea service, the display of framed photos. Hiding in plain sight on a cushioned chair is the pointy-eared Scottish terrier who must be the cute black puppy pictured in the earlier informal photos seen playing at Hill Top with Josie and Bert.

The very last page shows their bedroom, which is mentioned in a reminiscence provided by Josie's dearest college friend Margaret Barker, who wrote that the apartment was "just what she had always dreamed of, especially the chintz in her bedroom and the dressing table" pictured here as a curved, skirted "vanity" placed between their twin beds. However typical for her generation, the arrangement seemed discrepantly old-fashioned for this all-too-modern bride whose prim newlywed dream life was already being eclipsed by the opposing force of her secret, passionate, alternate universe.

These two realities converged in Detroit with Josie's surprise visit to Margaret, with whom she'd shared an apartment in New York during her gap year between dropping out of Bryn Mawr and marrying Bert. By that next December, Margaret had a small role in a play called *Sun Up* that was touring the midwest. This appeared to have been Josie's motivation for the trip to Detroit, but as Margaret described it to Mrs. Rotch:

> She arrived Tuesday morning, telephoning from the station, having so much to say that we both stuttered and giggled and made nothing out at all. Dashed up here for breakfast – I was in a double state of excitement, a chance to tell her all about my opening the night before in 'Sun Up' and the realization that she was actually here. I'd had no warning telegram and had never been positive just when she was coming.

Josie attended the next day's matinee performance and, as Margaret reveals:

> She had talked of getting back to Bert, saying she supposed she should not have come, really, but thought I had been so grand to be out here and she wanted to see how I was getting on.

Harry's diary entry for December 5th observed merely "she sees someone she knows and is upset," a detail merging directly with his vivid description of the opium that made Josephine "sick as a cat" on the overnight train.

The next day, December 7th, Josephine told Harry, and he agreed, that she should return to her husband. That she chose not to, and instead sent Harry a telegram I LOVE YOU I LOVE YOU I LOVE YOU, gave Harry's wife and friends a way to blame Josephine for the murder/suicide, as if it is irrelevant that, twice in those same days after Detroit, Harry had invited Caresse to jump with him into the sunset from the window of their hotel room on the twenty-seventh floor of the Savoy Plaza.

In the memorial book Mrs. Rotch reflected on her daughter's time in New York after quitting Bryn Mawr, when Josie and Margaret shared an apartment:

> She found New York life very fascinating. It satisfied her desire for new experiences and new ideas. She told me in the spring, at the time she decided to get married, that she could have been very happy in that New York life; it was getting a hold on her which she realized herself, but she also said that she felt that it tended to be both selfish and demoralizing, and would eventually unfit her for the kind of life which she knew she wanted in the long run. She said it was all right for those who had some definite and absorbing interest, but for her it would cease to satisfy her after a few years, and then she would have all the rest of her life to live.

Josie's analysis sadly perceives the crippling nature of her entitlement while overlooking the noteworthy model of her mother's and her aunt's public commitments to turning their advantage into opportunities for others through the League of Women Voters and Americans for Democratic Action. Although Josie had chosen to marry a man who proved capable of a remarkable lifelong investment in the nonviolent values he embodied, she was lured into Harry's postwar trauma-fueled addictive escapism. She embraced the worst rather than the best of Brahmin Boston.

With our own move to 128 Myrtle Street, from the rooftop deck and the stacked rooms on the front side of our little brick townhouse – the living room, my study, our own bedroom as newlyweds – we looked directly across the narrow street into the windows of the building at 127 Myrtle Street, the very apartment to which Josephine never came home.

In meeting new people in those years I would often insert the un-conversational topic of my first husband's death, if only to correct the default assumption that I was divorced. If anybody inquired further, I'd say he got sick in Africa and died suddenly, pausing to gauge what else to say, if anything.

I found most people would let it go at that, as if American travelers regularly got sick and died in Africa. But after marrying Jim, sometimes it was revealed that their seeming lack of curiosity camouflaged an embarrassment. They would then have to admit (those that did) to having assumed that, by virtue of Jim's having been a priest, I must have been a nun.

The first time this happened was at the Manhattan offices of the Book of the Month Club, the month Jim's *Mortal Friends* was chosen as a Main Selection. I was seated at lunch next to Clifton Fadiman, the eminent man of letters who became a judge for America's first national book club in 1944, the year I was born.

When I was growing up, Clifton Fadiman was less famous in our house as the popular radio and television host of the smart quiz program *Information, Please!* and the long-running *This is Show Business* than as the man my mother counted on to choose her reading list. I wished she were still alive so that she could have read Jim's novel on Clifton Fadiman's recommendation, and I told him this.

I can't really account for how our conversation proceeded from there, or why he may have had such a mistaken impression in the first place, but when he mentioned my having been a nun and I corrected his error, it proved to be too late anyway. The infallible Clifton Fadiman had already included this information in an encyclopedia of literary anecdotes, a just published volume he then presented to us.

On too many occasions I've heard myself explain, defensively, that I didn't meet Jim until after he'd left the priesthood. Sometimes I'd add, "And I'm not even Catholic!" which isn't the point either. The ignorance is bad enough, but the prurience is objectionable. When strangers invite themselves to picture sex between avowed celibates, between Jim and me as priest and nun, it's not just an ordinary "workplace romance" they're imagining. More to the point for me than that, though, is this. I also hear the implication that, in case I wasn't suspect enough as the wife of a suicide, I'll seduce a priest too!

This misperception of me as a former nun still happens even now after our forty-four years of marriage. By now I know that not everything beyond my control is my fault, but in that hectic first year of our marriage, when we were both so busy writing that we were mostly immune to any outside opinion that wasn't provided by the *Times Book Review*, it offended me to be misrepresented.

Meanwhile, the floor of my study was a mosaic of index cards fanned out in sequence to propel the momentum of my amateur research as I moved through the slow-motion observations of summer. The pond was decaying, short of oxygen in the heat of a day waiting for a storm to freshen the air and fracture the thick silence with thunder and lightning. With the approach of fall the beavers were active again felling trees to maintain their dams and lodges. As the pond's architects they were also responsible for its upkeep, so they were literally busy as beavers.

We renovated too, choosing geometric Mexican tiles for the kitchen and bathroom and green-patterned Laura Ashley wallpaper for our bedroom. Jim's *Mortal Friends* was a bestseller, and he set a good example. My *Gus in Bronze* was coming out in November, and Knopf had sold it to *Redbook* magazine as that month's condensed novel, a publishing event supplying hundreds of thousands of the magazine's subscribers and supermarket buyers as my first readers. I was one of them too, so imagine my surprise when I realized that "condensed" meant not only subtracting but adding. Here were phrases and sentences and even whole paragraphs that I guess the editors thought didn't go without saying. How naive could I be?

During the frigid winter months after my mother's death I'd used my experience of sitting for my own portrait to write my way into the depth of my loss of her, whose life on the page, as a younger woman and as someone else's mother, became a liberation. With my two beginner novels I'd learned to identify what I took to be my writing style, and while I held to the discipline Philip defined for me – to "swing back from the mawkish and hold to an emotion that I can't name, but that's okay" – one advantage in being self-taught was in not being as intimidated by this challenge as I ought to have been.

I channeled my own immaturity into the characters of the fifteen, thirteen, and two-year-old children of the dying young woman I'd imagined. The bossy eldest generates the story, so to speak, and though Daphni becomes insufferably managerial during the subsequent six weeks, it's the more timidly attentive middle daughter who attends to her mother at the moment of her death: "She's gone!" Maya gasped. "And I felt it happen! She kind of danced and then she just *left!*"

After two sleepless nights Gus's husband Andreas had fallen asleep on the cot beside their bed, but he nevertheless has the right answer to the question when he asks himself, twice, "And which meant more, his having been awake for her life or for her death?"

In creating Andreas I gave myself the occasion to feel less alone in, and less guilty for, my having fallen asleep the night Tim took a knife to his throat. In addressing the painful discrepancy between the real and the ideal, I thought there were possibly countless others who might feel similarly consoled. Which turned out to be true.

Katha Pollitt reviewed my novel in *The New York Times Book Review*: "It reduced me to tears at least once every ten pages." She called it "a *Love Story* about grownups, written by someone with a grownup mind," and since this was a reference to the then-current blockbuster novel and hit movie whose sales-pitch motto "love means never having to say you're sorry" was considered by me and many to be a ridiculous oversimplification, if not an outright lie, I felt deeply appreciated. I may never yet succeed in achieving a sufficiently complex rendering of my experience of Tim and his dying, but in *Gus in Bronze* I'd found my way into a portrayal of the grief at my core.

I was writing my thank-you notes to *Redbook* readers right up to our departure on the honeymoon trip to Europe that we'd delayed from May until January. The snowstorm that had been forecast turned into a blizzard, but we managed to take off with only a 24-hour delay. This was a one-day bonus for us because, as our wedding gift to each other, we were both giving up smoking at the start of our trip. I'd stopped smoking on the way to Ghana – and resumed when Dr. Beltman offered me a cigarette – but it was still true eight years later that only the tobacco executives knew about nicotine withdrawal. The weather event crossed the Atlantic behind us and was *"une tempête"* in France. And so were we, with each other.

We still like to tell those explosive stories, but only because we succeeded in quitting. It would have helped if we hadn't also made the miscalculation of staying in dirt-cheap hotels in order to splurge in a few special places, but after a few weeks of this we stopped resisting and found our harmonious rhythm again. On the overnight ferry from Italy to Greece, in steerage, we gave each other coral hearts that we'd bought separately in Florence. It was Valentine's Day.

The Grande Bretagne Hotel in Athens was where I had stayed with Jean and her parents, and I remembered the vast lobby for its carved marble columns. We stowed our backpacks and Jim approached the desk, where he asked the clerk for a room with a view of the Apocalypse.

On the island of Crete I told Jim I was pregnant. I'd agreed to stop taking the birth control pill in order to be "open" – Jim's word – to the possibility. My reluctance was based on the odds that it could happen immediately, when I wasn't yet ready, so I had to remind myself that in this interval since Ghana I'd become eight years older. Along the way I'd suspended my assumptions about automatically having children, but then was then and now was now. I felt confirmed when at a shop in Heraklion we bought a token pair of baby bibs, one pink and one blue, and the saleswoman returned my smile.

We relaxed our pace, taking our time by exploring a few of the smaller more recreational islands where we slept overlooking the lapis lazuli sea and woke to breakfasts of local honey on warm bread. Once we got back on the mainland we booked a room at the Oracle of Delphi in order to see from the Temple of Apollo on Mount Parnassus the sunset and sunrise that the day-trippers missed without knowing those were the times to be there. But on the bus ride into the mountains I felt dizzy with what I thought was motion sickness. The ride was rough, and by the time we got to Delphi I was nauseous with a harsher version of menstrual-like cramping that made me uneasy. I climbed into bed and visualized the Queen-Mother's immaculate birthing clinic in remote Wenchi, in an effort to reassure myself that I could probably find help here too if necessary.

The next morning I stood at the Oracle. The ancient Greeks considered Delphi to be the center of the universe, and the stone monument they built to signify this is called the *omphalos,* the naval. In the heat of the day the remnants of the temple complex look bleached, but in the first and last light the gray marble is golden. At this altitude the air is perfumed. Before the Greek nation states were unified, each had its altar here where the god Apollo slayed the dragon. Pilgrims brought offerings, journeying to consult the priestess whose hallucinations were interpreted as prophecy. I didn't need to invoke her to know my pregnancy was over.

"A VERY NICE LIFE"

It was a classic November day in New England, when even in a city park you feel the full glory of Nature's giving it all she has with her French blue sky and shapely clouds suspended above tangerine-colored maple leaves. Jim and I took the day off to walk through the Public Garden for lunch at Maison Robert, our favorite restaurant, then went down the street to be entertained at the movies by "Breaking Away," a breakout comedy. This pregnancy had almost achieved its due date, and we proclaimed ourselves ready. We had asked not to be told our baby's gender, but in approaching the sixth anniversary of my mother's death, I hoped for a girl to name Elizabeth.

Already a survivor for having outlasted my eighteen-hour labor, our valiant daughter was finally rescued by Caesarian section at "the mother of obstetrics hospitals," the Boston Lying-In. Then in its final year of operation before moving across the street into a state-of-the-art medical skyscraper, at its founding a century and a half earlier, in 1832, the Lying-In was restricted "only to married women, or to those who have recently become widows, and are known to be of good moral character." In its early years most "respectable" women still gave birth at home, but the pioneers in obstetrics at the Lying-In advanced women's healthcare for all with the introduction of pain relief during childbirth, the establishment of a prenatal clinic, and the first trials of oral contraceptives.

As Lizzy and I were released together into our future as mother and child, I recall that day for the true breath of fresh air it provided. And when

Tim's mother suddenly appeared at the hospital entrance, intending to visit, we invited Helen to follow us home. With Stevie Wonder's "Isn't She Lovely?" on the stereo, Helen became the first in the family to meet our daughter. From her complete joy, and mine, you might never have guessed that she wasn't my mother and Jim wasn't her son.

A few days later my father and stepmother arrived from New York for the Thanksgiving holiday, which coincided that year with his birthday. In my favorite photo of him, as he holds his new granddaughter in his lap he appears almost shocked, as if by an electrical charge, by what appears to be his first-ever experience of such an enormity of feeling.

Betty already had a granddaughter, and as my father prepared to move out of our family home into his new wife's house, I'd discovered in the attic my prized collection of Madame Alexander dolls carefully preserved in their stack of distinctive blue boxes. I offered them for her granddaughter to love the way I had.

I'm told that when Betty then presented the dolls to her daughter, my new stepsister asked, "But won't Lexa want to keep them for her own daughter one day?"

To which her mother answered, "Oh, no. Her life is over."

Still Waters was beautifully published and well-received, but I was eager to find my way into a new novel. Lizzy was already a dedicated sleeper, so I could be at my desk instead of still sitting around in my bathrobe. I was frustrated, until one morning my interest was unaccountably seized at the breakfast table by a pair of face-to-face full-page newspaper ads that were written in the form of dueling letters to the stockholders of a copper company. They were only being asked to sell or not sell their shares, but the language was so extreme in its contradictory accusations and promises that it read like a parody. I was curious enough to phone my dad for his interpretation, and he explained that a corporate takeover – a so-called tender offer – was no longer considered "ungentlemanly." Announcing a takeover bid in the pages of the *New York Times* represented that shift. This got my attention.

You could say it was *his* attention I was really after, but this wouldn't be enough to generate a novel, no matter how realistically I might render the world of corporate finance. Without a means of stimulating my invention of characters there wasn't enough to work with, and what did I have in common with the players in a takeover scenario? Unless you count that one day I had control over my writing life and, the next day, I was a wife and mother. It wasn't just that I was overcommitted but that the life I'd so carefully constructed now had to compete for my attention. No, it wasn't quite that either. It was that my good life was by my own choice – you could even say it was my reward – but, even so, it was a threat to the solitary writer's life by which I'd been rescued and upon which I relied for my sense of wellbeing.

So I imagined a protagonist who re-starts her life after divorce by turning her specialty fudge into a small business, only to have it succeed so well that a larger, richer company wants to own it. Today's billionaires would probably ask what's not to like about that, but then, when woman entrepreneurs were more of a rarity, it was nobody's ambition to be forced out of a job. As part of my research I visited the Connecticut corporate headquarters of Pepperidge Farm, whose legendary founder got her start in 1937 by baking bread for her asthmatic son from a recipe remembered from her Irish grandmother. Margaret Rudkin developed her product into a company with a 50% annual growth rate and sold it in 1960 to another family-run food business called Campbell's Soup.

In the alternate universe of an unfriendly takeover, I wondered instead what it might be like to have your grown children approached to sell the company stock you'd given them for each of their birthdays. Or to be given good reason to distrust the loyalty of your mentor and first investor. What if your original fudge recipe proudly and faithfully contains all-natural ingredients and the name of the takeover company is Syncorp? What if such a merger feels like another divorce? My protagonist was the founder and CEO of her own company, and "Phoebe realized the only other time she'd known this rage was when Dwight left, or no, not when he left but when he announced his decision to leave, and yes, this was the same. She hadn't been consulted. Someone else had made a decision about her life without even asking her opinion. And then had the gall, in both cases, to call the telling a courtesy."

My dad read the manuscript to make sure it qualified as verisimilitude – a concept I had to explain to him, so unbusinesslike was it – while schooling me in the subtleties of corporate raiding. I'd seen a statement from Steve

Forbes, the high-profile owner and editor of *Forbes* magazine, explaining, "Every issue of our magazine deals with one aspect or another of this tender offer process. And why? Because every month more companies are raiding and being raided." My dad and I both felt proud when an editorial *Nota Bene* on the *Forbes* table of contents page quoted my *Tender Offer* description of a businesswoman more typically receiving her company by inheritance from a father and husband who leave her "like a hammock suspended between two dead trees."

In the writing process I had discovered, to my surprise, what it was like to have the present gradually become more dense – more present – than the past. I'd become so accustomed to the weight of my burdened past that I'd literally had to set it down in order to pick up and carry the demands of my day-to-day life. In fact I welcomed the opportunity to relegate Tim to his new status as a minor character in my story, and while I feared I'd never fully uncover the secret of his death if I let go of it, I let go of it.

Tender Offer also became a *Redbook* novel, its condensed version a welcome commercial benefit, especially now that I knew to expect the text would be modified. While it was unlikely that this or any future work of mine would engage the magazine's readers the way *Gus in Bronze* reportedly had, I was glad for the vote of confidence.

I got the call when Jim and I were in Florida visiting Dad and Betty for his sixty-fifth birthday and Thanksgiving. Our daughter Lizzy had just turned one, and I could see her out on the spongey grass, barefoot, while I was on the phone in the kitchen.

The *Redbook* editor wanted me to insert at the end of my novel a newspaper headline from the day after the shareholder vote, to make it absolutely clear whether or not the corporate takeover succeeds.

I calmly answered, "Ah, but no, sorry, that won't be possible. I've deliberately left the ending ambiguous."

She told me my publisher had already agreed to it.

"I really can't do that. Sorry."

She argued more.

"Well, yes, I too want readers to be satisfied with how it turns out, which is why I wrote it this way. I don't believe any resolution is completely secure, but I've come as close as I can to rewarding both my character and my readers. There's no such thing as an entirely happy ending."

I had my eye on Lizzy in her pink gingham dress, her chubby legs sturdy as she let go of Jim's finger. "Wait. Right now while I'm talking to you I'm watching my daughter take her very first steps. Oh, no! She just took them!"

Our son Patrick arrived in an early April blizzard, two weeks after his due date. He was named for Jim's dearest friend, Lizzy's godfather, whose heart had stopped at age forty-one, before Lizzy turned one, while he rested after a training run. At this intersection of sorrow and joy, all I had to offer Patrick's widow Marianne was my own example. "In a mere dozen years," I told her with a caustic laugh, "you'll be better."

I've never taken an official break from writing, but after Patrick's birth and our move into another Beacon Hill townhouse with twice the square footage, the writing process became more resistant, like walking through knee-deep water rather than on firm ground. One day I watched with a mix of admiration and apprehension as our eighteen-month-old gymnastic baby vaulted over the side of his crib to land on his feet, his infancy done. Before turning three Patrick was ready for a two-wheeler without training wheels, so alarmingly precocious that the skeptical bicycle salesman made him prove he could handle it. A series of photographs evidence my dressing Patrick in red for the next several years in order to keep an eye on him as he rushed on ahead.

At my desk I was investigating the writing of Aimé Césaire, the distinguished poet-politician from the island of Martinique who, with Léopold Sédar Senghor, poet and President of Senegal, and the Guyanese poet Léon-Gontron Damas, is credited with developing the concept of *Négritude* as a counterforce to colonialist assumptions of superiority. My reading of their work kept me fluent in the language that I'd had the luxury of freely adopting but which had been imposed in West Africa and the *Antilles Françaises* as another form of ownership.

During my Crossroads summers I'd experienced the lasting legacy of the British in Ghana and Antigua with the imposition of afternoon tea, and the Dutch in Sint Eustatius with twice-daily coffee breaks, hot drinks that were mandatory despite the climate. The attitude of the French colonizers had been reported to me by a fellow graduate student at Columbia, a recently returned Peace Corps Volunteer. He was writing a paper on racism in the country of his service, Dahomey, but when he went to the French Consulate in New York and announced his topic to the librarian, she dismissed him by saying, as if it were true, *"Le racisme? Il n'y en a pas."* There isn't any.

I'd taken a mere snapshot of Senegal from our refueling stop on our flight to Ghana in 1970, and of Martinique only a thirty-six-hour impression of its capital, Fort-de-France. Before becoming Mayor – a job he held for fifty-six years – Aimé Césaire was a teacher at the *lycée* where the brilliant literary rebel Frantz Fanon was his student. I toured the domed Library named for the French abolitionist Victor Schoelcher, a masterpiece exhibited at an 1889 exposition in Paris before being dismantled and shipped to Martinique for reassembly. But I also witnessed a disheartening juxtaposition in the town center on the *rue Schoelcher,* whose facades are adorned by the decorative ironwork used as ballast in the slave trade that Victor Schoelcher had dedicated a half-century of his life to abolishing.

I became immersed in the efforts of *"Les Trois Pères"* Césaire, Damas, and Senghor to transform NÈGRE into NÉGRITUDE, rehabilitating a slur into the slogan later translated as BLACK IS BEAUTIFUL. The insight was that civilization is a continuum encompassing both sub-Saharan Africa and Europe, an argument against exclusivity and in favor of dialogue. I was familiar with some of the literature of the Harlem Renaissance but learned more about the conversations between those writers and their counterparts from the African diaspora. They convened in Paris in the 1930s to advance the dialogue in meetings brokered by an English-speaking Martinican named Mademoiselle Paulette Nardol, who edited her bilingual *Revue du monde noir* and whom Césaire credited as an *initiatrice* of the movement.

The intent of *Négritude* was to unify and liberate, but it was also to fight against the denigrating myths and stereotypes of French imperialism. Support came naturally from a cohort of white French intellectuals and artists, but so too did criticism from without as well as from within, including Césaire's protégé Frantz Fanon, whose 1952 book *Peau noir, masques blancs (Black Skin, White Masks)* dismissed *Négritude* as simplistic. Among later French Antillean writers a celebration of what came to be defined as *Créolité* was developed to acknowledge a plural ethnic and cultural identity, including Amerindian, Chinese, and Indian influences in addition to African and French.

I'll never know where this research might have taken me because I only got as far as a proposal for the novel I wanted to write, which my editor gently discouraged me from pursuing because later that season Margaret Atwood was to publish a novel similar enough in theme, she said, to make mine seem derivative. I must have been so flattered to find myself in the same sentence with Margaret Atwood that I capitulated without arguing that, by definition, no two works of the imagination are alike. Indeed, when Atwood's *Bodily Harm* appeared it was set on a fictional Caribbean island, its protagonist a travel-writer in a combative romance with a revolutionary during a political uprising. Her book jacket featured a spiny sea urchin.

The very different novel I had in mind might have been represented by an image of the breadfruit tossed from the decks of the *Bounty* whose slave cargo famously mutinied, sending its British Captain Bligh overboard with their detested starchy food supply. The fruit itself is enormous, its bright green skin reptilian, and while you won't find a French preparation for its dry dense flesh, the breadfruit fed to a slave population has now been rediscovered as a miracle food.

I started over. With my recognition of colonialism as the ultimate corporate takeover I saw that I had been continuing to exploit the jolt of my own loss of independence. But since I had a parallel set of feelings – the opposite of displacement being the sense of *belonging* that comes with loving and being loved – didn't I have another starting place? And, by extension, another destination?

I wrote a romance. And because my lovers were refugees from prior lives, *The Brass Bed* was about putting a new mattress onto an old frame. As a writing assignment I challenged myself to create a male protagonist in a coming-of-age story about deferred adolescence, risking reader indifference and/or irritation if I couldn't find the balance between likable and unlikable. Similarly, my female lead wasn't happy being lost, but neither was it her wish to be found. It turned into a romantic comedy.

The Brass Bed was part one of a two-book contract, the other work an unwritten novel to be called *The Child Widow*. My father and I were alone in a car on a simple errand when I told him I finally felt ready to write it. I also said I planned to have a tubal ligation. Our opportunities for such intimate conversation had become rare, but I wanted him to know how secure I felt, with the two healthy children aged three and five that I shared with Jim in a life no fiction writer could have imagined for either of us. His manifest pride in Jim and the authentic pleasure they took in each other's company had a welcome spillover effect upon me. The intrinsic conservatism prompting his advice to choose work I could go back to once the kids were in school was probably how he still felt, but I appreciated his endorsement of my ambition. Only he could fully understand why I still needed to keep trying to find the words. Indira Gandhi's murder was recent enough proof of that.

In November of 1984, fourteen years after Tim's death, when I asked my dad if he'd seen the televised cremation of the assassinated Prime Minister I learned that he too had watched it again and again and again. Her shrouded body was placed on top of the same tower of wood as was built for Tim, and when her son Rajiv touched a torch to the pyre he created the same shimmering explosion of fire, its dense black exhaust shockingly immediate. No matter how surreal the cremation in Kumasi had been for us, could this re-experiencing maybe confirm that the horror was still somehow *normal?* At the time we'd both struggled to make it seem so, but to revisit it these years later was to confirm for us both that, though this moment of setting Tim's body on fire may be normal for others, for us it was foreign. It was as purely foreign as anything could be, only more so.

With the approach of the fifteenth anniversary I felt prompted to reconnect with Crossroads, and was invited by Judy Manning, the West Indies Program Director and my old pal by now, to accompany her on her summer rounds of the projects in Turks & Caicos, Jamaica, and Haiti. I wanted to remember the impulse behind my original urge to volunteer – to be of service – and while I also thought of this trip as a research assignment for the ever-elusive novel I had underway yet again, the article I proposed to the editor of the *Boston Globe Magazine* was intended to account for why Judy's program for high school students had grown by nearly 75% since the previous summer.

One guess was that the current mega-hit anthem "We Are the World" was a call to action for teenagers to follow their rockstar heroes over the rainbow and into the deserts where people were starving. I admit, however, having grown up when the rule was not to trust anyone over 30, that I'd grown suspicious of those *under* 30. In Reagan's America weren't they all either Yuppies-in-Training or nihilist punkers? I was also cynical about the fact that in 1985 American college admissions officers suddenly seemed to be favoring students with "community service" experience. Elite summer programs competing for applicants were adding new features, such as getting hikers to plant trees in national parks or bicycle adventures that included spending time on tribal lands. But Operation Crossroads Africa was so truly the real thing – JFK's "progenitor of the Peace Corps," remember – that not even the slick tone set by our "Teflon" President Reagan could undercut the value of service. A third possibility, and my wish for them, was that – *plus ça change* – these kids were no different from me and all the others who feel compelled to correct the imbalance of equality.

For travel to Haiti my preparation included a prescription for an antimalarial medication, as before in going to Ghana. Perhaps because the protocol was familiar to me, it was without any particular fanfare – that is to say, with an inch of tap water from my bathroom sink – that I took the first tablet. The acid bitterness was the quinine, I quickly remembered, but I'd forgotten the force of it, not just the taste but the horrible *after*taste. It was so strong that it knocked me into such a vivid act of remembering that I understood Proust.

Reading Marcel Proust in high school, prematurely, the universe he'd found in fragments of cake dissolved in a single sip of tea had seemed forced. I didn't get how that one sip could bring him not only back into a summer childhood but simultaneously back and forth between past and present into a state beyond time. Proust described the event as creating in him a most powerful joy, so that for those few moments he ceased thinking of himself as *"médiocre, contingent, mortel."* I didn't know what he meant by that either.

But with the antimalarial, I did. The drug's unique bitterness was both familiar and unfamiliar, at once routinely prescribed and possessing a complexity entirely of my own making. I felt so dizzy I had to sit, for such a long uninterrupted time that it almost felt permanent.

I recalled the doctor in Accra saying that even though it was only our third day there, my young, always healthy husband had malaria. Since Tim didn't even outlast malaria's 16-day incubation period it was some other even more ferocious thing that broke him, including the antimalarial medication itself. My disbelief, the vigorous and naive disbelief that he could become sick enough to die, was fresh again. It all was.

And while retrieving this horror, in the midst of that overwhelming "remembrance" I had an even more powerful sensation, of the sort of joy Proust wrote about. My sense of myself as *"médiocre, contingent, mortel"* – I knew what he meant by that at last – was suspended in favor of the knowledge not only that I've had a life, but that it has been My Life and could only have been lived by me. In that moment of learning Proust by these triggered associations, I fully opened my heart to Tim. With my own comfort sabotaged, I was sharing – with my body – a measure of the depth of his panic.

It was with this mix of the known and the unknown that I boarded that plane. I was forty-one, soon to publish my fourth book and under contract for a next novel. I had a loving marriage, two healthy children, and I'd dared to claim my future with a tubal ligation. I wasn't accustomed to feeling this safe, but I liked the novelty.

Anniversaries are anchors, providing stability by preventing drift. In the first few years after Tim's death I threw myself at July 10th as if performing an historical reenactment geared to be both horrible and illuminating. The desired revelation rarely occurred, but something else always did. On one of those anniversaries I was caught by surprise – but as in "catch and release" from a fishhook – when I was in a bookshop writing a check at the cash register and had to ask what the date was. To step out onto the sidewalk that afternoon was to recognize that my future no longer hinged on a definitive knowledge of why Tim slit his own throat. The sky that day was cartoon blue. The air tasted so great I drank it in.

On that fifteenth July 10th when I woke up to a golden Grand Turk sunrise on a buggy cement balcony already saturated with heat, I was less eager to record my dutiful impressions than to get in line for a quick cool shower. As opposed to leading my own Crossroads groups, I was not only an outsider but a mere observer. It went without saying, in fact, that my own history was beside the point. This felt like progress.

As a novelist, however, and specifically as the author-to-be of a new-

and-improved version of *The Child Widow,* I needed to open my mind to it. The journey itself reinforced this aspect of the mission, and while I can't say I was conscious of conversing with my ever-patient muse, it usefully occurred to me to create the analogy of the Peace Corps as President Kennedy's *Child Widow.* The agency had been generated out of a spontaneous promise on a late-night campaign stop, and its high ideal was powerfully realized by that first group of volunteers setting off from the Rose Garden in their dressy clothes and landing in Ghana to sing the new national anthem – in Twi – for their astonished hosts. Out of this felicitous beginning, before their two-year term ended, their hearts were broken by their president's death. Needless to say, I knew the feeling.

So all that fall I borrowed a desk at the JFK Library to sit with files of volunteer reports from Peace Corps posts around the world. I searched for adventures and misadventures to take me outside my own frame of reference while making use of what I already knew. I thought about setting my novel in Senegal, to incorporate my notes about Sénghor, but decided instead to focus on the more controversial political figure of Julius Nyerere in Tanzania. I studied enough Swahili to learn the difference between the words for socialism and freedom. But guess what?

Though the odds seemed remote I got a home pregnancy kit to eliminate that explanation for why, despite my tubal ligation, my symptoms were so familiar.

I was told that there could be no medical understanding of "what went wrong" until a postpartum exam (when the imaging later clearly revealed that only one tube had been ligated). But what felt entirely *right* about this surprise pregnancy was the way the reaction of Jim and our excited kids was made unanimous by my own joy. Of course it was entirely destabilizing to ricochet from an embrace of voluntary sterility to an instinctive acceptance of the opposite outcome, but I felt eager to meet this baby who had been conceived against what I guessed to have been impossible odds. With such an uneventful first trimester I felt none of the apprehension I'd known with my other pregnancies. I will never be a fan of surprises, but I fully embraced this one.

Such a radical reversal presented an obvious opportunity to resume therapy, where I could watch myself let go of absolute control as an absolute value. When I asked the doctor who had performed my procedure to review his notes he graciously apologized for this unintended outcome. But we'd switched insurance providers during this interval – perfect timing to be eligible for that punishing "preexisting condition" loophole – so his plan and mine no longer overlapped anyway. I asked a friend for the name of her obstetrician, and while on my initial office visit to this new doctor I noted the framed "grateful patient" tributes competitively crafted in needlepoint or calligraphy and displayed like diplomas, I let go of my reflexive need to call out what I saw as bad politics. Top priority was that my prenatal examination was already several months overdue.

The rooms of our house required reclassifying too, so we reclaimed the nursery from its brief experiment as a computer room and had rolls of cute cloud-patterned wallpaper really to install on the ceiling. The baby was due in June, and it was late April's school vacation week when I drove the kids into town for their dental checkups from our Cape house ninety minutes away. I'd also scheduled a therapy appointment for that afternoon, and as I sat still for those fifty minutes I noticed, and mentioned, a regular pattern of what felt like mild contractions. From there I went directly to the doctor's office where, without being examined, I was told by the receptionist that these were only false contractions so it would be fine for me to go back out of town.

But don't get your hopes up.

By the time I got through to the doctor (at dinner in a restaurant, he let me know) my water had broken. He advised me to get back to Boston, and although my contractions were now coming at shorter intervals, I lay across the back seat of our car for the ride back to the city. It was a race we lost by Jim's veering off the highway into a local hospital's emergency room, where, with no obstetrician on duty, an anesthesiologist presided over the birth. Because the hospital was also without a neonatal intensive care unit, our baby lived her entire life in the delivery room, where Jim held her in his arms and looked into her open eyes as he baptized her.

Although I've withheld the names of certain others who pass through my narrative characterized in ways they might dispute, I choose to broadcast the name Warren J. Becker, M.D., unforgivingly. Not even post-delivery did he examine me, a failure evidenced three weeks later when it turned out that, because the placenta wasn't properly removed, I'd developed uterine clots the size of another baby. This time it was my own life that had been placed so casually up for grabs.

I still marvel that Jim and I survived the utmost trauma of burying our child, her name Jenny Marshall Carroll carved into granite with a single date to mark her perpetual prematurity. A loss this profound is often sufficient to wreck a marriage, but we managed to live our way through it. There were no survival lessons to re-learn. I already knew that the mere passage of time *doesn't* heal all wounds, just spreads out the depth of a loss the way a spill across a kitchen floor extends beyond its original dimensions to become shallower.

It goes without saying that I gave up on *The Child Widow* yet again. Each day of that calendar year I would try to "get to my desk before I did" and every day I would watch my compound-complex sentences collapse under their own weight.

When the sorrow I already lived with became eclipsed by this fresh grief that caused half my hair to fall out, the wisdom I was given, on a massage table rather than in a doctor's office, was that I must find a way to forgive my body. Told that grief lodges in the lungs, I saw why it sometimes became too painful to breathe. When I couldn't sleep, I understood. I grieved by breathing.

Jenny's body was buried in a small mahogany chest crafted overnight by a dear friend, and at the insistence of our then four-year-old son Patrick it was he who struggled to carry it, and didn't drop it. The hilltop plot that will now be ours as well one day overlooked a pond within the cemetery, and while there were gravestones as far as the eye could see in all directions, there were no immediate neighbors. I knew I was grasping after a belief that I have never actually held when I tried to imagine my enterprising mother somehow getting the news and finding her way to her newborn granddaughter. I struggled like this to have faith, and couldn't.

Might it help to get revenge against Dr. Becker for his negligence? We had a meeting in his office, and when Jim asked him to give us a reason *not* to sue, he said nothing. We then met with our lawyer and a young associate (who distracted me, by no fault of her own, by being six or seven months pregnant) but decided not to go forward when it became too easy to picture my tubal ligation used by Dr. Becker's lawyer as evidence against me, and finding me guilty as charged.

The holidays were rushing at us without a plan, a gap we bridged with a week at Sugarloaf Mountain in Maine to introduce our kids to the sport we'd each separately loved. It was there that I gradually allowed myself to rediscover the art of skiing, the form of dance where gravity does most of the work. I would never aim to perfect it again, but by forcing myself to focus – or fall – I rarely fell.

This period was productive for Jim because he was all the more driven. His novels appeared like a sequence of train cars, until he switched tracks with an invitation to write a weekly *Boston Globe* opinion column, which led to a fellowship at Harvard's Shorenstein Center on Media, Politics, and Public Policy. While there he considered and reconsidered the relationship between antisemitism and the Catholic Church, an argument later developed in his masterwork *Constantine's Sword*. Called "the conscience of Boston" by some and a troublemaker by others – such as Cardinal Law, for Jim's steady criticism of Catholic failures to reform – he rallied readers by both railing like a peacenik and devising proofs like a bench scientist. He was on a roll, like a locomotive, and he owned his *Globe* column, voicing his values, for the next quarter-century.

With my own writing involuntarily paused, I gave myself to directing the Ploughshares International Writing Seminar that Jim and I co-founded with another writer couple, Robie Macauley and Pamela Painter, and ran with treasured colleagues from Copenhagen and Paris and Boston. We brought it to Kasteel Well, a genuine Renaissance castle in The Netherlands that was leased from the Dutch government by Emerson College. A cohort of the participants were Emerson MFA students, but the majority weren't. These more mature writers came from a variety of cultures and brought the stories of their interesting lives to our workshops, but I worried about the inherent problem in encouraging a writer whose work may never see publication. It took a stopover in Ireland for me to find the solution in an analogy. Driving past a golf course I realized what a writing teacher and a golf pro have in common: you mostly provide practical pointers to increase the player's enjoyment of the game, but every now and then along comes someone with a natural swing.

One year, just as the seminar was concluding, I spoke to my father on the phone for the last time. After holding steady he was failing fast, his emphysemic lungs making it harder to expel his breath. The retained carbon dioxide caused him to confuse "hospital" with "hotel," as I realized when he told me in that call that he was getting very good room service.

I told him we were on our way home to him and asked him to hold on if he could. And although we rushed back, we failed to arrive before a first dose of morphine administered to ease his struggle instead abruptly ended it.

He'd prepared himself to die from the disease he thoroughly researched, underlining his textbook *The Lung* like a medical student. Throughout his seventies his definition of life was how far he could get on a breath, as he bravely measured his own decline. He'd had another lifetime beyond the eclipsed span of my mother's, including a good second marriage and a well-deserved retirement that he managed as diligently as if still at work. He'd seen certain of his law partners sink into alcoholic afterlives and devised the alternative of carefully calibrated journeys cruising the Inland Waterway back and forth between New York and Florida. Their two boats were given the un-nautical names *Carousel* and *Caprice,* and while this was never Betty's ideal way to spend time, she was a willing first mate and a very good sport. Increasingly less mobile, Dad compensated by being the first in the family to embrace computer technology. I don't think he ever stopped worrying about me and my brother, which I understand better now that my own children are close to the ages we were then. I wouldn't have thought I had still more to learn about death, but the new lesson for me was that, when it came, my dear dad's death at seventy-nine felt no less premature than the premature deaths of my husband at twenty-eight, my mother at fifty-eight, or my daughter at zero.

His one instruction for his funeral was that he wanted that ritual "Cravath Walk" where his law partners would march down the aisle in formation, so I was disappointed for him when only a modified version of this request could be met on the Friday of Labor Day weekend. In the same conversation he'd let me know his wishes for the burial of his ashes in the churchyard where my mother's had been placed along with a now mature

Star Magnolia. He nodded when I asked, "Next to Mom?" and gave me time to register my reaction – I was shocked, and thrilled – before adding that Betty's ashes would be buried there too, on his other side.

So he would be buried next to his first wife, yes, but also next to his second wife. It was as if to correct for that first Christmas with Betty when he couldn't acknowledge the day as the anniversary of his first wife's death. I attacked him that night for being linear rather than circular, excluding rather than inclusive. And he heard me.

When Lizzy was in third grade she studied reproduction. Her progressive elementary school was founded with the explicit mission to create a community reflecting Boston's racial and economic diversity, a city school committed to social justice and "a culture of collaboration where every child has the confidence to take action." The academics were quirky, in a good way, and her insightful teacher began the academic unit with insect reproduction, introducing the kids to the dramatic flourishing that I hadn't learned to appreciate until I wrote *Still Waters*. From there they set up an incubator in the classroom and watched the hatching of chicks, which prepared for the groundbreaking news my daughter brought home from school one afternoon, bursting through the door to announce, "Mom! Mom! Ms. Schoene lays an egg every month!"

Around that time Lizzy and I were crossing into the Boston Common, holding hands on an already beautiful day when the emerging linden leaves were still chartreuse against the rain-darkened bark. It wasn't yet warm in New England, but the potential was apparent. As I'd learned from the invisible abundance of life at the *Still Waters* pond, this season would have to be called something else if it weren't a coil ready to spring open.

"I'm very proud of myself," she announced.

What more could I hope for? But I nevertheless wanted to know what made her proud of herself.

"I have a very nice life."

At age nine, she not only valued her life but already knew to credit herself for it? That afternoon I seized upon Lizzy's insight as my permanent definition of Upward Mobility.

"Copyright 1988" is typed by her teacher onto the title page of the fifteen books Lizzy wrote and illustrated that year, volumes upholstered in scraps of interesting fabric, the pages hand-sewn with yarn, her vivid drawings colored in Magic Marker. Each one has a dedication page – she dedicates *The Two Friends* to her brother – and each one displays a profound self-confidence. In *How to Make Sandpaper* she asserts, "The way that you make sandpaper is quite simple. First you need an elephant and a pelican."

In *Liquid Nitrogen* a lesson is bluntly delivered: "WARNING: Don't ever stick your hand in liquid nitrogen." Jim's bench-scientist brother Dennis had performed an experiment for Lizzy and Patrick by freezing an orange for a mere instant before dropping it onto the concrete floor of his lab, where it splintered like glass. She writes, "Now if you should happen to get your hand in liquid nitrogen Do Not bang your hand on Anything or your hand will shatter and you will have only one hand."

In the compound wisdom of *Chili and Angolia Learn a Lesson* she tells how "Once deep in the jungle, there was a toucan named Angolia. She was the queen of the jungle. Her king was a lion named Chili." The story is about how the king collects taxes from all the houses in the jungle, so that soon "The only animals that had any money were the king and queen. They had tons of money." The plot shifts when a lizard named Sydney comes along. "One day Sydney got fed up with having to give all his money to the king." He gives a speech and, in a tradeoff that could be scripted by today's 99% against the 1%, he and the king switch places. The moral of the story is that "Everyone lived happily ever after, except Chili and Angolia."

These books held their prominent place on our shelf alongside the beloved children's classics collected by every household, and there they sat for another twenty years, until it came time to pack them up. We were giving up our address in the precious neighborhood embodying Boston's carefully preserved past for a part of the city – still mostly unbuilt – representing its future. The move across town seemed more charged than your typical age-appropriate downsizing, and while my thick ambivalence was no doubt predictable, and while I was able to take satisfaction in recycling our family's accumulated belongings, I wanted the move to feel more momentous than the mere sum of these parts. And then it did.

My now-grown daughter and I faced each other on couches in the library room whose wall-to-wall bookshelves were mostly sorted into cartons. As we paused to rediscover together this collection of her own books, I sensed the opportunity for a profound revelation of my own, and I grabbed it.

I said, "If I were dead you'd be doing this alone."

From Lizzy's pained expression it seemed possible that she had so far avoided imagining ever losing me, and while I didn't want to force such a reckoning on an otherwise tender moment, I added, "All I mean is that, instead of my leaving behind all these bookshelves for you to empty, we get to do it together."

She nodded.

I felt caught between her clear wish to let it go and my own preference not to. "So I'm able to relive your childhood *with* you." Our paging through her handmade books one by one was giving us this chance not only to feel exceedingly fortunate for the life we'd shared together, but to say so.

So much had remained unspoken between my mother and me that I'm always surprised to realize this isn't the case with my own daughter. It's been my life's work to reinvent that wheel, but with such a perpetual longing for forgiveness, no matter how perfectly well I know I'm not responsible for my mother's cancer, I've never felt entirely entitled to resolution. A year to the day after losing Jenny I graduated from stop-and-go psychotherapy to psychoanalysis, where I endlessly traveled the short distance back and forth between the known and the unknown. It was exactly then when Lizzy was writing these fifteen books that offer a better definition of mental health than all my own spiral notebooks.

On the wall opposite our paired couches hung fifty framed family photos, rendering fifty thousand words redundant. Still, I remembered her Upward Mobility declaration from when she was a girl, and I repeated it back to her. "I have a very nice life."

Despite the disabling losses I'd struggled against, here was my own revelation: "I'm not dead." I allowed myself to say this out loud too, to not only claim my existence but to define it by this moment. Perhaps it was even my impulse to credit myself for being alive, the way, at the elegant age of nine, on our walk in the Common, holding hands, Lizzy had claimed the creation of her own very nice life.

She seemed to be waiting for more from me.

So, quoting her again, I added the sentence I had never expected to hear myself say, "I'm very proud of myself."

"AKWAABA!"

The antimalarial I was prescribed for my long-deferred return to Ghana failed to melodramatize the experience the way it had fifteen years earlier, but I overreacted to the letter I was given to carry, which read:

> Alexandra Marshall, M.D. has been given permission from the Travelers' Advice and Immunization Center, at the Massachusetts General Hospital, to carry needles and syringes in case of an emergency. If there are any questions, please contact us at (617) 724-1934. Thank You.

At the Massachusetts General Hospital travel clinic the physician explained that this was just a precaution in case I needed blood. In case I needed *blood?*

He meant in the event of a car accident, but beyond the clear message that it was considered unsafe to trust a local hospital was the reminder that I already had! And, sure, AIDS had come onto the scene in the meantime, but by the year 2000 even AIDS wasn't what it used to be. I felt both offended and uneasy.

With the approach of the new millennium I had finally gotten up the courage to mark that thirtieth anniversary by revisiting Ghana. I got back in touch with Crossroads and was given the contact information for that summer's planned projects, but without knowing how to alert those with whom I most wanted to connect, I decided I would simply arrive in Wenchi.

Again, as when I toured the Crossroads projects in the Caribbean fifteen years earlier, I wanted to claim that thirtieth year as a challenge to learn something new about the impact of Tim's death. If I was always trying to keep Tim alive to compensate for what more I might have done when I had an actual chance to, wasn't I also trying to keep myself alive to the radical difference between life and death? I'd been shaken by my own more recent experience of that boundary.

This time I'm not referring to my postnatal emergency twenty days after Jenny's birth, but a more recent car ride home after a dinner with friends, our kids dozing in the back. We were sideswiped and projected across the four-lane highway to land upside down on the grassy median after flipping over a time and a half. I was driving, and when in the side view mirror I saw the pickup bearing down on us in the breakdown lane, I said, "Look at that asshole," two seconds before the accident happened.

I was only unconscious long enough that when I found myself hanging upside down in my seatbelt, like a bat, I thought maybe I *was* a bat. Jim and Lizzy could be quickly accounted for by the same crazy means, while it took a minute more to realize that Patrick had not only flown out the back window in a rain of glass but remained exempt from the ultimate rule of cause and effect. The law of gravity meant that he was on his feet. We all were.

My point here isn't only to note my relief at finding that we were all still alive, but to admit how stunned I was to recognize – after all my supposed experience with it – how little separates death from life, how little protection we have from it, and how deeply angry that made me. *Angry?* Yes, that such a great divide as there is between the living and the dead is in fact only separated by the thinnest of membranes. How could I not have known that? I felt deceived.

I wanted to feel empowered to make an authentic return to Ghana without worrying about getting into a car accident. Or if I did, without pretending I was someone I wasn't – Alexandra Marshall, M.D. – someone better than me. Wasn't the point of a reckoning to make an honest claim on identity? For thirty years, wasn't this my ever unrequited desire?

My traveler's luck kicked in like an insurance policy when I saw among the disembarking First Class passengers being moved through the chaos of the terminal in Accra that a dear friend, a member of my book group in Boston, had been on my flight from London. Dr. Juliette Tuakli was being met by her godfather, Ambassador Kojo Amoo-Gottfried, a retired diplomat who had served as Ghana's representative to China, Italy, and Cuba. He kindly invited me along to take a plush seat in the draperied VIP lounge while helpers saw to baggage handling and passport control. I thought of Tim's brand new passport with its first and only stamp marking his arrival in Ghana.

Over the muffled noise of an American-style television show featuring two Ghanaian men in a rowdy cooking contest, I overheard part of a conversation about the likelihood of Kofi Annan becoming the next U.N. Secretary General. I was introduced to the editor of the national newspaper called the *Daily Graphic,* and I shook the hand of the upcoming election's opposition candidate, J. A. Kufuor, who would win a decisive victory later that year and serve two terms, reclaiming power at last for the political party founded by Prime Minister Busia. When the Ambassador turned his attention to me with the polite conversation starter "Is this your first trip to Ghana?" my shorthand answer invited more questions.

The Labadi Beach Hotel is set back from the Gulf of Guinea, but through the trees I could hear the steady movement of the water when I opened the slider and stepped onto the narrow balcony. After two long-distance flights bracketing an extended layover at Heathrow, I wished simply to humidify – to naturalize – the artificially refrigerated air of a room smelling too strongly of disinfectant. Of course I noticed on my bedside table the plasticized sketch of a "Dusk to Dawn" mosquito with a diagonal red line bisecting it, but I was protected by the latest prophylactic antimalarial medication prescribed by the tropical disease unit at the Massachusetts General Hospital. I'd seen on my way through the lobby that the hotel's balmy outdoor terraces were filled with guests blithely enjoying their tropical drinks.

I slept densely, anticipating the recuperative potential of this long-postponed journey to acknowledge the trauma of my young husband's death. In this desire, I didn't yet know that I wasn't alone.

The next day the desk clerk delivered a message from Juliette to say she would pick me up that night to meet her godfather for a drink. Under a fluorescent full moon, when the Ambassador arrived on the large terrace of an outdoor nightclub a mile or so down the beach from my hotel, I would learn why Juliette's twin daughters' nickname for him was "Mr. Fix-It." He was accompanied by Nana Akua Busia, a fashion designer of my generation whom he introduced to me as the niece of the late Prime Minister and his brother and sister, Wenchi's Chief and Queen-Mother.

"Nana" means "ancestor" and is an honorific for all members of the Ashanti Royal Family, including the King, and though the live music made it nearly impossible for us to talk, when I thought I understood Nana Akua to be saying not only that the Chief and Queen-Mother were both still alive but that her aunt happened to be in Accra just then, I asked if she thought the Queen-Mother might be willing to meet with me. By her leaning toward me as she nodded yes I felt relieved, but I also felt deeply embarrassed to have arrived in their country so unannounced. And so long overdue.

I overdressed, and my long black sheath proved to be a fortunate choice when the Queen-Mother crossed my hotel's lobby the next night in a floor-length ivory satin strapless dress with a matching stole over one shoulder. She wore a four-strand pearl necklace and matching bracelet, but her vibrant face seemed unchanged from the only other time we'd met, when on that day in 1970 she had impressed me indelibly, being at once traditional and cosmopolitan, by wearing the crisp uniform of a nurse-midwife.

Nana Frema and her niece and I were seated at a small round table in the hotel's formal dining room. There were too many waiters with not enough to do, but the setting proved conducive and was made cozy by the candlelight that prompted the Queen-Mother to ask why they would waste candles when the electricity hadn't gone out. In Wenchi the power had been rationed by the use of a town generator that was cut off at night, and I would never forget holding the flashlight when the nurse came to administer the supposed narcotic cure for Tim's radical sleep deprivation. Because all these years had elapsed, I realized that I had no concrete idea, none at all, of what I would find there.

When Nana Frema inquired about my intentions for this return I told her that I wished to revisit Wenchi to pay my respects to her brother, the Chief, to express to him my regret and profound gratitude. If I was improvising, I was also in fact summoning up my truest feelings. She asked to hear more.

So I began by describing who my young husband had been, the Scholar/Athlete ideal and gifted teacher who so quickly and unaccountably became completely debilitated and demoralized. I talked about the fever and the provisional diagnosis of malaria that was then compounded by dysentery and sunstroke. I mentioned the Gulf's undertow on that first afternoon and the greater undermining fear of failure. I told her his saying he'd never again play tennis ought to have meant more to me than it did. I wanted her to have some sense of Tim other than the terrible way his life had ended.

She listened to all this with the attentive compassion of a nurse. And then she asked, "But don't you think it was a bit selfish of him?"

The next day I bought a book called *The Political Biography of Dr. Kofi Abrefa Busia* and learned that at the center of the Busia family story in Ghana was the bright boy known as Joseph Fred Busia until 1939 when, in going to England to further his studies, he changed his name at age 26 to Kofi Abrefa Busia. He is quoted as having reached the decision matter-of-factly: "After deep consideration I convinced myself that it is ridiculous that having neither a Hebrew nor a German ancestry I should, nevertheless, be called 'Joseph' 'Fred.'" An excellent student educated in Kumasi by British Methodist missionaries, his university training in the field of anthropology would yield a Doctor of Philosophy degree from Oxford. When he was named to become Wenchi's Chief, Dr. Busia deferred in favor of his younger brother, and entered national politics.

The former Gold Coast Crown Colony established by the British in 1874 was no less plundered of its mineral wealth and savaged by slavery than the rest of the continent, and yet its legacy since achieving its formal independence in 1957 has not been one of genocide or the lethal economic instability that has undermined its close neighbors in the region. Ironically, one reason is that the British and Missionary boarding school systems insured that the children of the four main ethnic groups not only received the same education but would learn to live together as schoolmates. This structure mimicked the British model, but because the largest and most influential group in the Gold Coast colony was the Akan, whose people were descended from the ancient Ashanti Empire, the collaborative governing principles of that matrilineal culture proved unifying. They would even famously trick their colonizers into stealing a fake Golden Stool, the sacred Ashanti throne, in the foiled 1896 British attempt to upset that indigenous power structure.

An Akan named Kwame Nkrumah became the eventual leader of the newly independent Ghana and governed for nine years – excessively, many thought when he gave himself the honorific title *Osagyefo* meaning "savior" – until the military overthrew him in a CIA-assisted coup. Busia had become an opponent of Nkrumah, who was the once-popular architect of pan-Africanism but later a dictator whom Busia compared to Hitler. After Nkrumah was ousted, Dr. Busia returned from political exile in England to serve as the top civilian in that military government until his Progress Party won a landslide victory in a democratic election. In becoming Prime Minister of the Second Republic of Ghana he took office in October of 1969 for what was to have been a four-year term. But during a visit to London for treatment of his diabetes, Busia was ousted in another military coup, in 1972, on charges ranging from financial corruption to a lack of charisma.

The military government that overthrew Busia was itself overthrown, and though elections were set for the next year, there were two more coups brought in rapid succession by Flight Lieutenant Jerry Rawlings, who ruled Ghana for a decade as a military man and for most of another as its self-appointed President. One of the accusations raised against Busia was that he'd paid – all in cash – for the construction of a grand house on the grounds of the royal compound in Wenchi. I would see for myself that next to Dr. Busia's gravesite was that building, then derelict and only recently restored to the family, which Rawlings had summarily requisitioned as a police barracks. When I asked the Ambassador about this, he described Rawlings disdainfully as a man so personally insecure that he needed to inflict insult even upon the dead.

The Chief and Queen-Mother were also to suffer the indignity of having their roles in the royal pyramid-shaped power structure challenged, even to the extent that, as the Queen-Mother told me at dinner, she read one day in the *Daily Graphic* about a Queen-Mother being de-stooled – de-throned – and discovered that the newspaper article was about *her!* In explaining to me that in those days it wasn't possible to resist such a decree (this was about 1980, she believes, when she would have been around 52, a decade older than when I'd first met her) she was required to give up the stool she'd been named to at age 24.

In detailing the suffering Nana Frema's family endured in the decade after the Prime Minister's ouster, she told me she was later able to retrieve her standing as Queen-Mother, but that in the meantime she was forced to make a portion of her home income-producing. In my British *Guide to Ghana* – "If you need to spend a night in Wenchi," is typical of the guidebook's condescending tone – Nana Frema's K.A.A.F. Guest House is described as the lesser of Wenchi's two hotels, with "more basic rooms in the US$2-4 range."

I felt ashamed to have gone back to my own country as if the tragedy of Tim's suicide had only occurred to us North Americans. My failure to know the Busia family's story was as great a loss to me as my ignorance of Bert Bigelow's heroic life. And though I knew my apology to the Queen-Mother was inadequate, I offered it with all I had.

As we approached the end of our dinner in Accra, Nana Frema invited me to stay at her home in Wenchi, writing her instruction on a scrap of paper for me to present to her housekeeper in case she became detained in Accra:

> Take good care of the bearer of this note, put her upstairs. She is my guest. Take good care of her, take her upstairs and give her a fan. Take her to greet Nana Kusi. Thank you.

The express bus from Accra to Kumasi made numerous unscheduled stops and became so densely packed by the end of the extended journey that I only hoped the driver had enough legroom to hit the brakes. I'd made a reservation in Kumasi for what turned out to be the comfortable Roses Guesthouse, and after a shower and dinner at Chopsticks, the nearby Chinese restaurant that came recommended, I felt readier to be reintroduced to this pretty city whose tourist sights were unknown to me. I hired a car for the next morning and while, yes, I surely wanted to visit the *Asantehene*'s Manhyia Palace, my itinerary required a word of explanation since my first request was the morgue.

"Did something change here?" I asked as we entered a traffic rotary that I recognized. "It doesn't feel quite familiar."

My young driver couldn't guess what I was talking about.

Before I saw the sign for the Komfo Anokye Teaching Hospital I knew it by the blue benches, all of them still occupied, around the edges of a large open-air waiting room. Of course I also took in the gated low building to its left, with its fresh yellow and white paint.

"Is it possible that the direction of the traffic in this roundabout has been reversed?" Or was I Alice in Wonderland?

"Yes, madam," he answered, pulling the car off to the side of the road as he explained in morbid detail how many accidents there once were, mostly due to the lorry drivers crossing the border from one of the Francophone countries to the north, who wouldn't know or notice the difference until too late.

I wanted to think I was brilliant to have figured this out, but first I had to ask myself how come I *hadn't* seen, until then, that nobody in Ghana drove on the left anymore. I'd already been here long enough to have noticed something this obvious, and it made me feel like I not only didn't know what I didn't know, I didn't even know what I *knew*.

I took a photo of the sign stenciled onto the exterior wall of the morgue. It detailed the fee structure for cold storage: the first three days were free, but after that there were different rates for those dying "in hospital" or "outside of hospital." It instructed that "corpses from outside the hospital for preparation should be routed through the casualty unit." I noted that "coroners cases" were also free "until bodies are identified," after which there seemed to be a higher rate than for the others. The gate was partway open, but I did not enter.

From there we drove to the Kumasi City Cemetery, where I noticed for the first time the decorative wrought iron archway at the entrance, which may or may not have been there thirty years earlier. A cemetery guide seemed to know where to find what I was looking for, and when I saw where he took me I understood why. Instead of an unmarked site, as before, off to one side there was a shoulder-high metal sign reading "Ghana Cremation Society." Next to it was what registered as a dwelling, but without walls or a roof, with four tall brick columns – looking like chimneys – on each corner of a raised cement slab. Its hilltop location remained the one essential, to allow that choking smoke to escape.

I summoned my dad in his Wall Street suit and Victor Badoo in his white robe. I supplied the bouquet of colorful tropical flowers that I distributed to the Crossroads volunteers and Hélène and Jean, who stood here with me. In this moment I could feel that blast of heat from the pyre.

And recall with vivid precision how, in telling Tim's family what happened, I began here and told the story backwards. I saw that I wanted them to know, first, that Tim was honored.

The straight road from Kumasi to Wenchi was now tarred, but it still took many hours to travel. I wasn't looking forward to sharing another meal with my driver after our stop for lunch at a roadside stand featuring the local delicacy he relished. The specialty food put before us was round and brown and as large as a coconut, but turned out to be – a *what?!* – a snail.

In fact the Queen-Mother had managed to arrive home ahead of me, and while accommodating my driver at her kitchen table, at her lace-draped dining room table upstairs she served the delicious multi-course meal that she'd prepared for me but said she wasn't up to eating herself. Our after-dinner coffee was accompanied by yellowish condensed milk which I then realized had been slowly seeping throughout dinner from a barely visible crack in its small pitcher, soiling the lace. I didn't know if she had noticed this or not but decided not to violate her refined impromptu hospitality by drawing attention to the problem, too late.

Nana Frema then showed me to her hot pink-painted guest room, and I spent that long night, wide awake, lying on brand new lilac-patterned sheets and listening to my table fan spinning against the background of Methodist hymns from a church choir practice. These measured tones alternated with distant drumming and the staccato of an insistent rooster.

The following morning she took me next door to greet her brother the Chief, and having refreshed my memory of the protocol, I'd purchased a good bottle of schnapps for libation to offer along with an envelope containing American dollars. I knew that the traditional exchange of greetings began with a welcome – *"Akwaaba!"* – and my being asked to state the nature of my errand. I articulated the reason I had come as my wish to offer the Chief my profound respects, and to thank him for having so kindly cared for my Crossroads group after the death of my husband. Because this meeting took place in a reception room at his home rather than in public, as on the day of our official welcome to Wenchi, we were now permitted to speak back and forth in English without the cumbersome intermediate presence of the Royal Linguist.

Before leaving Accra I'd hired a driver to bring me to a nearby village famous for its woodworkers, where I bought a freshly carved traditional stool. The popular Ashanti proverb *Sankofa* is represented by a bird with its head on backwards, a reminder that "there is no shame in retrieving from the past that which has been forgotten, in order to move forward." The stool I selected was carved with a *Sankofa* bird in profile supporting the perfect curve of its seat. The proverb refers to the importance of preserving ancestral tradition in order to learn from the past, but the supplemental translation I favored is the one about correcting mistakes.

Across the road from those stool carvers were the "Fantasy Coffin" carpenters whose designs are strictly contemporary and so customized that they're more sculpture than furniture. My favorites were the lipstick-red hibiscus, the plaid golf bag, and the silver rocket eternally poised for takeoff. It grieved me to see the child-size toy-themed caskets, but I had to admire the craftsmanship.

In this encounter with the Chief he was seated on a couch across a low coffee table from my chair, and he was wearing a lime-colored embroidered cotton dashiki with matching trousers. The first thing he asked me was if I knew that he had paid for Tim's coffin. Which I did not.

I'd assumed that Tim's coffin was ready-made in order to be provided so quickly, but I realized only now that its flamboyant gold paint and those porthole-like windows, whatever their significance, must have made it expensive. The souvenir photograph of my visit to the Chief shows us sitting side by side on his couch, my smiling face expressing the boundless thanks that were, however sincere, absurdly belated.

Nana Frema next asked if I would like to visit the house where Tim died, so after our visit to the Chief she took me to the place I'd scarcely inhabited. The main road ran right by it, this I remembered, but in 1970 the packed clay was only interrupted by a token stretch of fresh black tar at the crossroads, to give Wenchi the respect it deserved as the birthplace of a chief of state.

In one of the earliest of our centrifugal conversations filling the immediate days and nights after Jim and I met, when I introduced the distant subject of Ghana Jim told me that he too had traveled the road west from Kumasi, so he must have gone by the house in Wenchi on his way to Wa in the Upper West Region.

He'd gone there at the invitation of the Catholic Bishop of Kumasi and was offered the job he thought might make him want to remain in the priesthood, an assignment he said he would have accepted if not for the condition that he'd be required to commit to being there for at least twenty years in order to make a difference. Established as a trading post on the trans-Saharan route, Wa was a town of small-scale farmers, predominately Muslim, who were 75% illiterate, twice the national average. The chill that zipped along my spine took the form, "But if you were in Wa around the time I was in Wenchi, *what if* we'd met?" I imagined us as those magnets that repel each other until you flip them over and they adhere, which is a better way of saying timing is everything.

In my encounter with the Chief I promised to bring Jim back to meet him, which I did the next year. And whether or not the Chief understood why I had needed to come here alone this time, I knew Jim did. It was so I could stand at the edge of that highway, with my back to that road, and make myself look, just look.

The top floor of the square beige two story building was accessed as before by an exterior staircase that had been made more safe by the solid new railing leading to the narrow empty balcony outside the room where Dr. Beltman pronounced Tim's death. It was there that he told me, "Your husband is died. Dead," as I watched our volunteers head off to the construction site for their second day of work. Now the balcony was edged by a raised planter containing a row of spiky succulents, and the four poles supporting the roof were painted bright blue.

The Queen-Mother's conventional request for permission to enter was answered by the current resident's melodic *"Akwaaba!"* We stepped through the open door into the hallway, which was painted the same "shocking pink" as Nana Frema's guest bedroom. I knew which closed door concealed the shower room, but we were first invited into a living room crowded with upholstered chairs and an oversized couch for such perfunctory conversation that I can only recall feeling nervous. I tried to imagine my being this welcoming if a foreigner appeared at my door without warning to see the place where her young husband had bled to death thirty years earlier, and had to hope my presence here wasn't too rudely inconsiderate. From where I sat I could look into the spare room where the Canadian strangers who were our hosts had made up the spare bed for Tim in the middle of his next-to-last night. I couldn't have invented the intimacy that would be forced upon us in the next thirty hours, concluding with Jean's summoning *"Viens! Viens!"* The walls of that little room were now blue, trimmed with the cheerful yellow woodwork that ran throughout.

The Queen-Mother encouraged me not only to look at the small shower room but to take a picture of it, which I did, like a tourist at any historical site. Those walls were now painted blue and tiled white to shoulder height, domesticating the cubicle I remembered as bare. There was a frosted glass-louvered window on the outside wall to provide light and air, and from that threshold I noted how the shower head extended in an arc from the left wall, with two corner shelves for bathing supplies and two thin towels hanging on a high rack. In a corner of the cement floor was a white enamel basin with a smaller blue plastic bowl inside it, and this became my focus. I knew I could never make myself cross that threshold, but from that same spot where I couldn't, before, I made myself examine the ordinary drain down which Tim's life had vanished. I looked, and I saw it.

On that other morning when I witnessed the formal procession of the Chief and the council of Elders robed in black *Adinkra* cloth, a bearer held a large black parasol over the Chief. They smoothly navigated that exterior staircase to enter the same doorway through which Tim's body had been removed from the building to the flatbed truck that took it to the Kumasi morgue. I could see now that their mission to purify this defiled space seemed to have worked.

I left the building this time struck by its mundane character, and by the nonchalance with which I'd been received. If the situation were ever reversed I doubted my ability to reciprocate this gracefully, but I vowed to. It was as if the terrible event that had taken place in that shower cubicle had passed into the realm of legend, which almost made me feel as if I were no longer held to blame. Or maybe never had been.

Before this journey I had published a novel I called *Something Borrowed*, a tragicomic worst-case-scenario wedding weekend having little to do with the bride and groom. To explain the novel's origins, I found myself theorizing about my generation's notorious 50% divorce rate, concluding that those of us who hadn't divorced were invited to wonder What If We Had? just as those who *had* were obliged to wonder What If We Hadn't?

Once I set the novel's conflict in motion with this pair of hypotheticals, the action obligingly followed. And since I'd lived in Boston long enough by then to claim the convenience of the city's familiar setting with relative authority, I could focus on my characters and their hectic interactions.

My epigraph was by the poet Denise Levertov.

> The ache of marriage:
>
> thigh and tongue, beloved,
> are heavy with it,
> it throbs in the teeth
>
> We look for communion
> and are turned away, beloved,
> each and each
>
> It is leviathan and we
> in its belly
> looking for joy, some joy
> not to be known outside it
>
> two by two in the ark of
> the ache of it.

After my career gap it felt like a comeback even to hold the losing lottery ticket when, on the same day and in the same number of lines, while *The Baltimore Sun* compared me favorably to Jane Austen, the omnipotent *New York Times Book Review* compared me unfavorably to Agatha Christie.

My millennial return to Wenchi had invigorated me to try yet again to write the novel I always called *The Child Widow*. And I did, but it was rejected. The editor of *Something Borrowed* termed it too "self-conscious," but the real reason seemed to be that "my readers" would expect and prefer to read something more like what they'd just read. I quickly came up with an apparently acceptable scenario – another semi-comic marital dilemma with serious consequences – and to my own great surprise was able to get right down to work, finishing in five months a draft of the Plan B novel I called *The Court of Common Pleas*. Its protagonists were a trial court judge facing mandatory retirement age just as his somewhat younger wife, a career nurse, applied to medical school.

In my research of schools likely to accept such a "nontraditional" student I discovered Case Western Reserve, and encountered other enlightened learning practices there, where class ranking had been abolished in order to teach its super competitive medical students how to better collaborate as doctors. Rather than a cadaver, their first-year students were given a pregnant woman to follow, in order to study the interlocking systems at work within the human body. And so on. I so loved everything about it that, when the dean invited me to visit, I found I could imagine being a student there despite my hard-won horror of blood.

The novel was scheduled for September of 2001, and I was invited again to a book event in the town of Exeter, where I'd returned two years earlier during the publication of *Something Borrowed,* for the first time since moving out of Bancroft Hall. On that visit I'd been introduced to the Timothy Lee Buxton Teaching Fellow who was supported by the fund I'd established at the Academy in Tim's name, and I had felt warmly received by those friends who had remained on the faculty. This Exeter event was planned for September 11th, the day *The Court of Common Pleas* died – but hey! it's only a *book!* – along with all the others being published that season.

A series of events had been scheduled for Cleveland and, though flights were grounded, since it was within driving distance of Boston I went anyway. But while it was the only place in the country where my novel was noticed, it made me uneasy to be so far outside the shared experience of the personal losses suffered as those hijacked planes taking off from Boston reached their catastrophic destinations. "You must be glad to be away from it," someone for whom I signed a book in Cleveland assumed. But as we were all to learn, from that day on there was no such thing as being away from it.

In that week of 9/11, Jim's newspaper column argued for "Law, Not War" in the form of an international tribunal to bring Osama bin Laden to justice, no matter that in that reflexively retaliatory moment very few others agreed. Of course Jim was proved correct about the war against Afghanistan that bled into the war against Iraq, as by now almost everyone has concluded.

My own wish for America was that a spontaneous antiwar movement would rise up across the country and around the world, so the new work I threw myself into was a novel about a singer-songwriter of protest songs. I called it *Tinted Windows* after the vehicles the US-funded government of El Salvador used to "disappear" civilians. I had gone to El Salvador with a human rights group in early October of 1989, just before the Jesuit priests and their housekeeper and her daughter were murdered. Their slaughter sparked the rebel offensive that brought the war to an end, and my investment in that hard-fought truce was my way into a story about a protest song's power to rouse outrage.

I imagined my character resuming her career with an antiwar anthem that became a hit song!

But I was no musician, so to better understand songwriting I took piano lessons. I wrote lyrics and, in the most enjoyable extracurricular event of my writing career, sat in on a recording session when the performer Faith Soloway's throbbing voice and thundering piano brought my song to life. The production of "Tinted Windows" came about because I wanted to hear, realized, one of the eight or ten protest songs I'd invented.

No matter how my *Tinted Windows* might have fared in a different political climate, nobody cared to publish a novel that sang its way into exposing the lies of the Iraq War. My miscalculation didn't entirely surprise me, not with President George W. Bush posing in a flight jacket on an aircraft carrier to promote his unjust war as if we wouldn't remember that his father was a real pilot during World War II. But I was still upset each time an editor returned the submitted manuscript to my agent with the CD's cellophane wrapping intact.

To fulfill my promise to Nana Kusi to bring Jim back to Ghana, our arrangements included the antimalarial recommended for travel upcountry, with a stay of a few days in Accra. Jim was coming from the annual interfaith conference in Jerusalem that he regularly attended, and which was all the more essential when anti-Muslim extremism was sanctioned by the President of the United States. The Labadi Beach Hotel measured up to its four-star rating.

On our bus journey from Accra to Kumasi, when the driver began the trip by offering a convincing prayer for the safety of his passengers, we couldn't fail to note the badly cracked windshield. His announcement that the AC was not working made my seat all the more precious, except for the diesel fumes and the deafening rush of air through my wide-open window.

The popular new King of the Ashanti, the cosmopolitan *Asantehene* Osei Tutu II, was considered "a complete modern traditionalist" for his encompassing vision and side interests in golf and cricket. On our way through Kumasi we went to view the public exhibits at his royal compound, happening to arrive on one of the occasional days when the *Asantehene* is paraded before the public in all his golden finery, too splendid a figure to picture dressed in casual sporting outfits.

For the last hundred miles between Kumasi and Wenchi we hired a driver who brought us there efficiently and who seemed very pleased upon our arrival to be fed at the Queen-Mother's kitchen table a plate of the "bushmeat" that turned out to be a rodent four times bigger than a rat.

It was mango season, and the red flowering acacia tree bloomed all along our route back to the now-familiar town where Nana Frema and her brother Nana Kusi would welcome me yet again, and all the more gladly because I'd sent word ahead that I wasn't alone. Nana Frema's dinner for us – not bushmeat – was served on her fine lace tablecloth, and when she led us down the hall to her guest room she proudly showed off an air conditioning unit that was so new it had yet to be used. The louvered windows wouldn't allow for its installation, however, so it sat on a table in the center of the room, not only not cooling the air but making it hotter with its exhaust. We were unable to correct the situation except by switching it off.

The next day the Queen-Mother escorted Jim and me past the gold-painted lions on their cement pedestals to call on the Chief. Nana Kusi's wife was present again too as we offered our gifts, observing the formalities of stating the purpose of our visit and being received. The Chief enjoyed hearing about Jim's first trip to Ghana and the seemingly uncomplicated coincidence that, during his own previous life as a priest, he'd passed through Wenchi on his way to Wa.

Nana Kusi was named to the stool in 1949 when the future Prime Minister declined the nomination in favor of him. And at Queen Elizabeth's coronation in June of 1953 – she was twenty-six and Nana Kusi twenty-eight, back when his country was still part of the British Empire – he represented the Gold Coast as one of four Paramount Chiefs, of whom he was now the sole survivor.

The public record reveals that Nana Kusi's title had been "nullified" in 1976 during the regime that seized power in the coup against his brother, when *"any recognition in any manner"* of Nana Kusi Apea I as Paramount Chief was deemed punishable by a fine of one million *cedi* or two years in prison, or both. That injustice wasn't mentioned during our visit, but we discussed the irony of the 2000 elections where, with greater odds against it in Ghana than in America, democracy prevailed.

Nana Kusi had lived to witness the long-awaited victory won by President Kufuor, Prime Minister Busia's distinguished political heir, and we joked together that with George W. Bush's unorthodox installation as our president, the Jimmy Carter Center would now need to send Ghanaians to monitor free and fair elections around the world. It was a light moment, but we each knew the situation wasn't the least bit funny, as history has proved.

In going to Ghana with Jim in 2002 it wasn't my intention to continue my search for a means to re-write Tim's dying, but I returned home with the desire to give it another try. It was perhaps predictable that not even this better-informed version would succeed as a novel, so to finally dispatch with it as fiction, to finally publish something under the title that had been Philip Roth's long ago *bon voyage* gift to me as he sent me off into the writing life, I decided to bypass all my previous drafts and collapse my energy into a short story, my first ever. It would feature a feisty young widow making her return to Ghana to reckon with it far sooner, and better, than I myself had.

The central image of this "Child Widow" was neither *Kente* nor *Adinkra* cloth, but lace, the fabrication whose delicate design depends on the interplay between presence and absence. On my young widow's return journey she brings a carton of lace samples requisitioned from a bridal shop, remembering that the Queen-Mother favored lace for her curtains and tablecloths. In my story, as the village women play at being brides by draping themselves with the lace, the intricacy of the patterns is made more obvious, and beautiful, against their dark skin.

I wrote the story quickly, passionately, and found that I liked my young protagonist's personality not only more than my previous inventions but more than my own self. It was published in an issue of *Ploughshares* guest-edited by Alice Hoffman, and after all my unpublished versions I find it ironic that this inaugural attempt at short fiction was then selected among "100 Other Distinguished Stories" named in *The Best American Short Stories 2004*. For me the reward, and the surprise, was the way my nameless character's evolving clarity of purpose comes to seem natural, with an unencumbered directness.

She rents a room at the one-star Riviera Beach Hotel where from her window she has an unobstructed view of a Gulf of Guinea sunset:

> Already, the sun spread its wealth, turning the water gold. This land continued to be mined for the precious mineral that lured foreign exploitation throughout Ghana's fierce history. Because Peace Corps Volunteers are descended from those same colonizers, our mandate was to give more than we got. This was why I mistrusted the feeling I had in my chest, a fist-like clamp releasing its hold. Was it possible to seize power without taking anything from anybody?
>
> I felt unsteady on my feet, so I focused again on the brightly fractured water surface. Martin's impetuous love, I saw, had the power to stay alive within me, if I only let it. Turning thirty, I could toss the rest of my twenties overboard – not like an anchor – like a fish.

With its publication I felt satisfied, at last, to have fulfilled Philip's writing assignment with something so intentional. I welcomed my protagonist's authorization to conclude my perpetual quest. Tim's mother was still alive then, and while her protective daughter read my "Child Widow," she chose not to share it with Helen. At the time, it mattered more to me that I could finally stop trying to write my way into and out of Tim's suicide. Or so I thought.

JUST SING

My brother Will defined himself as the skier who fled to Colorado, never to return. And because his body literally incorporated the extreme-sport injuries that incrementally crippled him, there was still no keeping up with him on the slopes.

He got an early start avoiding catastrophic harm, the first time so narrowly that it was written up in the *Dobbs Ferry Register*:

> William Marshall, Jr. six-year-old son of Mr. and Mrs. William Marshall of 67 Bellair Drive, Dobbs Ferry, has returned home from the Dobbs Ferry Hospital where he was a patient following an accident at his home. The boy fell out of the bedroom window eighteen feet from the ground and miraculously escaped serious injury. He was treated at the hospital for cuts on his head.

He and I were playing a game of not letting our feet touch the floor, which we achieved by jumping around the circumference of a very small room, from bed to bureau to chair to radiator to bed to bureau to chair. We stopped to rest, with Willy on the windowsill and me on the bureau, when I suddenly saw his feet go upside down and disappear like in our Saturday morning cartoons. I rushed to find our mom, in her bedroom, on the phone, and she and I raced downstairs. To make it my fault, not his, I explained that I'd told him a joke and made him laugh so hard he tipped backwards (as if that explained the lack of a screen on the window). By the time we reached the kitchen door Willy was crawling toward us on his hands and knees, reassuring – immortally – "I'm all right, Mom."

This defiance of death was a prodigious start, and once he began to really work at it he got good enough to repeatedly rescue himself from that brink. I probably still don't know the half of it, coming as I do from a tidier world where calculating the invisible difference between synonyms is a full-time job. I always wondered how he did it. And why. It's no exaggeration to admit that while this terrifying experience emphatically marked the end of my own desire for danger, it quite possibly signaled the beginning of his.

Many years after Wharton, a classmate of his exclaimed with delight "What a memory!" when he discovered that I was Will's sister. He then gleefully divulged a series of legendary frat-boy pranks, such as Will's popping up Greek godlike – naked – from a plastic bin filled with a liquid concoction to offer a cup of punch to the fraternity president's girlfriend. Did our parents know Will rode a motorcycle? No, and neither did I. So who knew what secrets were buried, once he relocated to Aspen, under the snow cover on Ajax Mountain?

But in fact I too came to understand the compensatory benefit of risk when, after our demythologizing loss of Jenny, skiing rescued us as a family. Our interminable drives through the dark to Sugarloaf Mountain always delivered, its granite peak proving nature's unique ability to create consolation for the brokenhearted. I'd come to this knowledge as we four formed links in a chain on the beginner slope from top to bottom and I first believed in the possibility of recovery. Jim and I together embraced the assignment to demonstrate the twin values of control and letting go, until very soon our children made it clear that they could outpace us.

From the top of Sugarloaf Mountain the view extends to Canada from one range to the next, the foamy daylight a white skirt unfolding to that horizon. In the near distance the wind-thwarted evergreens are fastened with brooches of new snow. The silver sun ricochets. It seems eerily moonlike at the top of our world in this first light, and while in truth it doesn't feel entirely safe to me, I have no wish but to be here. The air is too cold to breathe, however, so the four of us take off, now always the children leading our way down. It is New Year's Day, and the partiers aren't up yet. Look what they miss.

The action feels almost natural without ice to undercut stability, with the packed snow so reliable underfoot that it's possible to swish from side to side, as advertised. The snow skirt has pleats fabricated by the vehicles whose headlights are visible from the ground at midnight as they roam the trails. Our son shows off by finding the bumps and carving athletic designs with his landings, while our daughter waltzes. I'm aware of the difference between his flash and the mechanical grace of her rhythmic carved turns, and while I can attempt to follow in her tracks, his form of upward mobility means that, should he ever decide to run away from home, there's no way I'll catch him.

The snow cover is deep enough to make it safe to fall if necessary, but it isn't. I want to get to the bottom without stopping and, simultaneously, to be alert to sensation along the way. Because in so many forms Jim represents for me such a dynamic and humane example of the exercise of male power, I pause to wonder how I could be so lucky. But even this distraction – not a thought, just a flash of feeling – is contraindicated on a trail of this caliber. Just sing, I tell myself. So I do.

That year Jim and I shared a writer-in-residence niche at Emerson College and taught graduate courses on writing. "A writer is someone for whom writing is more difficult than for other people," Thomas Mann said in a *Paris Review* interview, but writing was still the most effective way I'd found, and more deliberate than the discouragingly cryptic dreams I brought to the couch, for discovering what I didn't know I knew.

My analytic takeaway could be distilled into the therapeutic 1-2-3 of seeing that the depth of my childhood distrust in the lack of continuity of my mother's care is sometimes dangerously compensated for by my *over*-trusting; of recognizing the desperate degree to which I'd wanted my mother to be who she was capable of being (and *was*, part of the time) *all* the time; and of embracing the fact that her terminal illness had generated a freedom whereby I could be the daughter I'd rather have been and she could be the mother I'd rather have had.

As for my father, when I came upon an odd volume at the Boston Athenaeum that was a collection of more than three-hundred Cinderella tales from around the world I discovered that, in each of its less familiar versions, Cinderella's father was seriously complicit, either passively or actively, in the stepmother's behavior. In my difficulty with my own stepmother, and hers with me, I saw that by my dad's great need not to rock the boat or fan the flames or up the ante – pick your poison – he'd abandoned both his wife and his daughter. This was true, as far as I was concerned, with both of his wives. He was passive, but it felt active.

My exaggerated identification with my father in that classic Oedipal Either/Or has ruined many a son and daughter. In so strictly aligning myself with him I resented my own powerlessness, so I covered it up, pretending to be "just like him" the way my mother accused. I profited from this illusion for many years, loving it until I had no choice but to hate it once my actual *lack* of power over Tim permitted his death. I know that this is another oversimplification, but it's all I've got.

My brother fared worse. In our era the male heir was able to profit from that inherent privilege except when he failed to measure up to that generation's conquering hero, who, home from the war, threw himself into his career so obsessively as to become the absentee father that could pretty much guarantee the son's failure to measure up. There you have it in Will's case: his case of unrequited love (and petty crime) that led to the disastrous decision to send him off to The Choate School in search of some sort of surrogate father. That rigorous experience may have given JFK the "Ask Not" refrain that he recycled so stirringly in his Inaugural Address, but for other, lesser Choate boys, the Headmaster set a punishing tone. My brother's revenge against the system was to mastermind ever more mischievous pranks, the most daring, and dumb, occurring the night before graduation when he and a coordinated team of other disgruntled seniors filled the Dean's office floor-to-ceiling with balled-up newspaper. Successfully eluding detection by the roaming night watchman, they still managed to get diplomas.

Will's college years at Penn's Wharton School were such a blur that none of the coursework was salvageable. In that ski bum interval between Will's two undergraduate degrees our dad dismissed Aspen as a "bubble society," and while it eventually became clear to our parents that denigration was the least effective way to get Will's attention, by then he'd made Colorado his permanent home.

The transcript of the Wharton classmate named Donald Trump has been concealed, but despite Trump's bragging that Wharton was "one of the hardest schools to get into in the country, always has been" – "super genius stuff" – to prove his claim "I'm, like, a really smart person," those of us who attended the 1968 commencement exercises know that not only did Trump not graduate first in his class, as he pretends, he's not listed in the program as having graduated with honors of any kind. He and my brother had this in common, and nothing else beyond the career successes of their fathers. Unlike Trump's automatic absorption into the family business, I'm not sure Will ever had any actual wish to practice law. But I understood his thwarted desire to measure up, and so I found it daring of him to pass the Colorado Bar and declare himself a Public Defender, at the opposite pole from being a partner at Cravath. To score another point, he then joined a high profile Denver law firm, and quit that too.

Now and then Will would return to measure his spindly mountain aspens against the greener landscape of the northeast, and while he always claimed our masses of venerable trees as the only thing he missed, like most refugees he never entirely left the old country. He never fully got the hang of living in a world without irony either, so that whenever we were together, especially when I visited him there, I was such a throwback for him that this alone had its charms.

Sometimes my bossiness was overbearing, but this was familiar too. He had waited before telling me he'd been diagnosed with cancer because he knew that the second he did I'd be all over it. Which I was.

"Lexine?"

"Hey, Willard."

"I have Multiple Myeloma."

"I'll be right there."

I don't want to say his illness was a gift, but it blew through any unfinished business the way a stiff breeze shakes the pollen loose so it can fertilize. No, he didn't want to come to Boston to be treated by the world authority on his disease – he didn't want to be our guest – and while this saddened me, I respected Will choice to be cared for in Denver. It was hard for me at first to honor the medical expertise of a doctor costumed in a snap-buttoned shirt and snakeskin boots. (Until I asked myself what, really, was so convincing about the silk bow ties at Mass General?)

This was the summer of 2010, when Lizzy married James. The wedding To-Do list consists of the sort of infinite detail that can threaten to overcome the event's significance, but it didn't. Although the bride's uncle was too at risk to travel that June, the day was otherwise splendid, if this can be said to be entirely true with such a grim diagnosis hanging over a ceremony promoting the illusion of happily ever after.

Will's stem cell collection yielded millions of them in clear plastic bags that made me gasp at the wealth they represented as they were carted off to the vault of a deep freeze. Their unique color challenged me to conjure an analogy, but this golden pink magical substance refused to be reduced to the mundane. Not to mention that when the next phase of the treatment was to kill Will's bone marrow with chemo and replace it with this, it wouldn't do to expect so much from something resembling our grandmother's recipe for tomato aspic.

There was a short course offered at the hospital for the next of kin, with a syllabus that ranged from the correct technique for hand-washing to how to inject an emergency antidote when a dangerously high fever occurs without warning, as it does in 95% of the cases. "Any questions?"

Well, yes, but how to ask it when my poor brother, still the most handsome man in the room, is slumped in the chair next to mine and I think it sounds like cowboy medicine for him not to be hospitalized during the grueling chemo countdown and total rebuilding of his immune system! I get it that the risk of infection in a hospital is just as high if not higher, but how was I supposed to convince myself that if he preferred to stay at home and could get his fear under control, so could I? What about the clear and crucial benefits in relying upon the skills of a highly trained staff instead of someone like me who has been tested, who failed?

When so little else in my brother's life was lucky, I can't say what accounted for his making it into that 5%, but I know we got there together, minute by minute during those day-by-day weeks while the killer chemo dropped his white cell count to zero – zero! – in preparation for its restoration. Every day we commuted from his bedroom to the outpatient clinic to study the numbers as if we were part of the medical team. On one of those mornings his two nurses literally pumped his life back into him in a formalized ritual, reciting aloud the matching identification numbers before thawing the pouches of stem cells and massaging them into an infusion tube with their own hands. As I sat near enough to hold Will's hand, I had a conversion experience. I became a believer in Science, and came as close as I expect I ever will to believing in God.

As a caretaker, I gave Will the help I wasn't allowed to give Tim. And with this successful – "textbook" – example of his carefully calibrated decline and renaissance it proved possible for me to have faith when they told us that he was good to go for the next eight to ten years. At the same time Will's intimate knowledge of his body's strengths and limitations obliged him to remain suspicious in spite of the unqualified verdict of the medical experts who hailed his transplant a total success. In this regard Will was more realistic than I was, so in effect we'd switched places.

I went back to work. When my *Tinted Windows* failed to find a publisher, I promptly wrote another novel I called *The Pull of Gravity*. Because it began with a death that was either a fall or a jump from a bridge, the investigation occurred on multiple levels. After my dedication to the foreign worlds of protest music and illegal war, it was like coming home again to write about suicide. And in placing it against Colorado's rugged setting, I'd already done that research too. The manuscript managed to get me another new agent, and while the search for an editor was broad, it was unsuccessful.

I then decided that, if I was going to try again with a novel that wouldn't be published, I may as well make it a vehicle for learning something I didn't already know. The standard advice notwithstanding, the great beauty and challenge of fiction is that it allows its author to become a temporary expert in any subject. I had in mind three alluring themes to pursue: Adoption, Figure Skating, and the Siege of Sarajevo. The puzzle was how to fit them together into a narrative.

Adopting Love gave me a visit to the heroic city of Sarajevo an unrecovered decade after its brutal civil war. I made my protagonist a sixteen-year-old figure skater adopted to America during the Siege, when Sarajevo's ethnically intermarried population turned against one another to permanently blight the larger meaning of identity. The climax of her return was a skating exhibition that I invented and placed at the destroyed and rebuilt arena. This was the site of the 1984 Winter Olympics that fixed the world's pride on this civilization where the universal ideal of ethnic diversity was realized. My heroine skated to the disco anthem "Staying Alive" and landed all her jumps.

You could call "Staying Alive" my own theme song, and ice the medium of choice for any writer, after Robert Frost – or was it John Updike, or was it Updike quoting Frost? – lifted up the perfect image of a poem being like an ice cube riding on its own melting. The adoption theme opened my eyes to the universal grief in those individual stories, and it goes without saying that Sarajevo's brutal atrocities broke my heart wide open.

This too failed to find a publisher, but because I refused to let it die even when it was declared dead, I carved out a substantial excerpt of *Adopting Love* and submitted it to be published in *Ploughshares*, where "Adopting Sarajevo" was featured, like my protagonist, as a SOLO.

What it comes down to for me is my stubborn superstition that I might lose my life were I to quit writing. It's arguable that I could have devoted myself to other pursuits with greater success, but in risking giving myself to writing I was given that second chance that I don't dare forfeit. To voluntarily give up a life – or even a *way* of life – is a form of suicide. And I'm not going there.

For the Thanksgiving after Will's transplant – "Day 0 + 104" since his "second birthday" in August – he was cleared to join us in Boston. The walls of our dining room were glazed a reddish-pink or pinkish-red that Jim described as "less Palm Beach, more Pompeii," a color coming so alive with the room ringed in candlelight that on this day it recalled for me the unnamable color of Will's stem cells. Our table was extended to its fullest length with the inherited silver platters and serving bowls and candelabra polished to shine like in the olden days at our mother's and grandmother's Thanksgiving tables. We offered so many side dishes that our plates were too crowded, and Will sat at the head of the table as the embodiment of this feast day.

Whatever the precarious future might hold was anybody's guess. We were mindful, after all, that this national holiday is also observed as a "National Day of Mourning" by Native Americans. We knew that six years after that famous first Pilgrim meal with the Wampanoag in 1621,

Governor John Winthrop of the Massachusetts Bay Colony proclaimed a first official "Day of Thanksgiving" to honor the soldiers who massacred and/or enslaved seven hundred men, women, and children of the Pequot tribe. Our family Thanksgiving acknowledged this native reality over the mythology of the colonizers.

And yet our own good fortune proved so durable that a few months later we celebrated our son Patrick in his Broadway debut in a play called *Good People*. His role as Stevie was both deceptively simple and a hinge for the plot, and he delivered on his promise with a deep authority that awed his Stage Mom. To me, Patrick's acting talent was an organic refinement of the life skills that he had always possessed, not just as an observer but as a sympathetic witness to human complexity, starting with his own. It meant everything to him and to us all that his Uncle Will was able to be in that Broadway audience for back-to-back performances.

The play was a hit, and the star of the show was Frances McDormand, who won that year's Tony Award for her anguished portrayal of a combatively resilient woman continually down on her luck in a system without a safety net for good people like her. She wore a plain cotton dress and a jean jacket to accept her Tony at the awards ceremony, where, ever sincere in her generosity, she offered praise for the acting ensemble that included "our own young Patrick Carroll."

We were able to see *Good People* a number of times because the play was extended well beyond its run, with the final Broadway performance on May 28, 2011. This was the same day that Helen's obituary notice appeared in the *Boston Globe*.

Tim's sister had long ago graduated from her itinerant life and settled into an evocatively named California town called Valley Center. With Helen living nearby, she provided her mother with such consistently tender care in the last years of her life that, when she called to tell me of Helen's peaceful death at age ninety-two, it was my reflexive impulse to remember Helen as 100% alive – paying tribute with denial of my own – by recalling the time she'd almost died from a careless pharmacy error. Rather than bringing a lawsuit against the drugstore chain for giving her ten times the dosage of her doctor's prescription, she'd preferred to get them to fund a family reunion, which they did. This meant renting a beautiful house overlooking the Pacific and flying in all her children and grandchildren to spend a week together. In the happy group photo she sent me she was wearing what I think of as her favorite color, and certainly mine for her: the blue that matched her eyes.

I loved this about Helen because her solution represented a compromise between total denial and the sort of confrontation that went against her nature. She was pleased with herself, and it seemed fitting that she chose to be compensated for her near-death with a living investment in the family she cherished. Like her sisters and their mother, Helen was a progressive in many ways. But not in telling it like it is.

Jim and I drove to Old Lyme, meeting Tim's siblings at the Duck River Cemetery. By mistake, the hole for Helen's ashes had been dug across the clearing from its designated spot between the gravestones for Tim and Helen's mother, so while this correction was made we all walked down the road to the Congregational Church. The last time we were there together was when Tim preached from that pulpit.

And now it was his sister who spoke, delivering her eulogy with a poise as a public speaker practiced in her current work in what Helen described as "life coaching." Using the skills perfected in her former life as a jewelry maker, she had crafted a beautiful beaded monogrammed tag for the antique basket that held Helen's ashes, which were laid to rest after this service by the church's current minister. I'd brought a bouquet of roses from my Cape Cod garden and a second bunch for Tim's grave, a gesture that was natural to me but which seemed to take his siblings by surprise. I wondered why.

After the service, at the gathering in the now comfortably renovated barn where Tim lived that summer when I studied dance up the highway in New London, Helen's many careful scrapbooks were on display. Jim and I were touched to find an album dedicated to preserved clippings referring to us or our books. On the adjacent table was an unfurled scroll prepared by her third son, the family archivist, an elaborate ancestral chronology representing his ongoing research.

With such precise accounting, I wanted all the more to know which of the three of them had written the three-inch-square paid obituary notice reproduced from the *Globe*. Did Tim's brothers and sister prepare it together? I knew Helen would have approved the smiling photo that accompanied the text, but why were the four sisters by whom Helen was predeceased mentioned by name – Josephine, Lydia, Katharine, Phoebe – while her surviving children and grandchildren were not? I read it again: "Mrs. Rose was predeceased by her sisters: Josephine, Lydia, Katherine, and Phoebe; and is survived by a daughter and 2 sons, 8 grandchildren and a great grand-daughter." I read it again. Why wasn't Helen also predeceased by the son who didn't survive her?

I thought of the night Lee died, when Helen allowed me to witness the depth of her sorrow. I now interpreted that seeming disjunction between the anticipation of her own death and the compensatory birth of an imagined grandchild as that age-old instinctive pairing of death with new life. This promise was the text of Tim's own favorite Bible passage, as everyone knew – "unless a grain of wheat falls to the ground and dies, it remains alone; but if it dies, it bears much fruit" – so I shouldn't have been as surprised as I was. With Lee's death, in letting go of her past, Helen was supplying a future. To my knowledge she never asked Tim or her other three children to have their kids call her anything more than whatever they chose to call her – not *Babushka* – so that wish vanished.

On the day of her funeral in Old Lyme I wanted to ask each of them if, possibly, their mother might have had a hand in preparing her own death notice. I didn't want to make Helen the one responsible for omitting her son's name, but by having known her as a lifelong citizen of the state of denial I would have understood it better.

Yes, it was more logical to assume Tim's siblings as the authors of that text, but it didn't seem right to challenge or even investigate the scripting of Helen's obituary on the day of her burial, so I waited a while. During those weeks I rehearsed confronting each of them by phone or email, separately or together, preparing myself to be told that it was either entirely deliberate or a terrible, painful mistake. I wondered if it had been noticed by anyone else who may or may not have brought it up to them, and found myself wishing for honest conversation.

But then, after what seemed like a decent interval, I realized to my surprise that it was no longer necessary for me to know which of them was capable of such an oversight, if that's what it was, or to determine, if not, what else accounted for the exclusion. It didn't matter anymore whether I was the only one to notice Tim's absence because, by not including him as his mother's son and their own sibling, he became mine.

For their mother's sake they couldn't have intended or foreseen – or sanctioned – this outcome, but by not claiming their brother for themselves they released him to me. And by forfeiting possession of Tim's story, they gave me permission to write this book.

Once again my life got to my desk before I did. In spite of the recuperative experience of rediscovering Lizzy's books as we emptied our bookshelves, the sale of her childhood home was a large loss. The timing might have seemed reasonable and even logical coming after her wedding the previous June, but what if in that first year of her marriage it was all the more important not to lose her home base? She never said this, but we did discuss the poignant grip of her assumption, both conscious and unconscious, that one day her own child would sleep upstairs in her bed, just as I had in that same bed at my grandmother's house before it came to be my mother's, then mine, and now hers.

I told her I understood, and I did. And yet, I asked her, when she was a child visiting her grandparents – no matter that neither the grandmother nor the house was what I'd imagined for her! – did this matter to her? Did she even know, or want to know? Though she would later learn from me about the grandmother for whom she was named, and be shown the house that was once my family home, hadn't she been given a loving alternative?

My little brother, the eternal boy with the movie star good looks and the jokey demeanor that had always made him such good company, had survived the hell of a bone marrow transplant with my help. Perhaps it ought to have been obvious to me that any voluntary upheaval was an insane idea, but in undertaking the demanding process of selling our house I must have needed to prove that everything was possible, including keeping my dear brother from dying.

If you go to that last week in September of 2011 in the DAYMINDER brand Weekly Academic Planner that I continued to favor as my yearly calendar, you can see what I mean. I would never look to find my brother's fate revealed this way, but because it struck me as a curious thematic coincidence, onto that week's actual events – 8 scheduled showings within 72 hours – I taped a series of little dated *Globe* clippings from that page of the paper where you can find the comics or "This Day In History" or your Horoscope.

I know it's only by coincidence that Jim and I have birthdays that are only days apart, but because the week we met happened to be *that* week, our coming together during those days seemed consequential, even fated. So every now and then I'll read our shared Horoscope out loud to him. He always shrugs, no matter how accurate it may seem. I kind of like it that I'm curious about this and he's not. Not at all.

Monday September 26

AQUARIUS: Get what you want by being open, receptive and to the point. Don't go overboard trying to impress others. There are dollars to be made, contracts to be signed and settlements to be reached. Finish what you start.

Wednesday September 28

AQUARIUS: You've got nothing to lose and everything to gain. The coast is clear to change your life. Explore any avenue that will lead to an improved lifestyle and better living arrangements. Money is in the stars, along with love and commitment.

Thursday September 29

AQUARIUS: Get your personal papers in order and focus on contracts that can help you prosper. Don't let emotional matters slow you down or cause you to make a mistake. Timing is essential.

Friday September 30

AQUARIUS: Be a leader, not a follower. Trust in your abilities. Invest in your future, not someone else's. Financial, contractual and emotional gains can be made. An unexpected turn of events will bring benefits far greater than you can imagine.

Jim regarded me across our narrow breakfast table and, as I expected, he shrugged. Among the twenty-one books that he has published, in addition to his twelve novels are the nonfiction titles *Constantine's Sword, Toward a New Catholic Church, Practicing Catholic, Jerusalem, Jerusalem, Christ Actually,* and *The Truth at the Heart of the Lie: How the Catholic Church Lost its Soul.* In that nicely non-judgmental way of his he asked the obvious question. "So I wonder why, if you can believe in this shit, you don't believe in God?"

We sold the house, but I immediately rushed to Colorado when Will's prognosis was abruptly revised from eight to ten years to eight to ten *months.* This was a collapsing of expectation that would make the last of our time together seem like running in place. He chose me to be his caretaker, and when one of the nurses complimented me one day by asking if I was a nurse – and I replied, "Oh, no, I'm not nearly friendly enough!" – I could still make him laugh.

I also took on his full-blown anger the way a soccer goalie leaps and dives to intercept the ball, and after a while he seemed to trust me not to quit on him the way he felt tempted to himself. The calm he then reached for and achieved was textbook Elisabeth Kubler-Ross, whose heroic *On Death and Dying* had been published in 1969, just in time for me to identify my own first "Five Stages of Grief." I'd also absorbed her passionate views on hospice care, a practice she'd imported from Europe in order to convince America that we too were mortal.

One day, when Will was in that "Willard 'n Lexine" mood, he felt like hearing me tell him again about meeting Jim. I guess my description wasn't flamboyant enough, because he made me go to his desk and bring him a file containing a letter from me to him, dated March 18, 1977, six weeks into it.

"Dear Willy" began with my news that *Redbook* magazine had paid $7,500 (50% more than Knopf's advance) for *Gus in Bronze* to be one of its condensed novels. Yes, I was excited about that, but here was the reason he'd saved it:

> And everything else continues to go at the same chaotic clip. Jim + I keep up the Love Overflowing action until I swear I'll not be capable of another juicy, diabolical, cynical, habitual word. I hardly even speak English anymore, so gushy is it all. I keep waiting for it to level out +

it just escalates. And so on. Exhausting, bewildering, thrilling. Listen to me: what it all feels like is being both floored and ceilinged, both at once. And me, of all people. Good old acid-lady Lexine. (Obviously I'm still image-conscious, however much my brain has turned to champagne + roses.)

More tamely, the next paragraph reads, "I'm still loving dance class + still pleased with the beaver pond project. Fallen by the wayside is the new novel but I should get back to it hopefully next week. Jim, meanwhile, has done 700 pages of a 2nd draft in 6 weeks."

I cherished Will's preserving this evidence of my fluttery exhilaration, and I still do. It proves that he wanted me to be beloved, the same wish I had for him.

Dear Willy!

Like savings for a rainy day you'd set aside a few Colorado "fourteeners" to climb in your old age, but now those powerhouse legs of yours are so knobby-kneed that you look like a marionette. Instead of the button-down Oxford-cloth shirts that our dad wore in his hospital bed so he could keep his mechanical pencils handy, you favor a succession of faded navy blue Beefy T-shirts that have so softened in the wash as to become lightweight. The rest of your uniform consists of similarly antique Brooks Brothers boxers and the wool scarf you've worn draped around your neck ever since the neurosurgical intervention that I coerced you into having in Boston many years ago, which either crippled you or spared you from quadriplegia, depending on the day. The new orange cashmere scarf you wear now was a gift from Jim, its color matching the jars of Paradise Peaches grown in a valley at the base of the Rockies and preserved for you by your former girlfriend, Susie B. Other friends visit too, including your former wife, Diane. Married at age fifty and divorced after only a few mismatched years, it's a tribute to Diane, and you, that she wants to share in your care and that you want her to.

You consent to sponge baths and the occasional shave, but when I once tried to convince you to change your boxers you refused, properly putting me in my place by replying, with the humor you never lost, "Fuck bacteria! I'm trying to die here!"

Because you choose to let death take you on its own schedule you are credited for your courage by your wise and compassionate Physician's Assistant in a last appointment on February 7th at the blood cancer clinic. This is when you say you've "reached the end of the road, with zero quality of life," and make the decision to discontinue treatment in order to enter hospice care. Megan tells you admiringly, "The situation changed and you changed with it," but your doctor then disappoints me with what seems like the opposite – macho – impulse when Jeff asks, "What was your best climb, Will?"

This seems altogether off-topic because you are so weak, but I am proven wrong when, instead, you firmly answer, "McKinley." You don't mention that the mountain happens to be named for our mother's great-uncle, the least known of America's assassinated presidents, but you describe for a full five minutes the expedition where you and your climbing partners came upon others who were either already dead or in urgent need of evacuation, and rescued them.

Your hospice nurse is named Joy, and while you and I trade one of our New York smirks when she introduces herself, I make the executive decision not to expose you to Joy's well-intentioned social worker colleague who takes me aside to mention that it is often comforting for the dying to imagine being reunited with their parents.

During the last weeks of your life, as you become ever more dependent, you also become ever more receptive. At the same time it's just as true that you wish to remain firmly in control – the *willful* Will, so aptly named – so that in this first meeting with Joy, when you demand "Who's in charge here?" and she promptly gives you the right answer "You are!" she nevertheless feels obliged to double-check that the decision to enter hospice care is indeed your own.

We ask Joy for more information, but all she has to offer are the three categories of hospice care: weeks to months, days to weeks, hours to days.

Dear Willy!

We have moved your king-size bed downstairs into the living room of your classic bungalow, so that with me on the foldout we can sleep toe to toe. Jim has now arrived from Boston to be with us, and when he and I meet with the funeral home to arrange for the cremation you request, I realize you haven't told me your wishes for where to settle your ashes. This worries me until I see that you are allowing me to make the choice for you, to bring you home with us.

Our first cousin, your dear Gaily, is on her way to you. So too your loving nephew and niece, Patrick and Lizzy, who made a recent visit to you together and are now rushing back to Denver again. The hospice timetable's imprecision means, alas, that they will miss their chance to say goodbye.

The only signal that this final assignment is arduous for you is a swift crescendo of anxiety that is soothed, at Joy's instruction when I call in for her advice, by two drops of Lorazepam under the tongue.

Jim and I keep vigil through your last quiet night and witness a progression of measured breaths that cause your bony chest to rise and fall and rise again, until it doesn't. With an almost imperceptible shudder, at 9:40 on the morning of February 24th, after an overnight snowfall that is rare for Denver for being so dense, you enter into your first and only *non*-near-death-experience.

Dear Willy!

When Joy arrives to pronounce it, it is also part of her job to collect all your remaining medications. The protocol for their proper disposal is to funnel them into a liter-size bottle to dissolve them in water, and as she realizes the need for several more containers, she tells me she's never seen such a stockpile.

I saw you sit for hours with the oversize pills you resisted all the more firmly the sicker you got, but only some of these are those skipped doses. I knew where you kept the others, and why, and though you talked it through with me thoroughly enough that it eventually went without saying as an option, when you gave me the explicit choice of whether or not you would tell my kids that you were considering suicide – "Please don't!" – you agreed you wouldn't, and then you did. This news upset them, and when I told you this, you claimed it was important to let them hear it from you.

I'd learned from Tim that this hardly helped, but I gave you the benefit of the doubt as long as you promised (and kept *this* promise) not to ask either them or me to assist.

As I hand your overdose stash to Joy I realize that her reaction is the first amusing thing your death prevents me from telling you. This makes me sad. And proud too.

Dear Willy!

The overnight snow was forecast, but it is so thick that the sun can't instantly melt it the way it usually does in Denver. Of course this makes it both familiar and inconvenient in an Eastern sort of way, but it is unusually beautiful too, and fitting, the way everything looks bandaged.

Joy contacts the funeral home we've chosen, and as she prepares you for this journey we prepare ourselves. We can assume their arrival will be delayed by the weather just as Joy's was on this slow-motion morning that has just lost its speedometer.

Accustomed to all varieties of sleeping bags for your expeditions, you are zipped into this standard-issue rubber body bag and lifted onto the stretcher that is almost too short for you. I walk you to the curb and stand there with snow up to my knees, until the black van disappears into the white landscape.

I am picturing you where you would want to be, on Aspen Mountain for first tracks.

Dear Willy!

We gather at your neighborhood branch of the Denver Public Library, which represents for your family and extended family the importance of books in your life. Never an easy reader, in fact, I love that your first and perhaps best job here in Colorado was as an Aspen Middle School librarian. Your living room was filled with wraparound bookshelves that you were required to empty before the stem cell transplant, but the stacked cartons went no further than to line the walls of your garage in order to make them conveniently retrievable.

On the back wall of the library's community room are stenciled the first two stanzas of an Emily Dickinson poem that speaks of your life and death:

> There is no frigate like a book
> To take us lands away,
> Nor any coursers like a page
> Of prancing poetry.
>
> This traverse may the poorest take
> Without oppress of toll;
> How frugal is the chariot
> That bears a human soul!

In my eulogy for you I call you a loner in life – "a boy with a dog" – and as I gesture at the enlarged photograph of you with your first and best Golden Retriever, Waldo, a diagonal shaft of sunshine highlights the two of you.

Dear Willy!

I've learned that the nature of grief with a foreshortened life is to lose not only what we had but what, consciously and unconsciously, we expected still to have. This is true now with you, just as it was with Tim and Mom and our baby Jenny, who still has birthdays – her thirty-fifth this year – no matter that she lived for just a fraction of time. With Dad it's been possible to believe he had a full life because his was so much longer than the others, but now that I'm approaching the age he was when he died, he seems younger than he did at the time.

I know too now that the afterlife of a suicide is the same as the afterlife of everyone else. I've struggled to get here, as has everyone whose life has been split in two by a deliberate death, but my shame has allowed itself to be transformed into love, however incrementally, the way the night gives way to daylight and the day to a finite darkness, one night after the next, until sunup. You can cue the violins, but I believe in the consoling power of symmetry. I refuse to discount its value when this balancing ultimately reveals, I think, what Philip tried to teach me about Rilke's definition of love.

I've learned that the function of grief is to alchemize itself into love, which can then become an enduring companion for the rest of our days. This transformation of grief into love exercises its vehement power until it too expires, according to Tim and his trusted sources, to make way for the newborn.

And here is the ultimate proof of this, dear Willy. Exactly nine months after your death, our Lizzy gave birth to a baby girl she named Alexandra.

THE AFTERLIFE OF A SUICIDE

When the Queen-Mother telephoned to relay the news of the death of Nana Kusi, Will's death was a fresh grief. So when Nana Frema mentioned a library room for the building she wanted to construct in her brother's honor, the convergence inspired me to send a memorial gift to fund it. It was a chance to honor the memory of my own brother while paying tribute to hers.

It was less than a year later that I received a phone call from Nana's Frema's younger daughter to tell me of the Queen Mother's death. This daughter, named Doris Nana Konado Osei, lives in Texas, and she and I had spoken on the phone on several occasions. I was surprised to learn from Nana Doris that six months had already elapsed and that the burial wasn't scheduled for almost three months. When I told her, impulsively, that as long as the Busia family would consider our presence appropriate Jim and I would like to be there, she didn't hesitate either.

The flight was direct, and after these too many hours in the white air between New York and Accra, the confetti of corrugated rooftops created a multicolored mix of red and green and blue, to match the clay earth or the tropical vegetation or the ocean we'd crossed. Since my last visit to Ghana the airport had been upgraded to generic, but in stepping outdoors, under the *"AKWAABA!"* banner, I knew where I was by the embracing way the passengers were being welcomed. The specifics of our travel plans from now on were unknown, until one of Nana Frema's eleven granddaughters introduced herself and guided Jim to the adjacent domestic terminal to get our Africa World Airways tickets for the connecting flight to Kumasi. The Busia family was assembling from far and wide for this royal occasion.

Sentimentally, I'd packed the long black dress that I wore when Nana Frema and I met for dinner in 2000, and Jim had bought a black suit, his first since leaving the priesthood nearly fifty years before. We'd been asked to send our measurements so that funeral outfits could be sewn for us from commemorative fabrics, but that's all I'd been given to imagine about these five days of ritually choreographed mourning and celebration.

In becoming Queen-Mother of Wenchi Traditional Area, Nana Afua Frema Tatuo II chose that name to honor the great-grandmother who served as both Queen-Mother *and* Chief during the mid-1800s. In this matrilineal society Nana Frema was prized as the first daughter after six sons, and having been sent to school by her eldest brother, the future Prime Minister, she was the first educated Queen-Mother in the Ashanti Region when she was named to the stool in 1951 at age 24. Her death occurred on January 13th – noted by a member of the royal family as the 44th anniversary of the "infamous coup" against "the ideas and ideals that Busia lived and died for" – on her way to a doctor's appointment just a few weeks before the family gathering planned for her 89th birthday.

When our flight landed in Kumasi we were met by a co-worker of Nana Frema's other daughter, Nana Amerley Awua-Asamoa. In a pickup truck with "Western Ashanti Region – Electricity" stenciled on the doors, he took us to what appeared to be the newly built home of a friend of Nana Amerley's, where we were to wait for her driver to come for us from Wenchi. Since it didn't seem possible to know more, we settled into a marble-tiled reception room decorated with large framed family portraits and furnished with Victorian-inspired gold brocade upholstered settees that nevertheless allowed us to stretch out and acknowledge our jet lag while we had the chance. As it turned out, we were there for the next five hours, looked in on intermittently by our absent host's cute little grandson, who was more curious about us than his shyer sister and whom I entertained by letting him swipe through all the photos stored in my phone. When total darkness came we assumed the plan for us had changed, but this was also exactly when Peter the driver arrived and, with only a bottle of water for the return trip, headed back into the congestion that had taken him – and would again – twice as long as it should.

I remembered Kumasi as a city of shopkeepers whose open shed-like booths are crammed together like cells, and as we crept along for a full hour I noticed how, at nine at night, every proprietor seemed engaged either in conversation or in the manufacture by hand of yet more merchandise, or both. After an hour of this slow-dancing reverse of the commute that had already stalled Peter on the way in, he dodged the plumes of pollution coming from the truck named "Y2K" and the bus named "God Is Great" and the van named "Say Your Prayers" and broke us out onto the freshly paved highway. From here on we were interrupted only by the frequent series of speed bumps to slow the traffic that would otherwise make it impossible for the citizens of villages and towns to cross from one side of their road to the other. One daring and clever man created a measure of safety by swiveling his head from side to side, the LED flashlight he held in his mouth signaling his existence to the oncoming vehicles.

At some point I began to recognize landmarks and, eventually, off to the left, elevated, the lights of Wenchi. Back at the airport in Accra, as we said goodbye to the local granddaughter and her three cousins from Dallas who also came in on our flight, we'd felt sorry for them that they were to travel by car the whole way, until we realized the chances were excellent that they'd arrived sooner. I reminded myself with this little lesson how useless it is to anticipate the future when there's always more to learn about the present.

A parallel message was reinforced the next morning when in the open-air restaurant of our hotel – where a pair of peacocks strolled through our breakfast – I admired the classically draped fabric worn by the extroverted man at the next table. He introduced himself as Nana Frema's nephew, a son of the Chief and a prince soon to be named to a stool in a nearby town. His *Adinkra* cloth was stamped with the symbols I recognized, and when I told him I had a favorite proverb, *Sankofa*, he offered to lend me his book of proverbs. I already knew that *Sankofa* "signifies the importance of returning in time to bring to the present useful cultural values which are needed today," that it "teaches the wisdom in learning from the past, which helps in building the future," and is "a symbol of positive reversion and revival." But instead of the symbol of a bird with its head facing backwards, *Sanko* ('go back') *fa* ('take') was represented here by its alternate image, a heart.

Dressed in our own black-on-black, we were taken to the Queen-Mother's house for a second breakfast of tea and eggs and meat pastries and two kinds of porridge. This was offered with an insistent hospitality, while on the adjacent balcony was an extensive buffet of African food that would be provided meal after meal for extended family and guests, but was understood as not our cup of tea.

The walls along the lane were draped with braided lengths of red and black bunting, and it was a short walk to the largest of the houses in the compound, where alternating rows of red and black folding chairs were set up on both sides of the surrounding verandah. This was the home built by the Prime Minister whose Progress Party won a landslide victory in Ghana's democratic election in 1969 but who was ousted after three years in a military coup. To further punish the family, as I'd been told, after its years as a police barracks the building was only recently released to his children for restoration.

We followed Nana Doris past a group of volunteers in T-shirts bearing Nana Frema's image, and as we moved around the freshly whitewashed perimeter we too shook hands with each of perhaps a hundred people sitting in the front row. This was a custom observed all this day and the next by a steady stream of people who shook hands, coming and going, as they filed by to view the body.

Our interpreter for the running commentary that proved necessary, both for what was being said and what was being done, was Nana Abena Busia, the daughter of the late Prime Minister. I was meeting Nana Abena for the first time but knew of her as a poet and a professor at Rutgers University. She spoke of her father's death in still vivid detail and with a mix of bitterness and resignation as she pointed out from the balcony of this home the location he had chosen for his burial. It was a place at the intersection of two aligned trees, which – on his own property – the family was prevented from using. His marble monument stood instead with a different outlook from the one he desired, but I was glad to see, at least, that the now mature orange tree had come into full fragrant bloom.

We'd been told that in their tradition there is a family whose designated role is to prepare the bodies of royalty, but this fact was by no means adequate preparation for the display of Nana Frema's body lying on a high brass bed under a blanket of flowers, her entire exposed right arm ringed with gold bracelets and wearing large gold rings on all her fingers. Stands of white flowers formed a headboard, and although she was protected by both ceremonial crossed swords and real sword-bearing guards, a number of the mourners took advantage of the opportunity for a souvenir photo, even a selfie.

By now eight months had elapsed since the Queen-Mother's death, so I was impressed by what I can only call the lovely quality of her skin, and by her peaceful expression. Indeed, to my surprise, what I felt in seeing her dead was a transformative tranquillity that endured throughout that day and the next, as we processed by twice more to witness her body dressed in an exquisite series of different traditional cloths, the bed linens having been changed too. In a corner of this reception room a conventional dark wooden casket with metal handles sat ready in an alcove, and looked quite out of place.

In the late afternoon of the second day for viewing the body, the required black dress was sporadically interrupted by the regalia of variously affiliated groups such as the Methodist ministers and church choir offering prayers and music, and a group of women wearing sashes denoting the Planned Parenthood Association of Ghana, which Nana Frema helped to establish in the region. The colorful highlight was the parade of artfully arranged gifts in large silvery bowls borne on the heads of six young women. This symbolic display was a generous offering by the in-laws to provide necessities for what is called "the journey to the ancestors," so it included bottles of water, cellophane-wrapped sweets, juice boxes, alcohol (a local liquor for libation as well as imported whiskies), a variety of rolled handkerchiefs (including representations of the flags of the US, the UK, and Canada to represent the Busia diaspora), and decorative pillows and blankets to keep the Queen-Mother comfortable for the rest of time. The procession ended with the drummers and dancers who were stationed by the entrance, and finally, the blue-uniformed workers from the rental company that provided the funeral tents and chairs.

We knew that today was part of a progression of ceremonies, but since we didn't know what was next, the immediate focus was all that mattered. For me, each aspect of this careful choreography informed me in ways I had no means of imagining, and while of course a royal death is its own category, it made my handling of Tim's body all the more foreign by comparison. It goes without saying that, originally, in this climate, no amount of lime could preserve a corpse for such an extended amount of time as is now considered standard. But this also put into perspective the relatively few days – just a week – that it took me to work out the complex arrangements for Tim.

The three-star Viglosam Lodge – "an oasis in Wenchi" – was set back from the main road on a red clay lane so rough that it would be difficult to access without a four-wheel vehicle. The roosters comically stretched up on tiptoe to disrupt the quiet with their round-the-clock crowing as we came and went past the one-room cement homes with outdoor cooking pots and washbasins. This created a harsh contrast with the "Spacious Car Park for Comfortability" or the "Beautiful Garden and 24 Hour Security Surveillance" to protect these gated grounds. Since Jim and I were the only visitors from abroad we were forgiven our reliance on powdered Nescafé, but like everyone else we enjoyed the highly chilled jumbo bottles of the Ghanaian Star beer that we each remembered from our first visits. The hotel's menu was a blend of local and "Continental" specialties, which gave Jim the large plate of deep-fried potatoes that sustained him at home too.

Our time apart from the family was relaxing for us all, as was made plain whenever we reappeared and they switched from Twi to English. In this cosmopolitan family everyone spoke fluent English, fluidly combining cultures so that the men wore Bermuda shorts under their traditionally wrapped cloths, their dressy flip-flop style sandals made of patent leather. All the women wore traditionally styled two-piece dresses, and while I knew not to wear pants, my knee-length black skirt on the first day felt immodestly short, my tanned legs glaringly white. On this second day I was told by Nana Abena that I was paying tribute to the Queen-Mother by wearing the same dress that I wore for our hotel reunion in 2000. Jim and I had yet to see our customized outfits for the next day and the day after, when I expected that we would look either tastefully homogenized or ridiculous.

I had been invited to write something for what was termed a "tribute pamphlet," an opportunity I welcomed as a way to honor Nana Frema as well as to account for my presence at her funeral. When I was later asked if I would be willing to read my tribute aloud, I agreed without any sense – except for being wholly disinclined to refuse anybody anything – of what this entailed. When it wasn't mentioned again I relaxed, until our ride to the church ended with my being escorted into a seat that felt too prominent, too much like a place of honor. I told myself with every exhale, "This is not about you," a strategy I latched onto as a way to keep breathing.

The dark casket was borne down the aisle and placed on what looked like a dining table dressed with one of Nana Frema's own lace tablecloths. In addition to the Presiding Methodist Bishop there were twenty other Christian clergy, all Ghanaian. In the balcony were two choirs, one dressed in cap and gown and the other a more informal group of singers called "Christ's Little Band," which Nana Frema helped to form. The Queen-Mother was described in the minister's opening remarks as a "mellow soprano" who gave her last solo performance just days before her death. And while with this introduction the first hymn seemed tame, this restraint proved only temporary.

The red and black cotton fabric commissioned for everyone to wear on this day had been crafted into a cuffed shirt for Jim and, for me, a long tight skirt with a flared top embellished with black lace sleeves. The cloth's design consisted of Nana Frema's royal name and dates encircling a stool carved with the Adinkra proverb, Gye Nyame (Except God) to designate that "there was no one present at the creation and there will be no one present at the end – Except God." I was relieved to find that this closely fitted cotton dress kept me cooler than my own synthetic travel wardrobe, and although our skin now looked even more pink, we blended in.

The "tribute pamphlet" turned out to be an elaborate 43-page book illustrated with a hundred glossy photographs. It wasn't clear how many of the tributes would be read, or in what order, but I was ready. Until, that is, there was a commotion when a man seated two rows behind me stood up to register a vigorous protest that rudely interrupted not only the reading of the first daughter's tribute but the effort of the second daughter, Nana Doris, to continue reading for Nana Amerley when she was overcome by emotion.

As the buzz subsided I asked the granddaughter seated next to me to translate, and she told me the man was asking why, with so many present who don't easily understand English, this wasn't happening in Twi.

So when I was introduced as the next speaker I came forward timidly. But in offering my honest if improvised apology for being unable to deliver my remarks in Twi, I heard the murmur of affirmation. The congregation seemed to settle into an unnatural quiet that gave me confidence as, word by word, I slowly recounted my arrival in Wenchi in the summer of 1970. I recalled the traditional welcome ceremonies that greeted us, and described my first impression of Nana Frema dressed in the uniform of a nurse-midwife.

And when my second paragraph began, "Two mornings later we awoke to discover that my husband had committed suicide," I heard the muted gasp to confirm that I was being understood.

If Tim brought dishonor to Wenchi, however unintentionally, I could sense that it was now within my quite deliberate power to bring honor. As I read my tribute I felt the force of the privilege I was being given:

> The compassionate support provided by the Queen-Mother and the Chief sustained me in the immediate aftermath, as did the kind concern demonstrated by their brother, Prime Minister Busia. I returned to New York, but our group remained to complete our work, and when I met their plane at the end of that summer, the reports of their excellent experience in Wenchi were gratifying.
>
> I can't adequately account for why it took me so long to return, but when I finally did it was precisely thirty years later. Nana Frema happened to be in Accra just then, so our long-deferred reunion took place there. In our encounter I felt enormous gratitude for her warmth and interest, and for her directness and openness in talking with me about her own life and the challenges the family had endured during those three decades. Her personal connection to my own difficult history was a larger gift than I could have imagined.
>
> The Queen-Mother then invited me to revisit Wenchi as her guest, and she took me to greet her brother the Chief so that I could pay my respects and offer my thanks for his generosity in caring for me and for our Crossroads group throughout our stay.

My text was accompanied by both a current picture of me and the sweet snapshot from 2000 that showed me with the Chief and his wife and sister, we four squeezed together onto his couch.

> The Busia family story is heroic, and I am proud to be associated with it. The Queen-Mother's long and loving devotion to her royal duties and to her family legacy are made evident by the universal grief felt at

her death. She was a strong role model in ways both traditional and contemporary, and it is a great honor for me to be given this opportunity to join her family and friends in paying tribute to Nana Frema.

In the printed version the only change to the text that I'd submitted was the addition by the family of this final sentence: "May she rest in perfect peace." I recited it like a true believer.

The service proceeded with a reading from *The Book of Revelation*, John's vision about "the rewarding of the saints" when "the Lamb will be their shepherd and will lead them to springs of living water; and God will wipe away all the tears from their eyes." And then the Bishop mounted the podium to give a long and rousing sermon, in Twi, with interspersed phrases in English that served to locate his text in Revelation.

I couldn't follow it in any literal sense, but I heard him say *"Write!"* The service for the "Burial of the Dead" in *The Book of Common Prayer* of the Episcopal Church in which I was raised includes a passage from *The Book of Revelation* that reads, "I heard a voice from Heaven saying unto me, Write," a command to John from God's angel to "Write the things which thou hast seen, and the things which are, and the things which shall be hereafter." At the end of my first novel, *Gus in Bronze*, I made reference to this "Write!" with Gus's husband hearing her voice saying:

> yes, Write, tell me all the news, tell me how the children are getting along [...] and whether you miss me, Write, and tell me what I'm missing.

I absorbed the improbability of this intersection with an almost dizzy joy in my being able to pay sufficiently close outward attention even while being drawn deeply inward. I understood how much I had already learned during these days in Wenchi about how the disruptive futility of anticipation undermines the present moment. It had never been my ambition to fully master this skill until now, when I recognized that I had spent the last days of Tim's life projecting his recovery.

What use is it to imagine a cure with no basis in fact? As I sat with this lesson I asked myself to wonder what might have occurred, instead of what did, if I'd focused on the actuality of his condition. I had understood the importance, but missed the significance, and isn't this a violation of the foundational commandment to Do No Harm? Tim's suicide was no less shocking today, except that by process of elimination – his, of himself – hadn't he given himself over not only to my care but, by extension, to the kindness of all these good people?

In the tangible company of this congregation I felt extended by the "bridges of friendship" that personify the mission of Crossroads. This experience was initiated with the series of interactions during our orientation, by Ghanaian-Americans tasked with instructing us in basic language skills and customs. From one of our orientation sessions my notes on the art of bargaining took up a page in my journal – Twi for "Please, I beg you, reduce the price for me!" – which helped me to grasp its meaning on my guided tour of Wenchi's open-air market in buying the ingredients for our first dinner here. Instead of the common American understanding of negotiating with a focus on being overcharged, I saw that the bargaining ritual was an exchange of recognition, of trust.

We Crossroads volunteers knew the positive impact made by that inaugural Peace Corps group who, upon landing in Accra, lined up on the tarmac to sing the Ghanaian national anthem, in Twi. Our own arrival was less noteworthy, and though we were provided with experienced contacts to help us navigate the first few days, our Crossroads group was paired with curious young local counterparts eager to work alongside us. These interconnections fulfilled the program's purpose, and while my sudden departure had deprived me of these friendships then, I could feel that, with my tribute to their beloved Queen-Mother, I had made them now.

During the Offertory we all danced up to the large collection basket, row by row, including the musicians who came down from the balcony and even the clergy who contributed, to boost the take, in Nana's name, for the building fund for the new church that was soon to be dedicated. In his pitch the minister singled out "the two white people" in the congregation, and although we couldn't know the rest of what he may have said about us, we gave over all the currency we had, without knowing that there were still two more offerings to come.

In those parts of the service when I wasn't straining for understanding I focused on the twenty Styrofoam blocks spelling out the Queen-Mother's name, Nana Afua Frema Tatuo II, each decorated with a dozen lifelike artificial white roses. These were carried in by the grandchildren dressed not in the red and black mourning colors worn by the rest of us but another specially commissioned black and white fabric crafted into a variety of distinctly artful outfits. This intricate and firmly prescribed attention to detail was so elaborate that it became astonishing to realize that this was the third Busia family funeral in less than two years: first the Chief and then another sister, with now only one sibling remaining, Hon. Ama Bame Busia, the last.

For the previous two days "Auntie Ama" had been seated on the porch of the house adjacent to where her sister's body was on display, confined to a wheelchair after being fitted only the week before for her prosthesis following a leg amputation. Diabetes has been a family disease borne with dignity and now, heroically, since it prevented the sole survivor of her generation from this progression of ceremonies essential to the balance of mourning and thanksgiving.

In the tribute book she wrote:

> Today, I painfully pay tribute as the only survivor of thirteen children of Nana Yaa Pokua of the Sofoase Yefere Royal family of Wenchi and Nana Kwasi Bame, of which you were the seventh born and the first daughter. [...] You were our leader and the matriarch of this our unique family, and as tradition will have it you became the "Mother" of Wenchi Traditional Area. [...] Nana it has been difficult. Nana it has been very difficult for me these days as I find myself hoping to hear that musical laughter of yours one more time. [...] But I can understand why our maker wants you by His side. I really do.

According to the program there are twenty-eight elements to the Burial Service, and we were at number fourteen when the Choir offered its stirring Anthem. The lyrics of the hymns were projected onto the wall above the altar, along with a charming series of photographs of Nana Frema that were reproduced in the tribute book. Now she and her brother and his wife and I were sitting together on his couch, larger than life, and the image was fixed there for what seemed like its own eternity. I felt myself giving way, giving in, giving myself over to it. I was being told that, here, I was accepted and embraced – I was taken at my word – and with this blessed recognition such a heat was generated within me that, for the first time in my life, I thought I might faint.

But instead the congregation rose for "A Prayer of Commendation" and the "Benediction" that signaled the bearers to carry the casket to the waiting hearse. I noted that the program included an additional prescribed set of rites, "At The Grave Side," but what I hadn't fully understood until now was that it is the custom for all members of the royal family, not only the King, that a burial be not just private but secret. The final resting place is not revealed to outsiders, and sometimes not even to the family. This is in order to ensure that the body will remain undisturbed – unspoiled by plunderers perhaps too – and why the Queen-Mother's burial will take place later, at a site selected by the royal funeral caretakers, under cover of night.

It was now the lunch break, and while the buffet was being assembled we relaxed with the relatives on the second-story porch. Jim joined the men in a bottle of Star that I declined in order to prevent the need for either a nap or a toilet. Our caution had so far allowed us to sit ever patiently motionless for many hours at a stretch, and it was as if Jim had the same thought when, after a few sips, he set the beer on the floor beside him, and left it there.

We were given the alternative of resting up between events, so we didn't stay for the lunch of unidentified spiced meat boiled in a banana leaf wrapper, choosing to rejoin the group later. Once again, the schedule wasn't precise and didn't need to be. The imported Christian rites would resume the next morning with a Memorial Service to conclude these days of observances, but this afternoon was dedicated to a significantly larger and, to us, more exotic gathering. Now the assembled dignitaries would pay their respects according to the ancient tradition of the ancestors Nana Frema was rejoining.

The procession past the seated family took place in a vast open field encircled with thirty black and red peaked tents that suggested to me the set of a Shakespearean battlefield, especially once the parade got underway, with each Chief's entourage including his royal Linguist, a stool bearer, and a token warrior. In a few cases the Chief's official umbrella was large enough to become its own tent, so once these more elevated Chiefs had moved around the perimeter to a designated location, having shaken hands all along the way, they set up camp, so to speak.

There didn't otherwise seem to be a formal program, but there was an offstage MC and a booming sound system to announce the special guests, including a prominent cluster of Muslim clerics whose pastel robes created a striking contrast with the black business-suited delegation sent by Ghana's current President. In this crowd of 1,500 or more we were seated in the second row next to Nana Akua the fashion designer and Nana Abena the poet-professor. Their running commentary was welcome, but we needed no translation when we ourselves were announced periodically throughout the afternoon as "the two white people who have come all the way from America to mourn with us."

There were male drummers and female dancers, and then came a male dancer ritually dressed and decorated as a woman. In what we were told was an uncommon gesture of respect, one of the Chiefs performed a mourning dance as he processed by the extended family. But the most expressly plaintive dance was when the Queen-Mother's two daughters and eleven granddaughters formed a tight knot and slowly moved as one. Bending and straightening together, they were flowers on separate stems from the same root, the focused drumming providing an almost isometric momentum for their gliding back and forth across the open field to dance for their Nana.

The overall atmosphere was neither solemn nor festive, but a comfortably natural blend of set and spontaneous. Professional photographers moved among the guests, and while I would have loved to make a video of these entire proceedings, I refused to embarrass the family or myself by acting like a tourist. Meanwhile, the large laminated photos that were for sale demonstrated how difficult it is to flatter skin tones so vastly different from the norm as ours. We had the same washed-out look as the official pictures from a state visit made to Ghana by Queen Elizabeth. We laughed at this, and we were maybe still smiling when one of the men with whom we'd sat on the porch at midday passed by, shaking hands all along the way but leaning in with a smile of his own as he said to Jim, "I finished your beer."

This open field was located off the dirt lane called Hospital Road and, sure enough, the yellow building that I could see from there was where I had brought Tim, seeking help because, as only he and I knew him well enough to know, he wasn't himself. I don't know what Tim believed about himself at that point, but this dramatic proximity to the hospital required me to recall how, as if to mutely refute the doctor's assurance that he wasn't sick enough to be admitted, Tim then entered into a reduced state that I misinterpreted as the good news of his enforced rest.

So little has advanced in the study of suicide, compared to the progress in deciphering the complex natures of cancer, or viruses, or genes, that Lee Buxton's self-diagnosis of his suicide attempt as having been caused by "a combination of things" seems no less state-of-the-art today than it was in his day. I knew Tim as anxious but not as depressed, and while in psychiatric jargon anxiety disorder and depressive disorder are termed "comorbid," they're not considered fatal. If Tim was "predisposed" to a "death wish" because of the "suicide family" he came from, why wasn't he as proactive – as *preventative* – as he was with so much else in his life?

Another large question remains unanswered: by what calamitous process does a breadknife become a murder weapon?

I have taken Jim's great patience with my persistent reworking of this sorrowful narrative as a mark of his love not only for me but for Tim too. Beyond the eerie coincidence of their rhyming names, they have in common, more substantively, the fact that in the 1960s it was in seminaries like theirs that to study theology and ethics was to agitate for Civil Rights and against the war in Vietnam. Though his ministry was brief, Jim's entire Catholic priesthood was as a rebel, and it was he, not Tim, who once spent a night in a DC jail with Bill Coffin in the next cell leading this younger cohort of protestors in a full-throated rendition of "The Hallelujah Chorus." It's oddly easy to imagine the two of them in conversation – they learned from the same books – about the shared passions and concerns that have always been more theirs than mine.

Jim and I have been married forty years longer, yet if I minimize the still immature love during my brief marriage to Tim, don't I also increase my responsibility for his death? I can see that Jim finds my calculations even more upsetting than I do. Am I too analytic? Am I heartless? I wonder if, in his identification with Tim, he ever fears for himself. Would I fail him too?

Jim's companionship on this journey, on my return trips to Wenchi as well as with his sturdy protection and support of my writing life, has been mine ever since the day he and I met, at the end of which, after our intense twelve-hour lunch, in order to fully introduce myself I needed to describe Tim's dying. Though words eluded me then, you could say that, ever since, I've tried to supply them.

The Queen-Mother's enduring gift to me was the ricocheting simplicity of her asking, *"But don't you think it was a bit selfish of him?"* No one else – ever – gave me this permission to be critical of the choice Tim made that morning not to trust the people charged with his wellbeing. At the time of this conversation three decades later – when I replied *"Yes!"* – it seemed not only entirely fair but essential, not only permitted but required, not only freeing but liberating, to tabulate the lasting damage. And it still does.

We were exhausted. The ceremony ended with the start of another evening when it was a relief to be offered a ride to our lodgings so that we could take a cool shower and change back into our own clothes. For the family, like any family at any family funeral, the chance for the relatives to reminisce comes only after the crowd disperses.

All the actual business needing to be conducted may well have been addressed in the preceding months, but because of a rival Wenchi family's assertion of its own claim to the stool, great significance was given to the presence of the Chief who was seated next to Nana Frema's son and daughters. We were told that he was not only a member of that other family but had elected not to participate in this afternoon's possibly coincidental but certainly unfortunately timed funeral of his brother's son. The royal succession appeared to remain open-ended despite the powerful show of allegiance that we witnessed. Will the Queen-Mother's son be named to the Chief's still vacant stool? We told Nana George Kofi Ashitey Ollennu that when this happens, if he invites us to his enstoolment we will surely come.

When Jim first went to Ghana he was given a book called *The Sacred Stools of the Akan*, written by the Catholic Bishop of Kumasi. Here is his definition of the stool's significance:

> The seat, which is in the shape of a crescent, symbolizes the mother's embrace. [...] The middle portion, besides determining the name of the stool, is the object of various patterns and symbols. [...] The base

normally has two or three steps. This symbolizes the success which comes out of the readiness to bear one's fair share of the responsibility of the society in which one lives.

It is clear that it is by reason of the stool that one is a chief and enjoys personal sacredness. [...] He is chief, first and foremost, to perform the religious duties. Other functions, which may be described as administrative, executive, judicial and military are all part of this holy duty which is so necessary that it may never be neglected. [...] The chief's stool is also believed to be the resting place as well as the symbol of the chief's soul.

It was in this "middle portion" that the character of the stool was defined by the Chief or Queen-Mother's choice among the "various patterns and symbols" – the alphabet of *Adinkra* used to express the proverbs – carved into its center. So the stool was an actual stool with a very comfortable curved seat, as well as a symbolic representation of royal lineage with all its accompanying duties and privileges.

I am continually comforted by my absolute trust in the unlikely fact that Jim and I found each other, and it's a resource for us both that right here in the capsule of this remote world we each have rich histories. But that didn't mean I was able to fall asleep. Nature's night sounds were an untamed cacophony that kept me spinning my own wheels, never quite reaching the crescendo from which my energy could recede.

During the church service I'd calculated that when Tim died he was roughly the age of Nana Frema's grandchildren, but did this make me old enough now to be Tim's grandmother? I did the math again. Yes. If I'd had a baby that year, at that age, the child of that child would now be the age Tim was at his death.

Though I have no photos of Tim taken during our ten days together here in Ghana, I can see him clearly as that handsome boy – "tall, well-built," as the Pathology Report observed – with his cosmic concerns and his girl-wife, oblivious. The images I do have of Tim are only a handful of scattered faded snapshots, plus our intact burgundy leather wedding album containing all those predictable poses. Because I've been shown pictures of Tim's siblings' children and grandchildren I can visualize the baby he and I might have had together. He probably wouldn't want me to pity him this loss, but I do. I also feel sad for his fragile but determined mother, just as I feel compassion for his father, the physician whose brave career challenged, and changed, the law against reproductive freedom for women. Two unstable lives undercut, each by the other.

This short night finally unfolded into the morning of the final memorial service, and we dressed in another set of form-fitting outfits sewn from a different commemorative fabric, now black on white. This time the Queen-Mother's royal name and dates surrounded the image of a stool with the *Adinkra* symbol *Akofena* (*Ako* – war, *Afena* – sword) to represent the power and authority vested in chieftaincy. A booklet called *Values of Adinkra Symbols* calls this image of crossed swords "very significant for swearing the oath of allegiance" as it "advises people to honor and show loyalty to their leaders. It also encourages statesmanship and gallantry."

Yesterday's "Except God" and today's "War Sword" symbols seem appropriate for a Queen-Mother sustained both by her faith and the valiant force of her determined will to serve. The church was again packed to overflowing, with the service including more pulsing music and multiple collections. Since this was to be a Liturgy of Thanksgiving, the tone was almost festive.

Differing theories were proposed to us about our return travel schedule, with the conclusion reached that we must allow an extra few hours for the drive back to Kumasi to catch our flight to Accra. And so we did, no matter that slipping away early meant drawing the Queen-Mother's son and daughters out of the church into the courtyard in order to exchange our final thanks and goodbyes.

Before getting into the car, though, we then also submitted to our hosts' impromptu desire for us to walk with them a short distance from the church to see the building project to which I'd contributed funds after the Chief's death.

The nearly completed construction was plainly visible from the road, but I hadn't noticed it and it hadn't been identified. And although they were unable to open the gate without a key to the padlock, I was content to press my face against the wrought iron posts. For me, this memorial to Nana Frema's brother was linked to the death of my own brother.

Adjacent losses, the sight of this freshly painted pair of joined buildings with overlapping pale blue corrugated metal roofing pierced my heart.

This moment was made all the more vivid because it both made no easy sense and had no need to. I returned to Proust, and Proust returned to me.

My awareness of this fresh jolt of joy verged on what I believed Proust meant when he ceased to think of himself as *médiocre, contingent, mortal*, when all his anxiety about the future – all doubt – dissipated. He asked himself where this sensation came from and how it came to him, but even if the simple taste of a madeleine didn't logically contain the reasons for the joy he felt, he felt confident in his sudden understanding that death now had no meaning for him. Situated outside of time, what can he fear of the future? A parallel freedom came with my own realization, the same as Proust's, that my life was unique and could only be mine.

A pattern of sequential reveals had so much become our own new rhythm here that when we unexpectedly arrived in Kumasi with several hours to spare before our flight, while I was developing a fallback sightseeing plan – the Kumasi City Cemetery, *again?* – Jim swiftly negotiated switching our tickets to a flight soon to depart. He ducked into a bathroom to change out of his formal clothes, but I didn't. Among our fellow passengers on the flight were a number of other women wearing their own versions of the black and white fabric that I now knew to recognize as memorial cloth. I fit right in.

After our upcountry travels the familiar Labadi Beach Hotel felt First World, and welcome. I had stayed here each time since my first return in 2000, always comforted by the mature tropical plantings surrounding the staged outdoor terraces, ever consoled by the memory of the Queen-Mother's lasting gift to me here, over dinner, with her encircling welcome and the sharing of our stories.

The hotel now counted among its directors Ambassador Kojo Amoo-Gottfried, and when I phoned Kojo from Kumasi to say we were on an earlier flight back to Accra, I learned from him that his planned business trip to China had been postponed by a day, freeing him as well to meet us for dinner after all. Our pair of suddenly altered itineraries felt to me like a related instance of the traveler's luck initiated by Kojo on my first return to Ghana. And our fond reunion on the hotel's spacious veranda was made all the merrier by the intervening encounters we've had, in Accra and Kumasi and with his visit to our home in Boston, that made for a continuous conversation. Over dinner Kojo entertained us with faded snapshots and fond stories of his vivid encounters with Fidel and Ché from the days of his diplomatic service in Cuba.

At the end of that day, the bathroom shower was steamy hot, and I then melted into the ridiculous excess of our bed's fleet of pillows. This contrast with Wenchi's harsh simplicity might seem radically discrepant, except for the fact that for the Busia family these two worlds are one. I felt the active presence of my own long improbable history here as another luxury, and I embraced it.

After an almost absurdly comfortable sleep and the hotel's morning buffet including a classic colonial breakfast alongside an array of appetizing tropical options, we made our way to the steadily rumbling Gulf of Guinea that was audible, but invisible, behind a dense screen of vegetation. The same winding sandy path led from the hotel to that shoreline where nobody swims, and while I noticed that a few meager signs had been posted on some of the palm trees, the flat gray sea still concealed its perilous tides and currents. A stripe of clotted debris had been left behind by the receding tide, plastics pulverized into colored micro-specks that looked unnervingly pretty. Down the way there were washed-ashore rubber tires standing upright in the sand like hoops, all the warning any bather should need to stay out of that water.

Almost instantly, a vendor with a handful of trinkets emerged from the vegetation in hopes of bargaining his tired wares for our small change. Despite our traveling clothes I communicated that we weren't tourists, having no better way to convey that I just needed to stand on that beach to stare at that water.

The polished lobby was outfitted with oversized chairs and couches grouped for the quiet conversations that were taking place. It was there that I had been introduced to one of Nana Frema's teenaged grandsons, who made me laugh out loud when I offered him a drink and, scrutinizing the menu with its prices listed in Ghanaian currency, he protested, "Ten grand? For a Coke?" It shouldn't have surprised me that when Nana Kofi and I met again in Wenchi for his grandmother's funeral he was now a grown man with a family, since in this same interval I'd become a grandmother.

I was sitting again in one of those cushioned mahogany armchairs, my funeral clothes packed in the rolling suitcase by my side. In making random notes like these I was reminded, as always, of Henry Adams's perception that the habit of expression leads to the search for something to express. I was writing down my impressions as if a larger thought might emerge if I let it. And so it did.

My breath escaped with the revelation that, even if I could ever reach a conclusion about why Tim killed himself, it would be incomplete. In that defining moment when his life was being lost, he was already missing from it. I have tried here to supply Tim's life and death to include him – to name him! – in order to correct the record of his mother's negligent obituary. More ambitiously, I have wished to claim Proust's wisdom for Tim, so that he too might have been released, at least, from fearing the future. Instead I have come to see, at last, that it was never within my power to create an afterlife for Tim.

The afterlife of his suicide – the life – is my own.

My parents on their honeymoon, June 1941.

I met my father for the first time in April of 1945, at fifteen months,
when he returned from the War in his Navy uniform.

Tim and I had a traditional wedding in December 1966.
(Credit: Bachrach Photography)

That year we helped a friend build a roof for his cabin in the Hudson valley.

Harry Crosby and Polly Phelps Peabody
on their wedding day in New York,
September 1922.

Harry kept this photograph of Josephine
on his desk, and it was in his wallet when
he died. It was said that they resembled
each other like brother and sister.

Josie and Bert on their wedding day,
June 1929, in Old Lyme, Connecticut.

Their wedding party included twelve bridesmaids and fourteen groomsmen, among them Bert's Harvard classmates with storybook names like Roosevelt, Carnegie, and Tiffany.

Bert Bigelow, second from left, skipper of the 30' sailing vessel "Golden Rule" in a peace action to protest the US government's 1958 nuclear test explosions.

Author photo for *Gus in Bronze*, 1977.
(Credit: KS Hand)

Jim and me in 1977
on the roof at 128 Myrtle Street, Boston.

My favorite photo of Dad,
with Lizzy in 1979.

Lizzy and Patrick in 1984.
(Credit: Patricia Pingree)

A boy and his dog:
my brother Will with his Waldo.

The Busia family included thirteen siblings. Seated here in 1971,
left to right, are the Chief, the Queen-Mother, and the Prime Minister.

The Queen-Mother in 2000,
the night of our dinner at my hotel in Accra.

With the Chief, his wife, and the Queen-Mother, in Wenchi, in 2000.

The cover of the Tribute Book for the 2016 royal funeral of Nana Afua Frema Tatuo II.

Jim and me in our mourning clothes.

At the ceremony following the church service, seated with the Queen-Mother's nieces, Nana Akua, left, and Nana Abena, center.

ACKNOWLEDGMENTS

"The Afterlife of a Suicide" appeared in the Winter 2020 issue of *The American Scholar*, and I am grateful to its Editor, Robert Wilson, and to Jayne Ross for her close work on the text. Ladette Randolph, Editor of *Ploughshares*, published "The Ultimate Alchemy" in the Winter 20/21 issue, and I am honored by her enduring support of my writing. I also wish to express my appreciation to Emily Firetog at *Literary Hub* for publishing the excerpt "And Then What?"

Askold Melnyczuk's invitation to publish the memoir from which these three pieces are drawn brought new life to this old story, and it is a gift to work with such a true Man of Letters. My thanks also to his partner in literature and life, Alex Johnson, and for the talent and very generous guidance provided by Ezra Fox at *Arrowsmith Press*. For their work on this book I'm grateful to Kippy Goldfarb for photography, Kristen Mallia for art design, and Justin Hargett at Kickflip Publicity.

In Ghana, I am forever indebted to the Chief and Queen-Mother of Wenchi Traditional Area, Nana Kusi Apea I and Nana Afua Frema Tatuo II, and for the enduring hospitality of the extended Busia family. I'm proud to acknowledge Reverend Dr. James H. Robinson for his visionary creation of the ongoing program Operation Crossroads Africa.

The Writers Room in New York provided me with welcome workspace during the writing of this book. Beyond my general research into the range of themes related to this narrative, I am grateful to Amy Ryan at the Boston Public Library and the Boston Athenaeum, and Charles Pierce at the Morgan Library, for giving me access to archived material. I have also depended upon the works referred to here by the authors A. Alvarez, Albert Bigelow, Abena P. A. Busia, Caresse Crosby, Harry Crosby, Kwaku Danso-Boafo, Marguerite Duras, Herb Gardner, John Lewis, Maria Rainer Rilke, Philip Roth, Barbara Sproul, and Geoffrey Wolff. I have incorporated the journals and correspondence of Timothy Buxton in portraying him and our foreshortened life together. And I have been accompanied throughout by the wisdom and trust of Dr. Judy Kantrowitz.

Over the years I am fortunate to have worked with dedicated editors, literary agents, and publishers and would like to thank in particular Helene Atwan, Donald Cutler, Merloyd Ludington, Elaine Markson, Nancy Nicholas, Wendy Strothman, and Ike Williams.

As a reader, I rely on the smart company of the women of the Ladies Literary Guild. As a writer, I am sustained by my many writer friends, with profound respect for their inspiring example. I am deeply grateful for the public endorsement of this book by my celebrated sister writers Susan Cheever, Alice Hoffman, Megan Marshall, Taiye Selasi, and Joan Wickersham.

My favorite writer is my dear husband James Carroll, whose twenty-one books are brave works of conscience. Jim's support of my writing has been steady and steadying. We have also shared a cherished family life with our son Patrick and our daughter Lizzy, who gave us James and their daughters Annie and Julia, the next generation.

Credit: Carolle Photography

Alexandra Marshall's essays and short fiction have appeared in *AGNI*, *Five Points*, *Hunger Mountain*, *Literary Hub*, *Ploughshares*, *The American Prospect*, *The American Scholar*, *The Boston Globe*, *The New York Times*, and in several anthologies. She has published five novels (*Gus in Bronze*, *Tender Offer*, *The Brass Bed*, *Something Borrowed*, and *The Court of Common Pleas*) and a nonfiction book, *Still Waters*. With the publication of this work, earlier versions of *The Silence of Your Name: The Afterlife of a Suicide* have at last achieved a Beginning, a Middle, and an End.

ARROWSMITH is named after the late William Arrowsmith, a renowned classics scholar, literary and film critic. General editor of thirty-three volumes of *The Greek Tragedy in New Translations*, he was also a brilliant translator of Eugenio Montale, Cesare Pavese, and others. Arrowsmith, who taught for years in Boston University's University Professors Program, championed not only the classics and the finest in contemporary literature, he was also passionate about the importance of recognizing the translator's role in bringing the original work to life in a new language.

Like the arrowsmith who turns his arrows straight and true,
a wise person makes his character straight and true.

— Buddha

Books by

ARROWSMITH
PRESS

Girls by Oksana Zabuzhko
Bula Matari/Smasher of Rocks by Tom Sleigh
This Carrying Life by Maureen McLane
Cries of Animal Dying by Lawrence Ferlinghetti
Animals in Wartime by Matiop Wal
Divided Mind by George Scialabba
The Jinn by Amira El-Zein
Bergstein edited by Askold Melnyczuk
Arrow Breaking Apart by Jason Shinder
Beyond Alchemy by Daniel Berrigan
*Conscience, Consequence: Reflections on
Father Daniel Berrigan* edited by Askold Melnyczuk
Ric's Progress by Donald Hall
Return To The Sea by Etnairis Rivera
The Kingdom of His Will by Catherine Parnell
Eight Notes from the Blue Angel by Marjana Savka
Fifty-Two by Melissa Green
Music In—And On—The Air by Lloyd Schwartz
Magpiety by Melissa Green
Reality Hunger by William Pierce
Soundings: On The Poetry of Melissa Green edited by Sumita Chakraborty
The Corny Toys by Thomas Sayers Ellis
Black Ops by Martin Edmunds
Museum of Silence by Romeo Oriogun
City of Water by Mitch Manning
Passeggiate by Judith Baumel
Persephone Blues by Oksana Lutsyshyna
The Uncollected Delmore Schwartz edited by Ben Mazer
The Light Outside by George Kovach
The Blood of San Gennaro by Scott Harney edited by Megan Marshall
No Sign by Peter Balakian
Firebird by Kythe Heller
The Selected Poems of Oksana Zabuzhko edited by Askold Melnyczuk
The Age of Waiting by Douglas J. Penick
Manimal Woe by Fanny Howe
Crank Shaped Notes by Thomas Sayers Ellis
The Land of Mild Light by Rafael Cadenas edited by Nidia Hernández

CPSIA information can be obtained
at www.ICGtesting.com
Printed in the USA
FSHW010027290721
83607FS